THE AMERICAN HEART ASSOCIATION

Low-Fat, Low-Cholesterol Cookbook

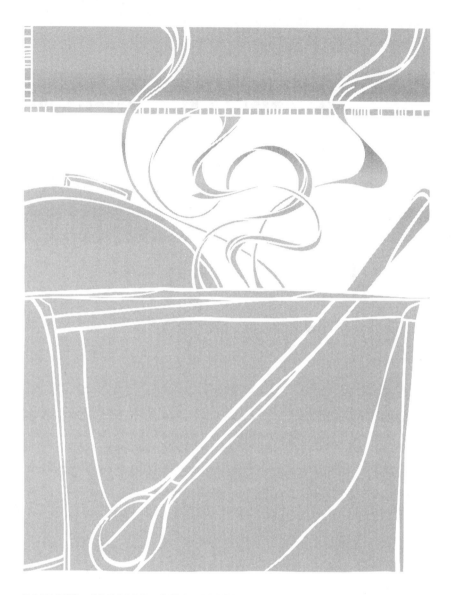

RECIPES CREATED AND TESTED BY
Laureen Mody, R.D.
Leni Reed, R.D.
Sherry Ferguson

RECIPES ANALYZED BY
Nutrition Scientific
Pasadena, California

ILLUSTRATIONS BY
Regina Scudellari

THE AMERICAN HEART ASSOCIATION

Low-Fat, Low-Cholesterol Cookbook

More than 200 delicious, heart-healthful recipes for the whole family

EDITORS

Scott M. Grundy, M.D., Ph.D.
Director, Center for Human Nutrition
University of Texas Southwestern Medical Center
Dallas, Texas

Mary Winston, Ed.D., R.D.
Senior Science Consultant
American Heart Association National Center
Dallas, Texas

TIMES BOOKS

Copyright © 1989 by American Heart Association
Illustrations copyright © 1989 by Regina A.E. Scudellari

All rights reserved under International and Pan-American Copyright
Conventions. Published in the United States by Times Books, a division of
Random House, Inc., New York, and simultaneously in Canada by Random
House of Canada Limited, Toronto.

The cooperation of David Burke of The River Cafe in Brooklyn, New York, in
the preparation of line art for this book is gratefully acknowledged.

Library of Congress Cataloging-in-Publication Data

Grundy, Scott M.
    The American Heart Association low-fat, low-cholesterol cookbook/by Scott
Grundy and Mary Winston.
        p.   cm.
    Includes index.
    ISBN 0-8129-1783-9
    1. Low-fat diet—Recipes.   2. Low-cholesterol diet—Recipes.
I. Winston, Mary.   II. American Heart Association.   III. Title.
RM237.7.G78   1989
641.5′635—dc19   88-36665
                                                                              CIP

Manufactured in the United States of America

B98765432

DESIGNED BY BARBARA MARKS
CUT-PAPER ILLUSTRATIONS BY REGINA SCUDELLARI
ART DIRECTION BY NAOMI OSNOS

PREFACE

For more than forty years the American Heart Association has been waging a war against heart disease. Our weapons are medical research, professional and public education and community programs. We continue to educate the public about the benefits of adopting a healthful lifestyle—to avoid smoking, control high blood pressure, maintain a low blood cholesterol level and be physically active. Incorporating these habits into your daily life and that of your family can greatly reduce the probability of having a heart attack.

This book is devoted to one of these major risk factors. It will show you how to reduce your blood cholesterol level in an effective, and even enjoyable, way. In the introduction, Dr. Scott Grundy, one of the foremost lipid specialists in this country and one of the AHA's most eminent science volunteers, explains the medical aspects of high blood cholesterol and the reasons why diet modification is the primary treatment for lowering it. Associating your diet with a treatment plan may conjure up thoughts of dull, unappetizing meals, but the two-hundred newly created recipes in this book will quickly dispel that notion. The cooking and shopping tips will help you modify your own favorite recipes so that they will contribute to a healthy heart as well. If you have to lose weight, this cookbook includes several tips for success.

Eating out may be a part of your daily life or something you enjoy only occasionally. Regardless, you need not give it up. Suggestions for various types of restaurant menu selections are also provided.

Finally, Dr. Grundy discusses various drugs and how they work. For some of you they will be a necessary part of your treatment along with diet modification.

As in everything, practice makes perfect, and provided you are willing to make an effort, your cholesterol-lowering diet can gradually become an enjoyable diet for life. The AHA recognizes that change is difficult for all of us, but acquiring a healthful lifestyle will become a reality if you introduce the needed changes slowly.

To the enjoyment of delicious meals, health and happiness!

Rodman D. Starke, M.D.
Senior Vice President
Office of Scientific Affairs
American Heart Association National Center

ACKNOWLEDGMENTS

This book is the result of the hard work, dedication and encouragement of many American Heart Association volunteers and staff.

I especially want to thank AHA Executive Vice President Dudley Hafner and Deputy Executive Vice President Cass Wheeler for creating an environment in which this project could be developed and for always finding a solution to apparently unsolvable problems.

I have much gratitude and admiration for my learned colleague and cookbook co-editor Scott Grundy, the director of the Center for Human Nutrition at the University of Texas Southwestern Medical Center at Dallas. His expert knowledge of lipid metabolism and diet and drug therapies for treating high blood cholesterol has made this more than a cookbook—it's a step-by-step blueprint for lowering blood cholesterol.

Besides offering an easy-to-understand eating plan, this book contains two hundred tasty, innovative recipes individually created and tested by nutritionists Laureen Moody and Leni Reed and food stylist Sherry Ferguson. I was in on the taste tests, and believe me, this trio has proven conclusively that meals can be both low in fat and delicious!

Each recipe in this cookbook has been expertly analyzed for protein, carbohydrate, fat, sodium and calories by Nutrition Scientific of Pasadena, California.

Kudos also go to Sam Inman, vice president, Office of Corporate Relations and Development, AHA, for skillfully negotiating the business aspects of the project, and to his assistant, Ann Yanosky, for following through on every detail. David Livingston, corporate counsel for AHA, provided legal expertise. My thanks to Pat Covington and Jane Ruehl for copy editing, to Jean Davis and Carol Boswell for their able secretarial help, always cheerfully given, and last but not least to my son, Rick, whose patience surpassed all understanding during the writing of this manuscript.

The most important thanks of all goes to the American Heart Association's Nutrition Committee for expertise, feedback and continued support and encouragement. It has been a delight to work with this team of professionals.

Mary Winston, Ed.D., R.D.
Senior Science Consultant
Office of Scientific Affairs
American Heart Association National Center

CONTENTS

THE AMERICAN HEART ASSOCIATION

Low-Fat, Low-Cholesterol Cookbook

INTRODUCTION

Heart disease is the number one killer of Americans. Despite recent advances in prevention and treatment, it takes the lives of almost one million of us each year.

Currently, about five million people in the U.S. are diagnosed as having heart disease. What's more, millions of others are at risk of heart attack or stroke and don't even know it. According to a landmark study completed by the National Heart, Lung and Blood Institute (NHLBI) in 1986, 80 percent of all middle-aged American men are at increased risk of dying prematurely from heart disease.

Now for the good news: The death rate for coronary heart disease in Americans began to fall in 1964—a trend that continues today. Physicians and scientists who have studied the reasons for the decline conclude that reducing the blood cholesterol level is the single largest contributor to improved cardiac health, followed by reducing or quitting cigarette smoking.

In 1985, Oxford University's Richard Peto said, "We know two things about how to prevent death in middle age: smoking and cholesterol. Each of those two things is responsible for about one third of all deaths in middle age." When these two factors are grouped with high blood pressure, the three account for 85 percent of all premature heart attacks.

There is no longer any question about high blood cholesterol's role in heart disease. Medical science has proven a causal relationship between high blood cholesterol and heart attack in a number of large clinical trials. The NHLBI landmark study referred to previously included 3,800 men with high blood cholesterol. Half were given a cholesterol-lowering drug called cholestyramine, and the other half were given an inactive medication or placebo. The men receiving the cholestyramine experienced significantly lower cholesterol levels than the men receiving placebos. The cholestyramine group also had fewer heart attacks. The results, reported in 1984, showed beyond a doubt that lowering blood cholesterol reduces the risk of heart attack. Other clinical trials using cholesterol-lowering drugs have had similar results.

In addition to clinical trials using drugs to lower cholesterol, a number have focused on cholesterol-reducing diets. One, conducted in Oslo, Norway, showed that modifying diet to lower blood cholesterol can indeed prevent heart attacks. Other diet-oriented trials reported from Los Angeles, Minneapolis and Helsinki, Finland, have provided similar results.

By averaging the results of all the clinical trials, it's now possible to estimate the degree to which lowering cholesterol reduces the risk of heart attack. As a general rule, a 1-percent reduction in total cholesterol level causes a 2-percent reduction in heart attack risk. This means that if you lower your blood cholesterol from 250 to 200 milligrams per deciliter (mg/dl), for example, you'll reduce your risk by 40 percent.

This cookbook has been developed to help you reduce your cholesterol level and lower your risk of heart attack by following a low-fat, low-cholesterol diet.

YOUR CHOLESTEROL GOAL

One of the most dangerous aspects of high blood cholesterol is that you don't feel it or see it. In fact, for 40 percent of heart attack victims, the first symptom of high blood cholesterol is death. That's why it's so important for your physician to check your blood cholesterol level as well as other coronary risk factors at least every five years. Be sure to keep a running record of your blood cholesterol (also known as serum cholesterol) so you can track any changes.

Your blood cholesterol level will fit into one of the following classifications. This makes it easy for your doctor to classify you according to risk. However, his or her advice will also take into account other aspects of your physical and medical history.

CHOLESTEROL (mg/dl)	CLASSIFICATION
Less than 200	Desirable
200 to 240	Borderline high
More than 240	High

If your cholesterol level is less than 200, blood cholesterol is not a major risk factor for you at this time. You should have it checked again in five years. Of course, if other major risk factors are present (smoking and high blood pressure), you're still in danger of heart disease and should follow the diet in this book. In fact, even if you have no other risk factors and your cholesterol is below 200, we recommend The American Heart Association Diet. After all, most authorities will tell you that when it comes to blood cholesterol, the lower the better.

If your cholesterol is between 200 and 240, you're in a borderline zone and face twice the risk of heart attack as people whose levels are well below 200.

And you're not alone: About 30 to 40 percent of American adults fall into this category. It's a situation that shouldn't be ignored, especially if you have other risk factors. In fact, even if you're in the borderline-high range, your doctor will probably advise you to follow a diet to lower your blood cholesterol level and ask you to return to have your cholesterol level checked.

Finally, if your cholesterol is over 240, you could be at high risk of heart attack, and further tests will be needed to determine the best treatment plan for you.

DIET: YOUR FIRST LINE OF DEFENSE

Since most cases of high blood cholesterol are caused by diet, it stands to reason that most cases can be reversed by diet. Most of the time, that logic holds true. However, a few individuals may not be able to reduce their cholesterol level to below 200 without medication. Remember, if you've had a heart attack or have other major risk factors, lowering your cholesterol to below 200 is extremely important. It is also important to reduce your low density lipoprotein (LDL) cholesterol, the kind that is most likely to build up in your arteries, to below 130. (For a complete discussion of lipoproteins, see page 267.)

If you have no other risk factors and have not had a heart attack, you should aim—at the very least—to reduce your cholesterol level to below 240 and your LDL-cholesterol level to below 160. But again, the lower, the better.

To accomplish this, you'll want to reduce your intake of fat, especially cholesterol and saturated fat, which tends to raise your blood cholesterol level. When you eat fats, stick to polyunsaturated or monounsaturated fats. They will not contribute to increasing your blood cholesterol level. You can reduce your fat consumption by eating more complex carbohydrates like fruits, vegetables, nuts, seeds and whole-grain breads, cereals and pastas.

How much will you have to change your diet to achieve your goals? That depends on a number of factors. For many people, some relatively minor changes can make a significant difference in cholesterol and LDL-cholesterol levels. For others, more extensive changes are necessary. That's why the American Heart Association has developed the Step-One Diet and the Step-Two Diet, which vary in the levels of saturated fat and dietary cholesterol they suggest.

USING THE STEP-ONE AND STEP-TWO DIETS

The Step-One Diet is similar to the program that the American Heart Association recommends for the general public. It calls for reductions in saturated fat and cholesterol and in total calories for those who are overweight. The components of this diet are outlined in the table below, with details discussed in Appendix C. All recipes in this book may be used for both the Step-One and Step-Two Diets.

STEP-ONE DIET NUTRITIONAL COMPONENTS

NUTRIENT	RECOMMENDED INTAKE
Total fat	30% or less of total calories
Saturated fatty acids	Less than 10% of total calories
Polyunsaturated fatty acids	Up to 10% of total calories
Monounsaturated fatty acids	10% to 15% of total calories
Carbohydrates	50% to 60% of total calories
Protein	10% to 20% of total calories
Cholesterol	Less than 300 milligrams per day
Total calories	To achieve and maintain desirable weight

Before advising you to adopt a Step-One Diet, your doctor will check your blood cholesterol level. Four to six weeks into the diet, he or she will check it again. Don't be discouraged if your cholesterol level has not changed much or even shows an increase. At this stage there can be a variation of plus or minus 10 percent. Have it checked again after three months. By this time your cholesterol level will have stabilized. If you've reached your target level for blood cholesterol, pat yourself on the back and stay with the Step-One Diet.

If the Step-One Diet doesn't lower your cholesterol to your goal, your doctor may refer you to a Registered Dietitian for additional help. The dietitian can help you review the principles and strengthen your resolve to stay with the Step-One Diet program. Once you've mastered the diet, have your doctor check your cholesterol level again. If you still haven't reached your target, the doctor or dietitian may recommend the Step-Two Diet.

STEP-TWO DIET NUTRITIONAL COMPONENTS

NUTRIENT	RECOMMENDED INTAKE
Total fat	30% or less of total calories
Saturated fatty acids	Less than 7% of total calories
Polyunsaturated fatty acids	Up to 10% of total calories
Monounsaturated fatty acids	10% to 15% of total calories
Carbohydrates	50% to 60% of total calories
Protein	10% to 20% of total calories
Cholesterol	Less than 200 milligrams per day
Total calories	To achieve and maintain desirable weight

As you can see from the table above, the Step-Two Diet is more restrictive in saturated fats and cholesterol and, consequently, will produce a greater reduction in your blood cholesterol. Once you've adjusted to the Step-Two Diet, ask your doctor to check your cholesterol level again. If you still haven't reached your goal, the doctor may decide that you're a candidate for cholesterol-lowering drugs. (See Appendix G for additional information on drug therapy.)

Both the Step-One and Step-Two Diets are based on a nutritious eating plan in which foods containing saturated fat and cholesterol are replaced with similar foods low in saturated fatty acids and cholesterol. The recipes offered are designed to help you include your new diet as part of an overall lifestyle change.

The diets are outlined in detail in Appendix C. Both, however, address the following general concerns.

TOTAL CALORIES. Obesity contributes to high blood cholesterol, and if severe (greater than 30 percent overweight), is a coronary risk factor in its own right. It's important for those who are carrying excess weight to reduce caloric intake, increase caloric expenditure or both. The fact is, many overweight Americans could lose weight simply by changing their sedentary lifestyles to include more exercise. Exercise alone or exercise combined with cutting calories is healthier than severely restricting caloric intake, which could result in deficiencies of important nutrients. The only successful weight-reducing diet is one that will allow you to lose weight and monitor it. A modest calorie reduction of 500 calories a day is best. As a rule of thumb, a reduction diet for men contains about 1600 to 2000 calories, and for women, not fewer than 1200 to 1600. This should allow you to meet all your nutrient needs, minimize hunger and promote a lifelong healthful eating pattern.

TOTAL FATS. In both the Step-One Diet and Step-Two Diet, total fat intake should account for no more than 30 percent of total calories. The American Heart Association has recommended this amount for years. Some investigators recommend reducing fat intake to 20 or even 10 percent of total calories, believing that the lower the amount of total fat in the diet, the lower the blood cholesterol level. However, recent research indicates that fat restrictions of 10 to 20 percent of total calories are not necessary to produce adequate reductions in blood cholesterol as long as the diet is restricted in saturated fatty acids.

To demonstrate the distinction between *total* fat and *type* of fat, compare the Asian diet, which includes just 10 to 20 percent fat, primarily monounsaturated, to the Mediterranean diet, which includes approximately 40 percent fat, primarily monounsaturated with some polyunsaturated. Both result in similarly low blood cholesterol levels. So, the type of fat—not just amount of fat—seems to be the most important factor in controlling blood cholesterol levels.

For most Americans, a diet that includes 30 percent fat is considered more palatable than a diet extremely low in fat. Either type of diet, though, can result in an adequate cholesterol reduction.

DIETARY CHOLESTEROL. The Step-One Diet calls for less than 300 milligrams of dietary cholesterol each day. The Step-Two Diet calls for no more than 200 milligrams of dietary cholesterol per day.

SATURATED FATTY ACIDS. The Step-One Diet recommends that saturated fatty acids be reduced to no more than 10 percent of total calories. Saturated fatty acids are found in animal products and in some plant products. Some animal sources are cheese, butter, cream, whole milk, ice cream, fatty beef, pork, lamb and poultry skin. Coconut oil, palm kernel oil and palm oil are plant sources of saturated fatty acids. In the typical American diet, 14 to 16 percent of total calories are provided by saturated fatty acids. That means most Americans should reduce their saturated fat intake by about one third to achieve the recommended levels. The Step-Two Diet calls for further reduction in saturated fatty acids, to less than 7 percent of total calories. Remember that this reduction applies to *saturated fats,* not all fats. So if you advance to the Step-Two Diet, you will not be required to reduce your total fat intake below 30 percent, although you are free to do so if you wish.

POLYUNSATURATED FATTY ACIDS. As you decrease your intake of saturated fats, you may substitute polyunsaturated fatty acids, up to a point. Substitute polyunsaturated margarines and oil for butter and lard. Use vegetable oils such as corn, safflower and sunflower and margarines that have one of these oils listed as its primary ingredient. These are high in polyunsaturates. However, polyunsaturated fatty acids should not account for more than 10 percent of your daily caloric intake, because no large population has ever eaten a greater proportion of polyunsaturated fat with proven safety. Without further knowledge, it is prudent to advise a limited intake.

MONOUNSATURATED FATTY ACIDS. For the visible fats in your diet such as salad dressings, spreads and cooking oils, choose products composed of poly-unsaturated and monounsaturated fatty acids. In fact, monounsaturates should account for between 10 and 15 percent of your total caloric intake. Olive oil and rapeseed (canola) oil are two major sources of monounsaturates.

CARBOHYDRATES. Approximately 55 to 60 percent of your calories should come from carbohydrates; most should be complex carbohydrates (starches and fibers) as opposed to simple sugars. Complex carbohydrates (provided by fruits, vegetables and whole grains) are rich in vitamins, minerals and fiber.

PROTEIN. The recommended protein intake in both plans is just 15 percent of total calories. Protein should be obtained from a variety of foods—such as dried peas, navy beans, tofu, meat, fish and poultry. Both plant and animal proteins provide a wide range of vitamins, minerals, fiber and other nutrients.

Some people misinterpret the first guideline to mean that *each food* or *each recipe* should have less than 30 percent of its calories come from fat. **The guideline applies to total calories eaten per day.** If it is applied to single foods, the "30 percent of calories from fat" guideline will cause many foods that fit into a well-balanced eating plan to be excluded. Examples of these foods include: oil and margarine (100 percent of calories from fat), regular and low-calorie salad dressings (75–100 percent of calories from fat), dark chicken meat without skin (43 percent of calories from fat), salmon (38 percent of calories from fat), lower-fat meats like turkey ham (34 percent of calories from fat), as well as many nuts and seeds (75–90 percent of calories from fat).

Applying the 30 percent standard to single foods greatly limits the variety of foods in the diet and can be misleading. **The only way to maintain balance, variety, and enjoyment of the American Heart Association eating plan is to interpret the guideline with emphasis on the word "total" for the day.**

WHAT TO EAT

DAIRY PRODUCTS

To lower your blood cholesterol through diet, substitute margarine for butter and skim milk products for cheese, cream and ice cream. It's important to reduce your intake of products containing butter fat substantially, including whole milk, butter, cheese, cream and ice cream. Butter fat raises the blood cholesterol level more than most fats because it contains large quantities of both saturated fatty acids and cholesterol. Since dairy products traditionally play an important role in the typical American diet, we'll look into each more closely.

WHOLE, LOWFAT AND SKIM MILK. Whole milk gets 49 percent of its calories from fat, and skim milk gets about .04 percent. Whole milk also contains a significant level of cholesterol. These are two persuasive reasons to virtually eliminate whole milk from your diet. While 2-percent lowfat milk is preferable to whole milk, it still gets an unacceptable 35 percent of its total calories from fat. And, again, that fat is highly saturated. That's why we recommend you choose 1-percent or skim milk. Both are rich in protein, calcium and other nutrients without having too much fat. Review the Dairy Products section of the Food Table in Appendix D, and the importance of choosing skim milk over whole milk will become obvious.

BUTTER, CREAM AND ICE CREAM. These dairy products contain even more fat than whole milk and should, therefore, be avoided. Unfortunately, butter and cream are often "hidden" in foods, especially in baked goods and desserts. It's important to make sure you know what's in the food you buy by checking the ingredients lists.

CHEESE. Cheese is mistakenly considered an acceptable high-protein substitute for meat. However, most cheeses are also high in highly saturated fat. In fact, 60 to 70 percent of the calories in cheese come from butter fat, about the same percentage as that in ice cream. For these reasons, select lowfat or part-skim milk cheeses.

EGGS

One large egg yolk contains almost the entire daily allowance for cholesterol. It's a good idea to limit your egg yolk consumption to three per week on the Step-One Diet and to one per week on the Step-Two Diet. Egg whites, on the other hand, contain no cholesterol and are a good source of protein. Feel free to eat as many egg whites as you wish and to substitute them for whole eggs in most recipes (see page 25).

MEAT PRODUCTS

A total of six ounces of poultry, fish or lean meat per day (in one or two portions) is quite adequate. If the meat is reasonably lean, six ounces will usually contain between 500 and 600 calories, which is about one third of total required calories, depending on the caloric intake established for your diet.

BEEF, LAMB, PORK AND VEAL. If you thought a cholesterol-lowering diet meant giving up red meat, you'll be pleased to know it's an unnecessary sacrifice. A three-ounce portion of red meat contains about 70 to 75 milligrams of cholesterol and an acceptable level of saturated fats, provided you take certain precautions. First, look for lean cuts of meat—those that contain a minimum of visible fat. Second, trim all outside fat from the meat before cooking.

PROCESSED MEATS. Processed meats, including sausage, bologna, salami and hot dogs, are rich in fat and calories, with about 70 to 80 percent of the total calories provided by fat. Processed meats should be used sparingly. Today, some processed meats are available with "reduced fat." Read the nutrition label and select those varieties with no more than 10 percent fat (by weight) or three grams fat per ounce.

ORGAN MEATS. These include liver, sweetbreads, kidney, brain and heart. All, except heart, which is really more like a red meat, are extremely high in cholesterol and should be eaten sparingly, if at all.

POULTRY. Often touted as a preferable substitute for red meat, poultry is in demand by the health-conscious. It is a good substitute only if the red meat is particularly fatty and the poultry is a lean variety, eaten without skin. Remember that chicken and turkey are leaner than goose or duck. Since the skin has the highest concentration of fat, it's a good idea to remove it before cooking.

FISH

While not free of cholesterol, fish generally contains less than red meat. For a cholesterol-lowering diet, this gives fish a slight edge over lean red meat and a definite edge over fatty red meat. For this reason, many authorities recommend that fish be eaten about two or three times a week. Fish can be either fatty or lean. Omega-3 fatty acids, found in some varieties of fatty fish, are currently being investigated for potential cholesterol-lowering benefits. Some fish high in Omega-3 fatty acids are Atlantic and coho salmon, albacore tuna, club mackerel, carp, lake whitefish, sweet smelt and lake and brook trout.

SHELLFISH

Shrimp, lobster, crab, crayfish and most other shellfish are very low in fat, although ounce for ounce some varieties contain more cholesterol than do poultry, meat or other fish. Even these, however, can be eaten occasionally within the recommended guidelines of less than 300 milligrams of cholesterol per day.

FRUITS, VEGETABLES, GRAINS AND LEGUMES

Foods in these categories have no cholesterol, tend to be low in fat and, in many cases, are high in fiber and vitamins. There are, however, a few exceptions. For example, coconut meat is high in saturated fatty acids. Olives and avocados are also high in fat, but since the fat is largely unsaturated, they need to be limited only because of their high calorie counts. Also, be careful to check the ingredient labels of processed foods made from vegetables, grains or legumes for fats or cholesterol added during processing. (Breads and pasta made with egg yolks, for instance, should be eaten sparingly.) Be aware that many processed and preserved vegetables contain excessive amounts of sodium. If your doctor has advised you to restrict your sodium intake, read the ingredient labels and buy only the many frozen foods (and some canned) without added sodium. Fresh produce is always a good choice. Generally, there is no reason to restrict your intake of fruits, vegetables, grains and legumes except to avoid excessive calories.

NUTS AND SEEDS

These tasty snacks tend to contain high concentrations of fat, and their caloric value is often greater than people realize. Nuts and seeds, though, do not contain cholesterol, and most of their fat is unsaturated. They are also good sources of incomplete proteins and can replace other high-protein foods to some degree. Incomplete proteins need other carbohydrate sources of protein to make them as nutritious a protein source as meat.

BAKERY GOODS

Foods in this category—cakes, pies, doughnuts, cookies and candy—offer few benefits to a cholesterol-lowering diet. They're typically high in calories and low in vital nutrients. Baked goods made with egg yolks and saturated fats not only lack nutritional benefits but are harmful to your diet. Commercially produced baked goods are usually the worst offenders. Homebaked goods prepared with unsaturated oils and egg whites instead of whole eggs are preferable. Still, baked goods of all kinds should be limited because of their high caloric content.

FATS AND OILS

SATURATED, MONOUNSATURATED AND POLYUNSATURATED FATTY ACIDS. These can come from either plant or animal sources. Fats and oils high in saturated fatty acids tend to become hard at room temperature: butter, lard and tallow from animals and coconut, palm and palm kernel oils from plants are common examples. These saturated fats raise blood cholesterol and should be avoided. Oils that stay liquid at room temperature are high in unsaturated fats. They include corn, safflower, sunflower, olive and rapeseed (canola) oils. All are low in saturated fatty acids and can be used to help lower blood cholesterol. Peanut oil has a somewhat higher level of saturated fatty acids, but can be used in cooking for flavoring.

HYDROGENATED OILS. These oils would ordinarily be found in liquid form at room temperature but have been artificially hardened to produce margarines and shortenings. Their effect on blood cholesterol depends on how much they are hydrogenated. It's best to look for margarines that have the hydrogenated oil listed as the second ingredient.

BEVERAGES

Very high consumption of coffee and possibly tea—that is, ten or more cups per day—is suspected of raising cholesterol levels. A modest amount of these beverages (one or two cups) seems to be okay. Alcohol has been erroneously credited with preventing heart disease. In moderation, alcohol does not appear to be harmful. But when excess alcohol is consumed, the ill effects are well established. Alcohol intake should, on the average, be limited to one ounce per day.

SHOPPING FOR LOW-FAT, LOW-CHOLESTEROL FOOD

Before you can effectively make healthy changes in the way you eat, you may need to make some changes in what you buy. The tips that follow can help you put the right foods into your cart and, ultimately, into your body.

BE A LABEL READER

When you see the words "No cholesterol" on a label, it means that the product does not contain any cholesterol, but be aware it may still contain saturated fat, which raises blood cholesterol. Basically, any product that does not contain ingredients from an animal source is naturally cholesterol-free. But coconut, palm and palm kernel oil are three plant sources that contain saturated fat.

A few product labels will give you the percent of calories from fat. Peanut butter and margarine labels often give this information, alerting you to the fact that these products contain primarily fat.

The words "low calorie" mean the product contains no more than 40 calories per serving. "Reduced calorie" means the product has at least one third fewer calories than the product for which this food is substituted. For example, reduced-calorie salad dressing is readily available.

When you shop, compare labels. Some premixed, frozen or prepared foods have a lower saturated fatty acid or cholesterol content than others. Now that many products list their fat and cholesterol content, shopping for low-saturated-

---

SOURCES OF SATURATED FATTY ACIDS AND CHOLESTEROL

Animal Fat	Cream	Palm Kernel Oil*
Bacon Fat	Egg and Egg Yolk Solids	Palm Oil*
Beef Fat	Ham Fat	Pork Fat
Butter	Hardened Fat or Oil	Turkey Fat
Chicken Fat	Hydrogenated Vegetable Oil*	Vegetable Oil**
Cocoa Butter*	Lamb Fat	Vegetable Shortening*
Coconut*	Lard	Whole-Milk Solids
Coconut Oil*		

* Sources of saturated fat only   ** Could be coconut, palm or palm kernel oil

fatty-acid, low-cholesterol foods is easier. With a little guidance, you can learn how to use these labels when you shop. First, look at the ingredients.

All food labels list the product's ingredients in order by weight. The ingredient in the greatest amount is listed first. The ingredient in the least amount is listed last. To avoid too much total fat or saturated fatty acids, limit your use of products that list a fat or oil first, or that list many fat and oil ingredients. The checklist on page 14 helps you identify the names of common saturated fatty acid and cholesterol sources in foods.

READ THE NUTRITION INFORMATION

Look on the label for the amount of total fat, polyunsaturated and saturated fatty acids, and cholesterol. The amount of monounsaturated fatty acids are not listed on labels. The following samples show you how to compare and identify products lower in saturated fatty acids and cholesterol. The labels give the amount of fat in grams (gm) and cholesterol in milligrams (mg) per serving.

COMPARING LABEL INFORMATION

NUTRITION INFORMATION PER SERVING	WHOLE MILK	SKIM MILK
Serving Size	1 cup	1 cup
Calories	150 kcal	86 kcal
Protein	8 gm	8 gm
Carbohydrates	11 gm	12 gm
Fat	8 gm	less than 1 gm
Polyunsaturates	less than 1 gm	0 gm
Saturates	5 gm	less than 1 gm
Cholesterol	33 mg	4 mg

NUTRITION INFORMATION PER SERVING	BUTTER, STICK	MARGARINE, TUB
Serving Size	1 tbsp.	1 tbsp.
Calories	101 kcal	101 kcal
Protein	0.1 gm	0.1 gm
Carbohydrates	0.1 gm	0.1 gm
Fat	11.4 gm	11.4 gm
Polyunsaturates	0.4 gm	3.9 gm
Saturates	7.1 gm	1.8 gm
Cholesterol	31 mg	0 mg

Note: The amount of monounsaturated fat is unlisted but can be approximately calculated by subtracting polyunsaturates and saturates from total fat.

You can see that skim milk has less fat and cholesterol than whole milk. Tub and some stick margarines have less saturated fat and cholesterol than butter.

The nutrition label also tells you what types of nutrients the product provides, the proportions of those nutrients and their contributions to the U.S. Recommended Daily Allowances for protein, vitamins and minerals.

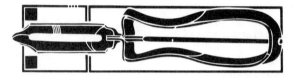

SHOPPING TIPS

With a little practice, shopping with these things in mind will become second nature.

- Plan your menus (if time is at a premium, confine this to the entrees) for the week and make a list *before* you go shopping to help avoid impulse buying of items that may not fit into your diet plan.
- Never go shopping on an empty stomach. Hunger may tempt you to reach for the wrong foods.
- Buy specials or sale items only if they fit into your food plan for the week and into your overall dietary program. Otherwise, they may go to waste. Or to waist.
- If you want to cut costs by trying store brands in place of your usual brand products, be sure to compare the ingredients lists and nutritional labeling to make sure you're getting what you expect.
- Check ingredients lists for salt and other high-sodium additives. Be alert to any food label that has the word "sodium" on it.
  —When you see the words "sodium-free" on a label it means the item has less than 5 milligrams of sodium per serving. "Very low-sodium" means less than 35 milligrams of sodium per serving.
  —"Low-sodium" means 140 milligrams or less per serving. "Reduced sodium" means the product was processed to reduce the usual sodium level by 75 percent.
  —"Unsalted," "no salt added" or "without added salt" means made without the salt that is normally used, but the product still contains the sodium that is the natural part of the food.

MEAT, FISH AND POULTRY

When you shop, choose USDA select or choice grades of lean beef such as round steak, sirloin tip, tenderloin and extra lean ground beef. Even the leanest ground beef has more fat than allowed in the Step-Two Diet Plan. Other things to remember are listed below.

- "Prime" grades are heavily marbled, making them high in saturated fatty acids.
- Liver, brains, kidney and sweetbreads are high in cholesterol and should be limited or omitted.
- Select lean pork such as tenderloin, loin chops, center-cut ham (fresh and cured) and Canadian bacon.
- All cuts of veal are lean except veal cutlets (ground or cubed) and breast. Examples of lean veal are chops and roast.
- The lean cuts of lamb are leg, arm and loin.
- Some wild game, such as venison, rabbit, squirrel and pheasant, are very lean; duck and goose are not.
- Processed meats should be eaten only if they contain no more than 10 percent fat or 3 grams fat per ounce. Many processed meats (luncheon meats, wieners) and sausage are high in saturated fatty acids.
- Because most fish is lower in saturated fatty acids and cholesterol than meats and poultry, it makes a better entree choice.
- All fresh and frozen fish are good selections, as is tuna, canned in water or rinsed. Uncreamed or smoked herring and sardines, canned in tomato sauce or rinsed, are good choices.
- Shellfish contains less fat than does meat or poultry. Although shrimp and crayfish are relatively high in cholesterol, they can be eaten occasionally in the Step-One Diet. However, since the cholesterol is further limited in the Step-Two Diet plan, these shellfish should be limited on that plan.
- Since much of the fat in poultry is in the skin, removing it greatly reduces the fat content. Select chicken, cornish hens and turkey for your entree. Avoid goose, duck and processed poultry products, which are high in saturated fatty acids.
- You will often see the words "lean," "lite" and similar terms used to designate beef, lamb and pork that have less trimmable fat (fat surrounding the meat) and sometimes, less marbling. These labels are also seen on processed meats and other foods. While the terms "light," "lite," "leaner" and "lower fat" generally refer to foods containing less fat, they can be confusing. Light may also mean light color, as in vegetable oil, or fewer calories, as in drinks. Such products are not necessarily low in fat.

DAIRY PRODUCTS

You don't have to give up all dairy products to lower your cholesterol—just follow these recommendations and choose carefully.

- Buy lowfat or skim dairy products such as skim milk, lowfat yogurt, nonfat dry milk and lowfat cottage cheese. And don't forget buttermilk! Despite its name and rich taste, buttermilk is very low in fat, since it's made from cultured skim milk.
- Look for lowfat or part-skim cheeses, lowfat or dry curd cottage cheese, farmer cheese, part-skim mozzarella or ricotta, or dry, grated cheese such as Parmesan or Sap Sago. Because they are made with skim milk, lowfat or imitation cheeses that have between two and five grams of fat per ounce are good choices. Creamy cheeses such as brie or processed cheese spreads are high in saturated fats and should be selected infrequently.

Individuals on the Step-Two Diet should select only skim, nonfat dairy products and cheese with two grams of fat or less per ounce. For desserts, choose frozen lowfat yogurt, ices, ice milk and sherbet.

- Cream substitutes—nondairy coffee creamers, sour cream substitutes and whipped toppings—often contain coconut, palm or palm kernel oil and are therefore high in saturated fatty acids. Read labels carefully and avoid those products high in saturated fatty acids.

FATS AND OILS

Selecting acceptable fats and oils will be easy if you keep these things in mind.

- Buy margarine in place of butter and always look for a margarine that lists liquid oil as the first ingredient or a diet margarine that lists liquid oil as the second ingredient (water is the first ingredient in diet margarines). Next on the list of ingredients should be one or more partially hydrogenated vegetable oils.
- Because diet margarine contains water, it is often difficult to use for cooking. However, it is still useful as a spread.
- Check the label of your vegetable oil and select safflower, corn, sunflower, soybean, olive or canola. Use peanut oil for a flavor change only.
- Buy nonstick vegetable sprays to use in place of butter or oil on pans and baking sheets.
- Because of their high fat content, some nuts, except coconut, and any variety of seeds, olives, peanut butter and avocado are listed in the category of fats. Because they are so high-calorie, select them only occasionally.
- Chocolate, coconut, coconut oil, palm kernel oil and palm oil contain more

saturated than unsaturated fat. When selecting commercial food items containing these ingredients, look for fatty acid information on the label. The foods you buy should contain more polyunsaturated than saturated fatty acids. Currently, information about monounsaturated fatty acids is not listed on the nutrition label, but they can be calculated approximately by subtracting polyunsaturates and saturates from total fat.

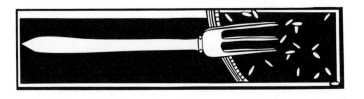

BREADS, CEREAL, PASTA AND STARCHY VEGETABLES

Most breads are low in fat. Some commercially baked products contain large amounts of saturated fatty acids, e.g., croissants, muffins, biscuits, butter rolls and doughnuts. The whole-grain types contain more fiber than others.

- Check the labels on baked foods. Many are made with whole milk and dried egg yolks, and should be only selected occasionally.
- Check the labels on crackers for fats and oils. Scandinavian-style rye crackers and other whole-grain crackers are often made without fats or oils and with little or no salt.
- Try buying brown rice, bulgur wheat, millet and other whole grains to cook in seasoned broth for a side dish. They're high in fiber, relatively low in calories and economical.
- Buy dried beans, peas and lentils to substitute for meats in casseroles, stews and soups. They're excellent protein sources and very economical.
- Check the ingredients lists on packaged cereals. Most of these are low in saturated fatty acids, but many contain large quantities of sugar, some contain salt, and a few even contain fat. Be particularly cautious of so-called natural cereals and granolas, which may contain all three. They often contain coconut or coconut oil.
- Look for reduced-salt versions of canned soups and canned vegetables. They may be found either in the diet section or on the shelves with their "regular" counterparts.
- Canned or dehydrated varieties of soup should have no more than two grams of fat per cup.

VEGETABLES AND FRUITS

Fresh vegetables and fruits have little or no fat, except avocados and olives. When shopping for processed foods, there are a few things to keep in mind.

- Vegetables prepared with butter, cream or cheese can be high in fat.
- Fried vegetables have several times more fat and calories than vegetables prepared without fat.
- Fruits that are fresh or canned in water are lower in calories than fruits canned in juice or in syrup. Drain fruits canned in syrup.

OPTIONAL FOODS

Before reaching for a snack, consider how it fits into your diet plan.

- A few types of commercially prepared cookies are low in fat, such as Newton-type cookies and gingersnaps. Plain angel food cake has no fat. If uncertain, choose only those labeled two grams of fat or less per portion.
- Desserts (cakes, pies, cookies and puddings) may be made at home with allowed margarine or oil, skim or 1-percent milk, allowed eggs, egg substitute or egg whites.
- Many snack products, such as chips and rich crackers, are high in saturated fatty acids. However, some chips are cooked in unsaturated oil. Choose only those labeled as having more polyunsaturated than saturated fatty acids.

FREE FOODS

These foods and drinks contain fewer than 20 calories and no fat per portion.

DRINKS

Bouillon or broth without fat *
Carbonated drinks, sugar-free **
Carbonated water
Club soda *
Cocoa powder, unsweetened
Coffee or tea
Drink mixes, sugar-free **
Tonic water, sugar-free **

FRUITS

Cranberries, unsweetened
Rhubarb, unsweetened

CONDIMENTS

Try flavored peppers, herb blends, spice blends, vinegars and other seasonings in place of salt.

**SWEET SUBSTITUTES **

Candy, hard, sugar-free
Gelatin, sugar-free
Gum, sugar-free
Jam or jelly, sugar-free
Sugar substitutes (saccharin or aspartame)

---

  * High in sodium. Look for seltzers or soda with no salt added.
** Sweet substitutes are listed for the benefit of those following a diabetic diet.

COOKING TIPS

Heart-healthy cooking is more than a matter of what foods you prepare. It's also a function of how you prepare them. The fact is, some cooking methods are better than others for cutting cholesterol, fat and calories while enhancing the nutritional value of your diet. As a rule of thumb, avoid all cooking methods that add fat or allow food to cook in its own fat. (Deep-fat frying or pan frying are two common offenders.) Instead, try some of the following heart-healthy cooking techniques.

Roasting. Always place a rack in the bottom of the roasting pan, so the meat or poultry doesn't sit in its own fat drippings. And be sure to roast at a low temperature, about 350°, to avoid searing the meat or poultry and sealing in the fat. For basting, use fat-free liquids such as wine, tomato juice or lemon juice.

Baking. Poultry, fish and meat can be baked in covered cookware with a little additional liquid. The moisture that the liquid adds makes this method particularly good for fish or chicken breasts, which tend to be a little dry.

Braising or Stewing. This method uses a little more liquid than baking does. It can be done in a covered container on top of the stove or in the oven. If you're braising or stewing meat or poultry, begin a day ahead of time and refrigerate the dish overnight. The next day, when the chilled fat has congealed, you can remove it easily before reheating. Braising is also an excellent way to cook vegetables.

Poaching. To poach chicken or fish, immerse it in a pan of simmering liquid on top of the stove. This method works especially well when you serve the food with a sauce made of pureed vegetables and herbs.

Grilling or Broiling. Placing food on a rack and cooking with these methods lets the fat drip away from meat or poultry. It's also a tasty way to cook fish steaks or whole fish. For extra flavor, try marinating food before putting it over the coals or under the broiler. Skewered vegetables also taste great browned over an open flame.

Sautéing. Fish, poultry and vegetable dishes can be sautéed in an open skillet with little or no fat; the high temperature and motion keep food from sticking. Try sautéing with a tiny bit of polyunsaturated oil rubbed onto the pan with a paper towel. Better still, use nonstick vegetable spray or sauté in a small amount of broth or wine.

Stir-Frying. Done in a Chinese wok, this method relies on the same principle as sautéing. The high temperature and the constant movement of the food keep it from sticking and burning. Try stir-frying vegetables and diced poultry or seafood with a tiny bit of cottonseed or peanut oil.

Microwave Cooking. This is a fast, easy cooking method that requires no added fat. You don't have to add fat to keep the food from sticking to the pan because foods don't tend to stick in the moist heat of microwaving. In fact, you can drain food of fat as it cooks by placing it in the microwave between two paper towels.

If you want to adapt a recipe for microwaving, try cutting the cooking time to one fourth to one third of the conventional time. If the food needs more cooking, increase it a little at a time. You might also look for a microwave recipe similar to the one you're trying to adapt. Keep the following hints in mind when microwave cooking.

- Choose foods that cook well in moist heat: chicken, fish, ground meat, vegetables, sauces and soups.
- Pieces that are about equal in size and shape will cook more uniformly.
- You can reduce the liquid used in cooking beverages, soups, vegetables, fruits and main dishes by about one third because less evaporates in microwave cooking.
- Choose a microwave-safe container slightly larger than the dish required for cooking the recipe in a conventional oven.
- Use a high setting (100 percent power) for soups, beverages, fruits, vegetables, fish, ground meat and poultry. Use a medium-high setting (70 percent power) for simmering stews and a medium setting (50 percent power) for baking breads, cakes and muffins, and cooking less tender cuts of meat.
- To create a crusty look on baked items, grease pans with an acceptable vegetable oil and add ground nuts or crumbs.
- Add lowfat cheese and other toppings near the end of cooking to keep the top from becoming tough or soggy.
- Stay away from coating meat with flour if you will be adding liquid for cooking. The coatings become soggy.
- Use quick-cooking instead of long-grain rice.

Steaming. Cooking food in a basket over simmering water leaves the natural flavor, color and nutritional value of vegetables intact. Try adding herbs to the steaming water or using broth instead to add even more flavor to the finished dish.

ADDITIONAL TIPS

There are many variables in making your food heart-healthy. There are lots of little ways to trim cholesterol, fat, salt and calories without trimming taste. There are also ways to enhance the flavors of your selected foods—and some special ways to handle food. The following tips may come in handy.

- Trim all visible fat from meat before cooking.
- After you roast meat or poultry, chill the drippings in the refrigerator. Once cooled, the fat will rise to the top and harden; you can remove it easily and save the stock to use in stews, sauces and soups.
- Buy only the leanest ground beef, pork and turkey (no more than 15 percent fat). After browning, put ground meat into a strainer or colander lined with paper towels. Allow fat to drain out. "Ground" meat is generally higher in fat than nonground meat. Even the leanest ground beef contains more fat than is recommended for those on the Step-Two Diet. Instead of buying prepackaged ground beef, have your butcher grind a sirloin steak for you. Be sure to have him remove all visible fat and clean the grinder to remove any fat from previous grindings.
- When figuring serving sizes, remember that meat loses about 25 percent of its weight during cooking. (For example, 4 ounces of raw meat will be about 3 ounces cooked.)
- To make gravy without fat, blend a tablespoon of cornstarch with a cup of room-temperature broth by shaking the two together in a tightly lidded jar. Then heat the rest of the broth in a saucepan and add the blended liquid. Simmer until thickened.
- Make a habit of skinning chickens before cooking and removing all visible fat below the skin. The skin will be easier to remove if you use paper towels or a clean cloth to take hold of it. Be certain to scrub the cutting surface and utensils well with hot sudsy water after preparing poultry for cooking.
- Fresh fish should be cooked for ten minutes per inch of thickness. Add five minutes if it's wrapped in foil. Frozen fish requires twenty minutes per inch of thickness, plus ten minutes if it's wrapped in foil. Cooking time may vary, depending on the cooking method used, but fish is done when the flesh is opaque and it flakes easily.
- Prepare scrambled eggs or omelettes so that only one egg yolk per portion is used. Add a few extra egg whites to the mixing bowl to make more generous servings.
- To remove oils or salty liquids, drain canned salmon, tuna or sardines. Then add water to the can and drain again to rinse.
- Seal natural juices into foods by wrapping them in foil before cooking. Or try wrapping foods in edible pouches made of steamed lettuce or cabbage leaves.

- Cook vegetables just long enough to make them tender-crisp. Overcooked vegetables lose both flavor and important nutrients.
- Clean mushrooms as you use them by wiping them with a damp cloth. A quick rinse in cold water is fine, but never soak them or they'll get soggy.
- Be sure to wear rubber gloves when handling hot peppers or wash hands thoroughly after handling. Skin, especially around the eyes, is very sensitive to the oil from peppers.
- Cut down on cholesterol by using more vegetables and less poultry or meats in soups, stews and casseroles. Finely chopped vegetables are great for stretching ground poultry or meat, too.
- Cut down on fat in creamy salad dressing by mixing it with plain lowfat yogurt.
- Sweeten plain lowfat or nonfat yogurt with pureed fruit or applesauce instead of buying prepared fruit yogurt.

RECIPE SUBSTITUTIONS

You probably have quite a few favorite recipes you hate to give up as you start your heart-healthy diet program. The happy fact is, you can salvage many of them simply by making a few simple adaptations and substitutions.

WHEN YOUR OWN RECIPE CALLS FOR:	USE:
Sour cream	Mock Sour Cream (see recipe page 26); lowfat cottage cheese plus lowfat yogurt for flavor; ricotta cheese made from partially skimmed milk (thinned with yogurt or buttermilk, if desired); one can of chilled evaporated skim milk whipped with one teaspoon of lemon juice; or lowfat buttermilk or lowfat yogurt.
Whipped Cream	Creamy Dessert Topping or Mock Whipped Cream (see recipes pages 193 and 234).
Unsweetened Baking Chocolate	Unsweetened cocoa powder or carob powder blended with unsaturated oil or margarine (one 1-ounce square of chocolate = 3 tablespoons of cocoa or carob plus 1 tablespoon polyunsaturated oil or margarine). Because carob is sweeter than cocoa reduce the sugar in the recipe by one fourth.
Butter	Unsaturated margarine or oil. (One tablespoon butter = 1 tablespoon margarine or ¾ tablespoon oil.) If you wish to substitute margarine for oil, use 1¼ cups margarine for 1 cup of oil. Use 1¼ tablespoons of margarine for 1 tablespoon of oil.
Eggs	Use commercially produced, cholesterol-free egg substitutes according to package directions. Or use one egg white plus 2 teaspoons of unsaturated oil for each egg.
	For each two whole eggs in baking recipes, substitute three egg whites. For one whole large egg, substitute two egg whites. The table on how eggs add up on page 277 will show you the approximate whole egg content of various prepared foods.
Whole Milk	Use 1 cup of skim or nonfat milk plus 1 tablespoon of unsaturated oil as a substitute for 1 cup of whole milk.
Cream Cheese	Blend 4 tablespoons of margarine with 1 cup dry lowfat cottage cheese. Add a small amount of skim milk if needed in blending mixture. Vegetables such as chopped chives or pimiento and herbs and seasonings may be added for variety.

MOCK SOUR CREAM

MAKES ABOUT 1 ¼ CUPS, CONTAINING ABOUT 200 CALORIES

2 tablespoons skim milk
1 tablespoon lemon juice
1 cup lowfat cottage cheese

Place all ingredients in a blender and combine on medium-high speed until smooth and creamy.

SOME ADDITIONAL SUBSTITUTION IDEAS

- Use evaporated skim milk for cream when making whipped topping. (Be aware that the evaporated milk won't whip unless it's well chilled first.)
- Substitute plain lowfat or nonfat yogurt for sour cream in baking recipes.
- Substitute plain lowfat or nonfat yogurt for sour cream in sauces. Mix 1 tablespoon of cornstarch with 1 tablespoon of yogurt and mix into the yogurt. It will prevent the yogurt from separating.
- Try plain lowfat or nonfat yogurt or buttermilk in place of sour cream or mayonnaise in salad dressing recipes.
- Substitute lowfat or skim milk for cream or whole milk in baking recipes.
- Thicken soups, stews or sauces with cornstarch or flour dissolved in cold liquid or with pureed vegetables.
- Substitute chopped vegetables for some of the bread when you make poultry stuffing.
- Since most recipes include more sugar than necessary, you can usually reduce the amount of sugar by one fourth to one third.
- Reduce salt in nonyeast baking recipes.
- Substitute herbs and seasonings for salt as you cook. See below for herb seasoning recipes.
- Substitute onion or garlic flakes or powder for onion salt and garlic salt.
- Add a drop of lemon juice to the water you cook pasta in and eliminate the salt.
- Substitute brown rice for white rice to add whole-grain roughage.
- Use a blend of whole-wheat flour and all-purpose flour in recipes that call for regular flour.
- Use wheat germ, bran and whole-wheat bread crumbs in place of buttered crumbs to top casseroles.
- Using vegetable oil for shortening in cakes that require creaming will affect the texture. Use margarine instead; use vegetable oil in recipes calling for melted butter.

HERB SEASONING

½ teaspoon cayenne pepper
1 tablespoon garlic powder
1 teaspoon dried basil
1 teaspoon dried marjoram
1 teaspoon dried thyme
1 teaspoon dried parsley
1 teaspoon dried savory
1 teaspoon mace
1 teaspoon onion powder
1 teaspoon freshly ground black pepper
1 teaspoon powdered sage

MAKES APPROXIMATELY ⅓ CUP

Use this in casseroles, stews or fresh vegetable dishes. It makes a great substitute for salt.

Combine all ingredients in medium bowl. Toss gently with spoon until well blended. Store in an airtight container in a cool, dry, dark place for up to six months.

LEMON HERB SEASONING

4½ tablespoons dried basil
3¾ tablespoons dried oregano
1½ tablespoons powdered black pepper
1½ tablespoons granulated onion
1½ tablespoons whole celery seed
1¼ tablespoons powdered basil
½ teaspoon granulated garlic
½ teaspoon lemon rind, grated (optional)

MAKES APPROXIMATELY 1 CUP

The flavors of the blended spices of this mix mingle well with the flavors of fish, chicken or turkey. For extra lemony flavor, add seasoning mix to meat and then sprinkle with fresh lemon juice.

Combine all ingredients in medium bowl. Toss gently with spoon until well blended. Store in an airtight container in a cool, dry, dark place for up to six months.

SALAD HERB BLEND

**MAKES
APPROXIMATELY
1 CUP**

For a salad bursting with flavor, sprinkle this on before adding dressing.

¼ cup dried parsley
¼ cup dried marjoram
2½ tablespoons dried basil
1½ tablespoons sesame seeds
1½ tablespoons chili pepper flakes
1½ tablespoons powdered rosemary
1¼ tablespoons powdered celery seed
2½ teaspoons dried savory
2½ teaspoons powdered sage
2¼ teaspoons dried thyme
2 teaspoons granulated onion
2 teaspoons dried dillweed
1¼ teaspoons powdered black pepper
¾ teaspoon granulated garlic

Combine all ingredients in medium bowl. Toss gently with spoon until well blended. Store in an airtight container in a cool, dry, dark place for up to six months.

HOW TO USE THESE RECIPES

The recipes in this book have been analyzed by computer. Each analysis is based on a single serving, except where indicated otherwise. The number of calories and the amount of protein, carbohydrates, total fat, saturated fatty acids, polyunsaturated fatty acids, monounsaturated fatty acids, cholesterol and sodium per serving has been calculated. The values for saturated, monounsaturated and polyunsaturated fatty acids will not add up precisely to the total fat in the recipe because the total fat includes not only fatty acids, but other fatty substances and glycerol. The values are as accurate as possible.

The caloric values are for physiological energy values. They represent the energy values remaining after the losses in digestion and metabolism have been deducted from the gross energy. Caloric values are based on the Atwater system for determining energy values.

In the recipes calling for vegetable oil, choose corn, safflower or sunflower oil because they contain polyunsaturated fat. Canola or olive oil are acceptable monounsaturated oils. You may also use peanut oil occasionally for variety.

The nutritional information for a serving of a particular recipe includes such additions as salad dressings and garnishes. However, nutritional information is provided for each salad dressing.

The calories in alcohol evaporate when heated, and this reduction is reflected in the calculations.

When a marinade is used, the total amount of the marinade is calculated.

Salt is not used in most of these recipes, and where it is used, the amount is very small. The analyses therefore also include salt where applicable, although salt is often marked as optional.

All serving sizes and figures for total amount made are approximate.

Specific ingredients listed were used in the analysis. However, use your own judgment when selecting ingredients. For example, when the recipe calls for fresh lemon juice and you have only reconstituted lemon juice, use it. Other ingredients can also be substituted if necessary. For example, yellow onions and red wine vinegar can be replaced with white onions and apple cider vinegar. Several recipes give optional ingredients. Let your individual taste be your guide —and enjoy the heart-healthy food you create!

RECIPES

Appetizers and Spreads

ARTICHOKE AND SPINACH SPREAD

1 10-ounce package frozen, chopped spinach
1 14-ounce can artichoke hearts, drained and
   rinsed
¾ cup Double-Thick Yogurt (see page 262)
½ cup coarsely chopped fresh parsley
⅓ cup coarsely chopped green onions, including
   tops
¼ cup prepared reduced-calorie ranch dressing
Freshly ground black pepper to taste

S E R V E S   1 0
¼ C U P P E R
S E R V I N G

*Use this versatile spread
instead of mayonnaise on
sandwiches. Also try it as
a dip with crudites or Pita
Crisps (see page 214).*

Thaw and drain spinach, squeezing out excess
liquid. In a blender or the workbowl of a food
processor fitted with a metal blade, combine all
ingredients and process until smooth, but not
completely pureed. Refrigerate for at least 1 hour
before serving.

**N U T R I E N T
A N A L Y S I S**

Calories	32.87kcal
Protein	1.77gm
Carbohydrate	5.62gm
Total Fat	1.76gm
Saturated	0.01gm
Polyunsaturated	0.04gm
Monounsaturated	0.01gm
Cholesterol	0.00mg
Sodium	71.35mg

ZUCCHINI SPREAD

SERVES 8
¼ CUP PER
SERVING

A food processor makes preparation simple! Serve with crackers, vegetable sticks or rounds of crusty French bread. Or, use as a sandwich spread. For example, line a pita half with zucchini spread and stuff with vegetables.

NUTRIENT
ANALYSIS*

Calories	38.14kcal
Protein	1.05gm
Carbohydrate	2.65gm
Total Fat	2.95gm
Saturated	0.36gm
Polyunsaturated	0.93gm
Monounsaturated	1.43gm
Cholesterol	0.00mg
Sodium	66.99mg

* For entire recipe.

3½ cups unpeeled, shredded zucchini, about 3
    small zucchini
1 tablespoon olive oil
2 tablespoons red wine vinegar
¼ cup finely chopped fresh parsley or cilantro
1 clove garlic, minced
¼ teaspoon salt (optional)
Freshly ground black pepper to taste
2 tablespoons finely chopped walnuts or pecans

Squeeze zucchini to remove excess water. In a blender or the workbowl of a food processor fitted with a metal blade, combine zucchini, oil, vinegar, parsley or cilantro, garlic, salt and pepper. Process until smooth, scraping down sides as needed. Spoon mixture into serving container and fold in nuts. Cover and chill before serving.

HUMMUS (CHICKPEA DIP)

1 19-ounce can chickpeas, rinsed and drained
½ cup fresh lemon juice
¼ cup tahini
2 cloves garlic, minced
1 teaspoon acceptable vegetable oil
½ teaspoon ground cumin, or to taste
⅛ teaspoon cayenne pepper (optional)
Freshly ground black pepper to taste
¼ teaspoon salt (optional)
¼ cup water
½ cup finely chopped fresh parsley

SERVES 8
¼ CUP PER SERVING

Hummus is a Middle-Eastern specialty traditionally served with flat Syrian bread, warm pita or as a dip for raw vegetables. It is an excellent source of protein, and this recipe is lower in fat than the usual version.

Tahini, a sesame seed paste, is found in health-food stores and some supermarkets. If unavailable, it can be made by blending together ½ cup sesame seeds, 1 tablespoon water, 1 tablespoon lemon juice and a few drops of vegetable oil.

In a blender or a food processor fitted with a metal blade, combine chickpeas, lemon juice, tahini, garlic, oil, cumin, cayenne, pepper, salt and water. Blend, scraping sides occasionally. If mixture is too thick, add more water, a few drops at a time. The mixture should be a smooth paste. Stir in parsley.

Hummus tastes best when refrigerated for 24 hours before serving, allowing the flavors to blend.

NUTRIENT ANALYSIS

Calories	176.57kcal
Protein	8.74gm
Carbohydrate	22.31gm
Total Fat	6.79gm
Saturated	0.86gm
Polyunsaturated	3.01gm
Monounsaturated	2.24gm
Cholesterol	0.00mg
Sodium	82.43mg

APPLE-ALMOND BUTTER

SERVES 20
1 TABLESPOON
PER SERVING

Apple butter is available in supermarkets and health food stores. Apple-Almond Butter tastes great on whole wheat toast or English muffins.

NUTRIENT ANALYSIS

Calories	70.99kcal
Protein	1.37gm
Carbohydrate	8.58gm
Total Fat	3.92gm
Saturated	0.31gm
Polyunsaturated	0.74gm
Monounsaturated	2.63gm
Cholesterol	0.00mg
Sodium	0.62mg

1 cup whole almonds, with skins
1 cup sweetened apple butter

Preheat oven to 375° F.

Toast almonds in a single layer on a baking pan for 5 to 10 minutes, or until golden, turning once. Put into workbowl of a food processor fitted with metal blade and process continuously, scraping sides as needed, until almonds become a thick paste. (At first almonds become powdery, like almond meal; then if you keep processing, you will get almond butter, a thick paste.) Add apple butter and continue to process, scraping sides as needed, until mixture is smooth. Refrigerate.

BETTER PEANUT BUTTER

½ cup peanut butter
1 cup carrots, sliced and cooked
¼ cup raisins

**SERVES 12
1 TABLESPOON
PER SERVING**

In the workbowl of a food processor fitted with a metal blade, process peanut butter and carrots until fully mixed. Place in a bowl and add raisins. Stir to mix thoroughly. Refrigerate 24 hours for the full flavor to develop. Use within two more days for best flavor and consistency.

Peanut butter is very high in fat. To reduce the fat and still retain the "peanutty" taste, mix a little peanut butter with a lot of carrots. Try it spread on bread, toast or crackers. Even teenagers may ask for seconds. Select a peanut butter that contains only peanuts, with or without salt. Avoid those with sugar and hydrogenated oils.

**NUTRIENT
ANALYSIS**

Calories	66.17kcal
Protein	2.41gm
Carbohydrate	4.95gm
Total Fat	4.60gm
Saturated	0.88gm
Polyunsaturated	1.32gm
Monounsaturated	2.16gm
Cholesterol	0.00mg
Sodium	117.48mg

RICE CAKE AND CHEESE SNACK

SERVES 2
1 RICE CAKE PER SERVING

Try this for an easy-to-fix snack. It's a great after-school treat for kids—and an anytime treat for adults.

NUTRIENT ANALYSIS

Calories	29.18kcal
Protein	1.22gm
Carbohydrate	6.13gm
Total Fat	0.20gm
Saturated	0.02gm
Polyunsaturated	0.07gm
Monounsaturated	0.02gm
Cholesterol	2.58mg
Sodium	31.60mg

2 rice cakes, unsalted
1 teaspoon prepared yellow mustard
¼ cup Defatted Cheddar Cheese (see page 261), grated

Preheat oven to 350° F.

Place rice cakes on baking sheet or aluminum foil and bake 3 to 4 minutes, or until crisp. Remove from oven, spread with mustard and top with cheese. Return to oven and bake 3 to 4 minutes, or just until cheese melts. Serve immediately.

STUFFED MUSHROOMS

18 large mushrooms
1 tablespoon olive oil
¼ cup minced onion
1 clove garlic, minced
¼ cup finely chopped walnuts
1 shredded wheat biscuit, crushed
1 tablespoon grated Parmesan cheese
½ teaspoon Herb Seasoning (see page 27)
Freshly ground black pepper to taste
½ teaspoon paprika (optional)

SERVES 6
3 MUSHROOMS
PER SERVING

This hot appetizer is an ideal party food. Prepare it an hour in advance and put it in the oven as guests arrive. The aroma is mouth-watering!

Preheat oven to 350° F.

Clean mushrooms with a vegetable brush or wipe with a damp cloth. Remove and finely chop stems. Heat oil in a nonstick skillet over medium-high heat. Sauté chopped mushroom stems, onions, garlic and walnuts until onion is tender, 4 to 5 minutes. Remove from heat. Stir in shredded wheat, Parmesan cheese, herb seasoning and pepper. Stuff mushroom caps, packing mixture firmly. Arrange mushrooms in a shallow baking dish. Sprinkle tops lightly with paprika. Bake 20 to 25 minutes, or until mushrooms are tender.

NUTRIENT ANALYSIS

Calories	86.08kcal
Protein	2.76gm
Carbohydrate	6.65gm
Total Fat	5.98gm
Saturated	0.88gm
Polyunsaturated	2.39gm
Monounsaturated	2.26gm
Cholesterol	0.82mg
Sodium	26.15mg

BAKED GARLIC

SERVES 6
⅓ GARLIC HEAD PER SERVING

This dish has a surprisingly mild taste. For a delicious appetizer, spread the garlic over thin slices of French bread or Melba toast.

NUTRIENT ANALYSIS

Calories	27.23kcal
Protein	0.93gm
Carbohydrate	4.63gm
Total Fat	0.78gm
Saturated	0.11gm
Polyunsaturated	0.08gm
Monounsaturated	0.55gm
Cholesterol	0.00mg
Sodium	2.86mg

2 large heads garlic
1 teaspoon olive oil

Preheat oven to 350° F.

Do not remove the paper skin from the garlic. Cut each head of garlic in half horizontally. Drizzle ¼ teaspoon oil on cut side of each half of garlic. Place halves together and wrap securely in foil. Bake 1 hour, or until soft.

Remove from oven and allow to cool slightly. When cool enough to touch, squeeze the garlic from the skin onto a small plate.

POTATO SKINS

4 teaspoons nonfat "butter" granules
6 medium baking potatoes, scrubbed and baked
½ teaspoon garlic powder
Freshly ground black pepper to taste

Preheat oven to 450° F.

Reconstitute the "butter" granules according to the directions on the package.

Cut each potato in half. Scoop out the center, leaving about ¼ inch of potato on the inside of each skin. (Use leftover potato to make Shepherd's Pie, see page 130.) Cut skins into quarters. Dab liquid butter substitute onto the white side of each potato skin. Sprinkle with garlic powder and pepper, if desired.

Place prepared skins, skin-side down, on a baking sheet. Bake 15 minutes, or until lightly browned. Turn skins over and bake another 5 minutes, or until crisp. Serve immediately.

SERVES 12
4 PER SERVING

These are perfect for entertaining or just for snacking.

NUTRIENT ANALYSIS

Calories	27.93kcal
Protein	0.74gm
Carbohydrate	6.32gm
Total Fat	0.06gm
Saturated	0.00gm
Polyunsaturated	0.03gm
Monounsaturated	0.00gm
Cholesterol	0.01mg
Sodium	29.40mg

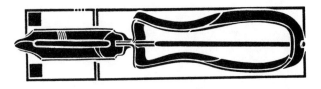

CHICKEN TRIANGLES

SERVES 12
2 PER SERVING

These are neat little phyllo triangles of ''garlicky'' chicken. They're great as nibbles, hors d'oeuvres or a side dish.

Phyllo is a paper-thin dough, available frozen in 1-pound packages of about 24 sheets in most large supermarkets and specialty stores. Phyllo should be defrosted in the refrigerator. Unopened, the defrosted dough will keep for a month, if refrigerated. Refreezing can make the dough crumbly. When working with the dough, keep it covered with a damp cloth to prevent drying.

NUTRIENT ANALYSIS

Calories	95.92kcal
Protein	8.76gm
Carbohydrate	5.83gm
Total Fat	4.05gm
Saturated	0.72gm
Polyunsaturated	1.13gm
Monounsaturated	1.87gm
Cholesterol	19.19mg
Sodium	94.56mg

*1 pound boneless chicken breasts, skinned, all
    visible fat removed*
½ tablespoon olive oil
2 tablespoons lemon juice
2 cloves garlic, minced
1 tablespoon minced fresh parsley
*1 tablespoon fresh or ½ teaspoon dried tarragon,
    oregano or basil*
¼ teaspoon salt (optional)
10 sheets phyllo pastry
3 tablespoons acceptable margarine, melted

Finely chop chicken. Combine oil, lemon juice, garlic, parsley, tarragon and salt in a small bowl. Add chicken and toss to coat. Cover and refrigerate for at least 1 hour.

Preheat oven to 400° F.

Lightly brush a sheet of phyllo with melted margarine. Stack a second sheet on top. Cut the two-layer sheet into five short strips, crosswise, with scissors or a sharp knife.

Place a teaspoon of chicken filling on a two-layer strip, 1 inch away from the bottom. Fold a corner across the filling and continue folding, corner to corner (the way a flag is folded). The filling expands during cooking, so do not fold the dough too tightly. Tuck the excess dough under the triangle, then place on a baking sheet. Repeat with the remaining eight sheets of phyllo and chicken. Lightly brush the prepared triangles with melted margarine. Bake 15 to 20 minutes, or until golden brown.

To freeze for later use, place unbaked triangles on baking sheets and freeze. Store frozen triangles in freezer in plastic freezer bags. To bake, place on baking sheets in a preheated 400° F. oven, 20 to 25 minutes.

SCALLOP AND HAM ROLL-UPS

24 sea scallops, about ¾ pound
6 ounces thinly sliced lean ham, visible fat removed
24 pineapple chunks, canned in their own juice,
    about ½ of a 20-ounce can
24 toothpicks soaked in water for at least 30
    minutes

Preheat broiler.

If the muscle is still attached to the scallop, remove it. Cut ham into approximately 6- × 1¼-inch strips. Wrap one strip around each scallop and skewer with a toothpick. Add one pineapple chunk to each toothpick. Place prepared toothpicks on a baking pan with sides.

Broil five inches from heat for 4 minutes. Turn scallops and broil another 3 minutes. Serve hot.

SERVES 12
2 PER SERVING

Soaking toothpicks before using helps prevent charring the wood when broiling.

NUTRIENT ANALYSIS

Calories	50.64kcal
Protein	7.48gm
Carbohydrate	1.85gm
Total Fat	1.35gm
Saturated	0.42gm
Polyunsaturated	0.21gm
Monounsaturated	0.49gm
Cholesterol	19.58mg
Sodium	140.27mg

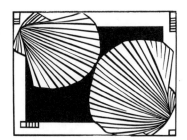

MELON BALLS WITH TURKEY AND HAM

**SERVES 15
3 BALLS PER
SERVING**

This is an easy-to-fix appetizer that combines fresh melons with ham, chicken and a tangy-sweet, minted mustard dip.

NUTRIENT ANALYSIS

Calories	89.07kcal
Protein	5.46gm
Carbohydrate	13.94gm
Total Fat	1.93gm
Saturated	0.51gm
Polyunsaturated	0.27gm
Monounsaturated	0.67gm
Cholesterol	13.33mg
Sodium	144.30mg

1 medium honeydew melon, cut in half and seeded
1 medium cantaloupe melon, cut in half and seeded
4 ounces thinly sliced lean ham, visible fat removed
4 ounces thinly sliced turkey

DIPPING SAUCE
¼ cup spicy brown mustard
2 tablespoons honey
12 fresh mint leaves, chopped

Using the large side of a melon-baller, make balls from the melons; set aside. Cut the ham and turkey into 4 × 1-inch strips. Wrap each melon ball in either a strip of ham or turkey and skewer with a toothpick.

In a small bowl, combine sauce ingredients. Serve with wrapped melon balls.

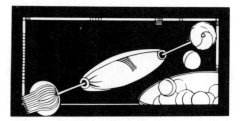

Soups

Country-Style Vegetable Soup
Light and Lemony Chicken and Spinach Soup
Lentil-Spinach Soup
Mock Condensed Cream of Chicken Soup
Mock Condensed Cream of Mushroom Soup
Mock Condensed Cream of Celery Soup
Cream of Corn Soup
Split Pea Soup
Tomato Soup
Tomato, Orange and Tarragon Soup
Fresh Melon and Mango Soup
Yogurt Gazpacho

COUNTRY-STYLE VEGETABLE SOUP

1 medium onion, chopped
4 large carrots, chopped
1 pound potatoes, scrubbed and chopped, about 3
    medium potatoes
3 stalks celery, chopped
2 medium zucchini, chopped
¼ teaspoon salt (optional)
Freshly ground black pepper to taste
2 bay leaves
¼ cup finely chopped fresh parsley
6 cups homemade Chicken Stock (see page 263)
6 ounces (¾ cup) Defatted Cheddar Cheese,
    crumbled (see page 261)

In a large heavy saucepan or Dutch oven, combine onion, carrots, potatoes, celery, zucchini, salt, pepper, bay leaves and parsley. Cover with stock, bring to a boil and simmer, covered, 45 to 60 minutes, or until vegetables are very tender. Remove bay leaves.

Serve hot, topped with cheese.

**SERVES 10
APPROXIMATELY 1
CUP PER SERVING**

A great anytime dish, this hearty soup is an excellent way to take advantage of an abundant supply of fresh vegetables. It can be served as an appetizer or a main lunch course.

NUTRIENT ANALYSIS

Calories	120.41kcal
Protein	9.08gm
Carbohydrate	17.20gm
Total Fat	6.00gm
Saturated	1.27gm
Polyunsaturated	0.15gm
Monounsaturated	0.40gm
Cholesterol	7.58mg
Sodium	147.36mg

LIGHT AND LEMONY CHICKEN AND SPINACH SOUP

SERVES 2 APPROXIMATELY 1 CUP PER SERVING

The unusual flavor combination makes this a wonderful winter soup.

NUTRIENT ANALYSIS

Calories	56.36kcal
Protein	5.76gm
Carbohydrate	8.12gm
Total Fat	0.88gm
Saturated	0.18gm
Polyunsaturated	0.30gm
Monounsaturated	0.17gm
Cholesterol	6.80mg
Sodium	208.78mg

2 cups homemade Chicken Stock (see page 263)
2 teaspoons fresh lemon juice
¼ teaspoon dried thyme, crushed
⅛ teaspoon salt (optional)
4 leaves spinach or other greens such as escarole,
  rinsed and torn
Top of 1 green onion, thinly sliced

In a 1-quart saucepan, bring stock, lemon juice, thyme and salt to a boil. Put torn leaves of fresh spinach into individual soup bowls and pour hot soup over them. Top with green onions. Serve immediately.

LENTIL-SPINACH SOUP

2 tablespoons olive oil
1 large onion, chopped
1 pound lentils, rinsed and drained
4 cups homemade Chicken Stock (see page 263)
4 cups water
1 pound fresh spinach, washed, stemmed and torn
  into bite-size pieces, or 1 10-ounce package
  frozen, chopped spinach, defrosted and squeezed
  dry
½ teaspoon freshly ground black pepper, or to taste
⅛ teaspoon ground allspice
4 ounces shredded part-skim mozzarella cheese or
  4 ounces lightly beaten, plain, nonfat yogurt

**SERVES 8
APPROXIMATELY 1½
CUPS PER SERVING**

*The cheese or yogurt
completes the protein in
the lentils, making this
delicious soup a
nourishing, high-protein
main dish. This is a good
recipe to double and
freeze. Omit the cheese or
yogurt when freezing.*

In large stock pot or Dutch oven, heat oil over medium-high heat. Add onion and sauté until golden brown, 3 to 4 minutes. Stir in lentils, stock and water. Bring to a boil, reduce heat and cover. Simmer 45 to 60 minutes, or until lentils are tender, stirring occasionally.

Stir in spinach, pepper and allspice. Simmer, covered, 15 minutes longer. Thin the soup with additional chicken stock or water, if desired.

Serve hot, topped with either shredded cheese or whipped yogurt.

**NUTRIENT
ANALYSIS***

Calories	135.43kcal
Protein	8.24gm
Carbohydrate	18.04gm
Total Fat	4.49gm
Saturated	0.65gm
Polyunsaturated	0.72gm
Monounsaturated	2.68gm
Cholesterol	3.65mg
Sodium	54.87mg

* Made with yogurt.

MOCK CONDENSED CREAM OF CHICKEN SOUP

MAKES ABOUT 1⅓ CUPS

Here is a recipe for a healthful condensed cream of chicken soup. It is excellent for use in other recipes—just use this when the recipe calls for the canned counterpart.

NUTRIENT ANALYSIS*

Calories	407.00kcal
Protein	32.66gm
Carbohydrate	29.84gm
Total Fat	17.10gm
Saturated	2.66gm
Polyunsaturated	8.79gm
Monounsaturated	4.25gm
Cholesterol	68.44mg
Sodium	643.19mg

* For entire recipe.

1 cup homemade Chicken Stock (see page 263)
1 bay leaf
¼ pound boneless chicken breast, skinned, all visible fat removed
1 tablespoon acceptable vegetable oil
3 tablespoons all-purpose flour
⅓ cup skim milk
1 tablespoon nonfat "butter" granules
Freshly ground black pepper to taste
⅛ teaspoon garlic powder
⅛ teaspoon salt (optional)

In a small saucepan, heat stock and bay leaf, uncovered, over medium-high setting until liquid simmers. Add chicken. When stock begins to simmer again, reduce heat, cover and simmer about 5 minutes, or until chicken is no longer pink inside. Remove from heat. Remove chicken from stock and set aside.

In a small saucepan, heat oil over medium heat. Add flour, stirring constantly for 1 minute. Gradually add the stock (with bay leaf), milk, "butter" granules and pepper, stirring constantly until mixture thickens, about 2 to 3 minutes. Remove from heat. Remove and discard bay leaf.

Pour into a blender or the workbowl of a food processor fitted with the metal blade and blend until smooth. Add cooked chicken, garlic powder and salt. Blend until pureed.

MOCK CONDENSED CREAM OF MUSHROOM SOUP

1 6-ounce can or jar sliced mushrooms
1 tablespoon acceptable vegetable oil
3 tablespoons all-purpose flour
1 bay leaf
⅓ cup skim milk
1 tablespoon nonfat "butter" granules
Freshly ground black pepper to taste
⅛ teaspoon garlic powder

MAKES ABOUT 1⅓ CUPS

This soup tastes incredibly similar to the store-bought version, yet it's lower in fat and sodium. Use this when a recipe calls for condensed cream of mushroom soup.

Drain the liquid from the mushrooms into a measuring cup and add water, if needed, to bring the total liquid to ½ cup. Set aside.

In a small saucepan, heat oil over medium heat. Add flour and bay leaf, stirring constantly for 1 minute. Gradually add mushroom liquid, milk, "butter" granules and pepper, stirring constantly until mixture thickens, about 2 to 3 minutes. Remove pan from heat. Remove and discard bay leaf.

Pour into a blender or the workbowl of a food processor fitted with a metal blade and blend until smooth. Add mushrooms and garlic powder. Blend until pureed.

NUTRIENT ANALYSIS*

Calories	274.44kcal
Protein	7.90gm
Carbohydrate	29.33gm
Total Fat	14.44gm
Saturated	1.91gm
Polyunsaturated	8.22gm
Monounsaturated	3.37gm
Cholesterol	1.68mg
Sodium	851.96mg

* For entire recipe.

MOCK CONDENSED CREAM OF CELERY SOUP

MAKES ABOUT 1⅓ CUPS

When a recipe calls for canned cream of celery soup, use this instead.

NUTRIENT ANALYSIS*

Calories	323.88kcal
Protein	11.36gm
Carbohydrate	37.57gm
Total Fat	14.99gm
Saturated	2.10gm
Polyunsaturated	8.24gm
Monounsaturated	3.51gm
Cholesterol	8.42mg
Sodium	782.82mg

* For entire recipe.

¾ cup homemade Chicken Stock (see page 263)
1 bay leaf
1 cup thinly sliced celery
1 tablespoon acceptable vegetable oil
3 tablespoons all-purpose flour
⅓ cup skim milk
1 tablespoon nonfat "butter" granules
Freshly ground black pepper to taste
⅛ teaspoon garlic powder
⅛ teaspoon salt (optional)

In a small saucepan, heat stock, bay leaf and celery, uncovered, over medium-high setting until liquid simmers. Reduce heat, cover and cook at a low simmer 10 minutes, or until celery is tender. Remove from heat. Remove celery from stock and set aside.

In a small saucepan, heat oil over medium heat. Add flour, stirring constantly for 1 minute. Gradually add the stock (with bay leaf), milk, "butter" granules and pepper, stirring constantly until mixture thickens, about 2 to 3 minutes. Remove from heat. Remove and discard bay leaf.

Pour into a blender or the workbowl of a food processor fitted with a metal blade and blend until smooth. Add celery, garlic powder and salt. Blend until celery is pureed.

CREAM OF CORN SOUP

2 cups fresh or frozen corn kernels
1 cup water
1 cup skim milk
¼ teaspoon freshly ground black pepper, or to taste
2 teaspoons low-sodium soy sauce
1 tablespoon cold water
1½ teaspoons cornstarch
3 egg whites from large eggs, lightly beaten
Hot pepper sauce to taste

In a blender or the workbowl of a food processor fitted with the metal blade, blend corn and water until creamy. Add milk and pepper.

In a 3-quart saucepan, heat mixture over medium-high heat to boiling. Reduce heat and simmer, covered, 5 minutes. In a small bowl, mix soy sauce and 1 tablespoon cold water; add cornstarch and stir to dissolve. Add cornstarch mixture to soup and stir to thicken.

Remove from heat and add egg whites, slowly, while stirring with a fork.

Serve hot. Season with hot sauce at the table.

**SERVES 6
APPROXIMATELY 1
CUP PER SERVING**

Try this recipe when fresh corn is plentiful. This flavorful and economical soup is a real family-pleaser—and easy to halve or double if you need to.

**NUTRIENT
ANALYSIS**

Calories	70.22kcal
Protein	4.92gm
Carbohydrate	13.44gm
Total Fat	0.36gm
Saturated	0.08gm
Polyunsaturated	0.15gm
Monounsaturated	0.08gm
Cholesterol	0.82mg
Sodium	121.40mg

SPLIT PEA SOUP

SERVES 10
APPROXIMATELY 1
CUP PER SERVING

*Traditional recipes for split
pea soup call for salt pork.
This recipe breaks with
tradition and uses ham
instead: you get the taste
without the fat. To cut
back on sodium, use low-
sodium soy sauce,
generally available in the
Asian or diet food section
of your supermarket.*

**NUTRIENT
ANALYSIS**

Calories	203.73kcal
Protein	14.68gm
Carbohydrate	34.50gm
Total Fat	2.57gm
Saturated	0.51gm
Polyunsaturated	0.85gm
Monounsaturated	0.64gm
Cholesterol	7.30mg
Sodium	310.93mg

1 pound dried split green peas, rinsed and drained
8 cups water
2 carrots, scrubbed but not peeled, cut into eighths
2 medium yellow onions, cut into eighths
3 cloves garlic, quartered
2 stalks celery with leaves, cut into eighths
*4 ounces lean ham, visible fat removed, cut into
    bite-size pieces*
3 tablespoons low-sodium soy sauce
*1 teaspoon chopped fresh oregano or ½ teaspoon
    dried oregano*
*½ teaspoon grated fresh ginger or ⅛ teaspoon
    dried ginger*
3 dashes hot pepper sauce, or to taste
Freshly ground black pepper to taste

In a large saucepan or Dutch oven, bring peas,
water, carrots, onions, garlic, celery and ham to a
rapid boil over medium-high heat. Reduce heat and
cook, covered, at a gently rolling boil, 1 to 1½
hours or until peas are soft.

Add soy sauce, oregano, ginger, hot pepper
sauce and pepper. Simmer 10 minutes to blend
flavors. In a blender or the workbowl of a food
processor fitted with a metal blade, process two to
three cups at a time, until puréed. Return to saucepan and reheat, if necessary. Serve hot.

This soup freezes well.

TOMATO SOUP

1 tablespoon olive oil
1 small onion, chopped
4 green onions, including tops, chopped
1 clove garlic, minced
2 tablespoons all-purpose flour
4 cups homemade Chicken Stock (see page 263)
3 medium ripe tomatoes (about 1 pound), chopped
½ teaspoon salt (optional)
Freshly ground black pepper to taste
½ teaspoon sugar
2 tablespoons chopped fresh dill or 1 teaspoon dried
    dill weed

GARNISH
½ cup plain nonfat yogurt, lightly beaten
2 tablespoons chopped fresh dill (optional)

SERVES 6
APPROXIMATELY 1
CUP PER SERVING

Fresh-picked tomatoes and fresh dill are perfect for this soup.

NUTRIENT ANALYSIS

Calories	109.21kcal
Protein	5.35gm
Carbohydrate	15.54gm
Total Fat	3.03gm
Saturated	0.43gm
Polyunsaturated	0.29gm
Monounsaturated	1.77gm
Cholesterol	4.85mg
Sodium	219.88mg

In a large saucepan, heat oil over medium-high heat. Add onions and sauté for 2 to 3 minutes or until translucent. Add garlic and flour; cook 1 minute, stirring constantly. Pour in stock and heat to boiling, stirring well to combine flour and liquid. Add tomatoes, salt, pepper, sugar and dill. Reduce heat and simmer, covered, 30 to 40 minutes, or until tomatoes are reduced to a pulp. Allow to cool for a few minutes, then purée in small batches in a blender or food processor. Reheat soup.

Serve hot. Drizzle about 1 tablespoon yogurt over each serving and sprinkle with dill.

TOMATO, ORANGE AND TARRAGON SOUP

SERVES 6
1½ CUPS PER SERVING

Establish your culinary reputation with this! A refreshing soup that can be served hot or cold is a sure winner.

NUTRIENT ANALYSIS

Calories	106.67kcal
Protein	3.46gm
Carbohydrate	17.68gm
Total Fat	2.76gm
Saturated	0.35gm
Polyunsaturated	1.41gm
Monounsaturated	0.60gm
Cholesterol	2.26mg
Sodium	105.83mg

1 tablespoon acceptable vegetable oil
1 medium yellow or white onion, sliced
3 small potatoes, diced
3 large tomatoes, about 3½ pounds, chopped
2 tablespoons chopped fresh tarragon or 1 teaspoon dried tarragon
1 clove garlic, crushed
2 cups homemade Chicken Stock (see page 263)
¼ teaspoon salt (optional)
Freshly ground black pepper to taste
1 cup freshly squeezed orange juice
1 teaspoon freshly grated orange rind

GARNISH

Few sprigs of parsley or tarragon

In a heavy saucepan, heat oil over medium-high heat. Sauté onions and potatoes 2 to 3 minutes, or until onions are translucent. Add tomatoes, tarragon, garlic, stock, salt and pepper. Bring to a boil, reduce heat and simmer, covered, 20 to 25 minutes, or until vegetables are tender.

In a blender or the workbowl of a food processor fitted with a metal blade, process in small batches until liquefied. Pass through a sieve to remove coarse skins. Discard the pulp that remains in the sieve.

Mix strained liquid with orange juice and rind. Reheat or serve chilled. Garnish with fresh tarragon or parsley.

FRESH MELON AND MANGO SOUP

2 medium peaches, peeled, pitted and cubed
2 large ripe mangos, peeled, pitted and cubed
1 small ripe cantaloupe, peeled, seeded and cubed
3 cups frozen unsweetened strawberries
⅓ cup frozen orange juice concentrate
½ cup plain, nonfat yogurt
Juice of ½ lime
⅓ cup port wine
2 tablespoons orange liqueur
1½ teaspoons raspberry vinegar (see page 90)

GARNISH
½ cup plain nonfat yogurt

In the workbowl of food processor fitted with a metal blade, process all ingredients until thick and creamy. Pour into a serving bowl and freeze for about 20 minutes. Spoon into individual bowls and garnish each serving with a heaping teaspoon of yogurt. Serve immediately.

**SERVES 14
APPROXIMATELY ½
CUP PER SERVING**

Soup made with melons?
You bet! With the wine
and liqueur, not only is
this soup beautiful, but it
has a delightful taste that
will surprise you.

**NUTRIENT
ANALYSIS**

Calories	72.46kcal
Protein	1.27gm
Carbohydrate	14.91gm
Total Fat	0.35gm
Saturated	0.03gm
Polyunsaturated	0.02gm
Monounsaturated	0.04gm
Cholesterol	0.14mg
Sodium	9.80mg

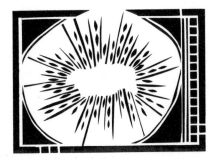

YOGURT GAZPACHO

SERVES 11
½ CUP PER
SERVING

You don't have to like yogurt to enjoy Yogurt Gazpacho. It's a sure hit when served as an appetizer before Chicken Fajitas (see page 116).

4 cups plain nonfat yogurt
¼ cup picante sauce
2 medium ripe tomatoes, quartered
3 green onions, including tops, quartered
⅛ teaspoon garlic powder
Fresh cilantro to taste

In a blender, process all ingredients. Pour into chilled stemware glasses and serve.

NUTRIENT
ANALYSIS

Calories	56.21kcal
Protein	5.16gm
Carbohydrate	8.46gm
Total Fat	0.21gm
Saturated	0.09gm
Polyunsaturated	0.00gm
Monounsaturated	0.03gm
Cholesterol	1.45mg
Sodium	119.83mg

Salads

Salad with Creamy Mustard Vinaigrette
Spinach Salad
Boston Lettuce with Grapefruit and Pecans
Crispy Tortilla Salad
Orange Blossom Salad
Warm Mushroom Salad
Potato Salad
Tabouli Salad
Marinated Vegetable Salad
Carrot and Cabbage Stuffed Peppers
Guacamole
Deviled Eggs
Cucumbers in "Sour Cream"
Cucumber-Melon Salad with Raspberry Vinaigrette
Fresh Fruit Salad
Fresh Fruit Salad with Poppy Seed and Yogurt Dressing
Herbed Chicken Salad
Ham and Rice Salad
Salmon and Pasta Salad
Seafood Pasta Salad

SALAD WITH CREAMY MUSTARD VINAIGRETTE

DRESSING
½ cup Oil and Vinegar Dressing (see page 87)
½ cup tofu, 4 ounces, drained
2 tablespoons water
½ teaspoon honey
½ teaspoon Dijon mustard

SALAD
1 head leaf lettuce or a mixture of lettuce greens,
    about ½ pound, rinsed and dried

GARNISH
3 dried apricots, slivered
2 teaspoons sunflower seeds, toasted

SERVES 8

This recipe makes a double batch of dressing (approximately 10 tablespoons). Use half for this recipe and save the rest for another salad.

NUTRIENT ANALYSIS

Calories	140.87kcal
Protein	3.45gm
Carbohydrate	5.69gm
Total Fat	12.41gm
Saturated	1.63gm
Polyunsaturated	1.44gm
Monounsaturated	7.92gm
Cholesterol	0.00mg
Sodium	15.93mg

Preheat oven to 300° F. Place sunflower seeds in baking pan and bake 12 minutes, or until very lightly browned. Remove from pan and let cool.

In a blender, process dressing ingredients until creamy.

Toss salad greens with 5 tablespoons of dressing and garnish with apricots and sunflower seeds. Refrigerate remainder of dressing for later use.

SPINACH SALAD

SERVES 6

This colorful salad makes a wonderful light lunch or a welcome accompaniment to dinner. The dressing is best made several hours ahead and refrigerated to allow the flavors to blend.

NUTRIENT ANALYSIS

Calories	90.19kcal
Protein	3.17gm
Carbohydrate	4.43gm
Total Fat	7.14gm
Saturated	0.93gm
Polyunsaturated	0.70gm
Monounsaturated	5.00gm
Cholesterol	0.00mg
Sodium	51.23mg

OIL AND VINEGAR DRESSING

3 tablespoons olive oil
3 tablespoons cider or wine vinegar
2 tablespoons water
1 to 2 teaspoons stone-ground mustard
1 tablespoon finely chopped fresh or ½ teaspoon
    dried herbs (parsley, basil, oregano, chives or
    tarragon)

SALAD

1½ pounds fresh spinach
2 hard-cooked eggs, whites only, chopped
12 cherry tomatoes, quartered
1 small red onion, cut into thin rings
Freshly ground black pepper to taste

Combine ingredients for dressing, mix well and refrigerate.

Thoroughly rinse spinach in cold water. Drain well. Remove and discard stems and bruised or tough leaves. Tear spinach into bite-size pieces, place in a large salad bowl and top with remaining salad ingredients.

Pour dressing over salad and serve immediately.

BOSTON LETTUCE WITH GRAPEFRUIT AND PECANS

1 large head Boston, butter or bibb lettuce, rinsed
   and dried
2 grapefruit
1 tablespoon fresh lemon juice
⅓ cup pecan pieces, toasted

Tear leaves for salad. Peel and section grapefruit, collecting the juice in a bowl. Mix in the lemon juice and pour over lettuce. Toss to coat evenly.

   Place lettuce on individual plates, and garnish each portion with several grapefruit sections and a sprinkling of pecan pieces.

SERVES 6

NUTRIENT ANALYSIS

Calories	88.56kcal
Protein	1.80gm
Carbohydrate	10.80gm
Total Fat	4.87gm
Saturated	0.41gm
Polyunsaturated	1.20gm
Monounsaturated	2.81gm
Cholesterol	0.00mg
Sodium	4.67mg

CRISPY TORTILLA SALAD

SERVES 6

This crispy, light Mexican-style salad is a favorite among chalupa lovers. Prepare the ingredients in advance and assemble them just before serving.

NUTRIENT ANALYSIS

Calories	276.35kcal
Protein	16.78gm
Carbohydrate	36.94gm
Total Fat	8.45gm
Saturated	4.27gm
Polyunsaturated	1.20gm
Monounsaturated	2.07gm
Cholesterol	20.93mg
Sodium	624.55mg

6 corn tortillas, 6-inch diameter
1 head iceberg lettuce, shredded, about 6 cups
4 ounces part-skim mozzarella cheese, shredded
2 ounces Defatted Cheddar Cheese (see page 261)
1 19-ounce can kidney beans, rinsed and drained
3 medium tomatoes, chopped
1 cup bottled or homemade Salsa (see page 191)

Preheat oven to 350° F. Bake tortillas in a single layer on a baking sheet for 10 to 15 minutes, or until crisp and lightly browned.

Top each tortilla with layers of shredded lettuce, cheeses, kidney beans, tomatoes and salsa. Serve with additional salsa on the side.

ORANGE BLOSSOM SALAD

3 navel oranges
4 large leaves of Boston, butter or bibb lettuce,
    rinsed and dried
Orange-flower water or orange liqueur (optional)
¼ cup slivered almonds, toasted

Remove the peel and pith from the oranges. Cut into ¼-inch slices. Place a lettuce leaf on each salad plate. Arrange orange slices on top. Put a few drops of orange-flower water or orange liqueur on each slice. Top with toasted almonds. Serve immediately.

SERVES 4

This recipe features orange-flower water, which is available at most Middle-Eastern markets and some liquor stores, pharmacies and supermarkets. This salad goes especially well with Marinated Steak or Poached Fish in Oriental Broth (see pages 127 and 95).

NUTRIENT ANALYSIS

Calories	125.94kcal
Protein	2.83gm
Carbohydrate	20.22gm
Total Fat	4.11gm
Saturated	0.34gm
Polyunsaturated	0.77gm
Monounsaturated	2.69gm
Cholesterol	0.00mg
Sodium	1.56mg

WARM MUSHROOM SALAD

SERVES 4
¼ CUP PER
SERVING

NUTRIENT
ANALYSIS

Calories	30.89kcal
Protein	1.84gm
Carbohydrate	3.98gm
Total Fat	1.17gm
Saturated	0.18gm
Polyunsaturated	0.38gm
Monounsaturated	0.43gm
Cholesterol	0.00mg
Sodium	23.40mg

2½ tablespoons balsamic or rice vinegar
1½ tablespoons water
3 tablespoons port wine (or any sweet red wine)
2 cloves garlic, finely minced
8 ounces fresh mushrooms, sliced into ¼-inch slices
1 teaspoon margarine
⅛ teaspoon freshly ground black pepper, or to taste
4 leaves of Boston lettuce, rinsed and dried
1 teaspoon chopped fresh parsley

In a nonstick skillet, heat vinegar, water, wine and garlic over medium-high heat until small bubbles begin to form. Add mushrooms and stir frequently 8 to 10 minutes, or until all liquid evaporates. Add margarine and pepper; stir to coat evenly.

Arrange mushrooms on lettuce leaves and sprinkle with chopped parsley. Serve warm.

POTATO SALAD

2 pounds potatoes, about 6 medium
2 green onions with tops, chopped
1 small red or green bell pepper, chopped
4 to 5 small radishes, minced
2 stalks celery, finely chopped
¼ cup finely chopped fresh parsley

DRESSING
¼ cup reduced-calorie mayonnaise
½ cup plain nonfat yogurt
2 tablespoons cider or wine vinegar
½ teaspoon salt (optional)
1 teaspoon Dijon mustard, or to taste
½ teaspoon celery seeds
1 tablespoon fresh dill weed or 1 teaspoon dried dill
   weed
Freshly ground black pepper to taste

GARNISH
2 tablespoons finely chopped fresh parsley
½ teaspoon paprika

Boil potatoes until tender. When cool enough to handle, peel and cut into ½-inch cubes. In a large bowl, combine potatoes with onions, bell pepper, radishes, celery and parsley. Mix together dressing ingredients and add to potato mixture. Toss gently.

Sprinkle parsley and paprika over the top. Cover and chill for at least 2 hours before serving.

**SERVES 8
1 CUP PER
SERVING**

A must for summer picnics and parties, this salad is best made at least a few hours in advance to allow the flavors to blend. The yogurt dressing is a low-fat version of an all-mayonnaise dressing.

**NUTRIENT
ANALYSIS**

Calories	113.25kcal
Protein	3.45gm
Carbohydrate	19.35gm
Total Fat	2.79gm
Saturated	0.54gm
Polyunsaturated	1.13gm
Monounsaturated	1.04gm
Cholesterol	5.25mg
Sodium	237.87mg

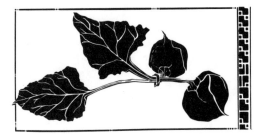

TABOULI SALAD

SERVES 6
**½ CUP PER
SERVING**

Make this dish well in advance—the flavors improve with age. Bulgar, a finely cracked wheat, is available at health-food stores and most supermarkets. To serve, place a scoop of the salad on a leaf of lettuce, or use it to stuff tomatoes, zucchini or peppers.

**NUTRIENT
ANALYSIS**

Calories	149.66kcal
Protein	3.64gm
Carbohydrate	23.39gm
Total Fat	5.06gm
Saturated	0.67gm
Polyunsaturated	0.57gm
Monounsaturated	3.37gm
Cholesterol	0.00mg
Sodium	6.02mg

1 cup bulgar
4 cups boiling water
2 tablespoons olive oil
¼ cup fresh lemon juice
3 green onions with tops, finely chopped
2 medium tomatoes, finely chopped
¼ cup finely chopped fresh mint or 1 tablespoon
   dried mint
¼ cup finely chopped fresh parsley
Freshly ground black pepper to taste

In a large heatproof bowl, combine bulgar and boiling water. Cover and allow to stand for 1 hour, or until most of the water is absorbed. Drain bulgar, using cheesecloth to help extract most of the moisture.

Combine oil and lemon juice. Add to bulgar along with onions, tomatoes, mint, parsley and pepper. Gently toss mixture with a fork and refrigerate at least 1 hour to allow flavors to blend. Serve chilled or at room temperature.

MARINATED VEGETABLE SALAD

1 16-ounce bag frozen mixed vegetables, defrosted
1 15-ounce can chickpeas, rinsed and drained
⅓ cup low-calorie Italian salad dressing
¼ cup frozen apple juice concentrate, defrosted
1 tablespoon acceptable vegetable oil
1 tablespoon rice or white wine vinegar
2 tablespoons fresh lemon juice
2 cloves garlic, finely minced, or ¼ teaspoon garlic powder
⅛ teaspoon freshly ground black pepper, or to taste
8 leaves lettuce, rinsed and dried

Combine frozen vegetables and chickpeas in a bowl.

In a jar with a tight-fitting lid, shake the salad dressing, juice concentrate, oil, vinegar, lemon juice, garlic and pepper to mix well. Pour over vegetable-bean mixture and mix well. Let marinate for a few hours in refrigerator. Arrange salad over lettuce leaves. Serve chilled.

SERVES 8
½ CUP PER SERVING

This salad is bright and beautiful. For a delicious sandwich, drain any leftovers and use the vegetables to stuff a pita. Garnish with a little Defatted Cheddar Cheese (see page 261) and lettuce.

NUTRIENT ANALYSIS

Calories	60.01kcal
Protein	0.92gm
Carbohydrate	8.61gm
Total Fat	2.85gm
Saturated	0.36gm
Polyunsaturated	1.65gm
Monounsaturated	0.63gm
Cholesterol	0.60mg
Sodium	85.32mg

CARROT AND CABBAGE STUFFED PEPPERS

SERVES 6
½ PEPPER PER SERVING

Stuff pepper halves with cool, crunchy carrots and cabbage for a refreshing salad. Serve with hamburgers, baked chicken or any barbecue dish.

NUTRIENT ANALYSIS

Calories	99.99kcal
Protein	2.42gm
Carbohydrate	12.82gm
Total Fat	5.11gm
Saturated	0.68gm
Polyunsaturated	0.63gm
Monounsaturated	3.37gm
Cholesterol	0.00mg
Sodium	41.02mg

3 cups finely shredded cabbage, about ½ pound
3 medium carrots, finely shredded
1 small onion, finely chopped
1 teaspoon poppy seeds
2 tablespoons olive oil
2 tablespoons cider or wine vinegar
1 teaspoon sugar
½ teaspoon Herb Seasoning (see page 27)
3 green, red or yellow bell peppers, split in half and seeded

Combine cabbage, carrots, onion and poppy seeds in a bowl. Toss lightly.

In a jar with a tight-fitting lid, shake the oil, vinegar, sugar and seasoning to blend. Pour over the cabbage-carrot mixture and mix well. Spoon mixture evenly into each pepper half. Wrap each pepper with plastic wrap and refrigerate. Serve chilled or at room temperature.

GUACAMOLE

1 medium ripe avocado, peeled, seeded and mashed
1 tablespoon fresh lime juice, about ½ of a large
   lime
¼ teaspoon ground cumin
1½ tablespoons Salsa (see page 191) or mild or
   medium picante sauce
1 medium ripe tomato or 8 cherry tomatoes,
   chopped, about 1 cup
2 tablespoons finely chopped onion
1 tomatillo, husk removed, finely chopped (optional)
2 tablespoons chopped fresh cilantro, lightly packed
1 clove garlic, finely minced
Freshly ground black pepper to taste

In a bowl, mix together all ingredients. Serve chilled or at room temperature.

SERVES 8
1½ TABLESPOONS PER SERVING

A tomatillo is a small green tomato enclosed in a thin, papery husk. It is available in Latin-American markets and also may be found in some supermarkets. Guacamole can be served with Corn Crisps (see page 213) as an appetizer. It is also a great accompaniment to Mexican foods. Place a small scoop next to a serving of Mexican Beef and Cornbread Pie (see page 134) or use it to garnish Chicken Fajitas (see page 116).

NUTRIENT ANALYSIS

Calories	48.00kcal
Protein	0.76gm
Carbohydrate	3.18gm
Total Fat	3.88gm
Saturated	0.61gm
Polyunsaturated	0.50gm
Monounsaturated	2.40gm
Cholesterol	0.00mg
Sodium	32.91mg

DEVILED EGGS

SERVES 12
2 HALVES PER
SERVING

To avoid the fat and
cholesterol of regular
deviled eggs, this recipe
uses tofu instead of egg
yolks. Flavorless itself,
tofu takes on the flavors of
the food mixed with it.
Deviled Eggs are a great
accompaniment to a picnic
lunch and can also be
served as appetizers.

1 dozen eggs, hard-cooked
10 ounces tofu, drained
3 tablespoons spicy brown mustard
1 tablespoon reduced-calorie mayonnaise
Paprika if desired

Remove shells from eggs. Slice eggs in half lengthwise; remove yolks and discard. Place tofu in a
large bowl. Using a fork, mash tofu into small bits.
Add mustard and mayonnaise and mix well. Stuff
into egg whites. Top with paprika if desired. Serve
chilled.

NUTRIENT
ANALYSIS

Calories	40.18kcal
Protein	5.34gm
Carbohydrate	1.31gm
Total Fat	1.58gm
Saturated	0.24gm
Polyunsaturated	0.78gm
Monounsaturated	0.42gm
Cholesterol	0.83mg
Sodium	108.35mg

CUCUMBERS IN "SOUR CREAM"

1 cup lowfat cottage cheese
1 small onion, finely chopped
¼ cup plain nonfat yogurt
1 tablespoon fresh lemon juice
1 tablespoon reduced-calorie mayonnaise
1 teaspoon sugar
3 medium cucumbers, peeled and thinly sliced

In a blender, process the cottage cheese, onion, yogurt, lemon juice, mayonnaise and sugar until smooth and creamy. Pour over cucumbers and mix well. Serve chilled.

SERVES 6
¾ CUP PER SERVING

This is a simple way to make a sour-cream-like sauce from cottage cheese, yogurt and a few other flavorful ingredients. Use the sauce on baked potatoes or anywhere you would use sour cream.

NUTRIENT ANALYSIS

Calories	60.32kcal
Protein	5.79gm
Carbohydrate	5.77gm
Total Fat	1.65gm
Saturated	0.65gm
Polyunsaturated	0.39gm
Monounsaturated	0.54gm
Cholesterol	4.67mg
Sodium	178.87mg

CUCUMBER-MELON SALAD WITH RASPBERRY VINAIGRETTE

SERVES 4
¾ CUP PER SERVING

Serve this refreshingly different dish as a salad or a relish. To make a relish, simply chop the ingredients finely.

NUTRIENT ANALYSIS

Calories	39.06kcal
Protein	1.36gm
Carbohydrate	9.15gm
Total Fat	0.33gm
Saturated	0.01gm
Polyunsaturated	0.02gm
Monounsaturated	0.00gm
Cholesterol	0.00mg
Sodium	15.89mg

1 cucumber, scrubbed and partially peeled to leave
    some dark green for color
½ large cantaloupe, seeded
1 bunch radishes, scrubbed
¼ cup raspberry vinegar (see page 90)
Freshly ground black pepper (optional)
4 leaves leaf lettuce, rinsed and dried

Cut cucumber into bite-size pieces. Cut cantaloupe into cubes or small melon balls. Thinly slice the radishes. In a medium bowl, combine cucumber, cantaloupe and radishes. Toss with vinegar and sprinkle with pepper. Serve chilled on individual plates lined with leaf lettuce.

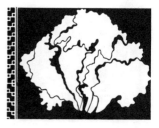

FRESH FRUIT SALAD

4 cups assorted fresh fruit, sliced
1 to 2 tablespoons raspberry vinegar (see page 90)

SERVES 4
1 CUP PER
SERVING

Slice fruit and arrange on a serving plate. Sprinkle with raspberry vinegar, cover and chill.

Choose seasonal fruit such as peaches, oranges, pineapples, seedless grapes or fresh or frozen berries for this refreshing dish. Purchase raspberry vinegar in gourmet stores or make at home.

NUTRIENT ANALYSIS*

Calories	87.26kcal
Protein	1.28gm
Carbohydrate	22.19gm
Total Fat	0.49gm
Saturated	0.06gm
Polyunsaturated	0.11gm
Monounsaturated	0.04gm
Cholesterol	0.00mg
Sodium	1.21mg

* Based on a salad made up of peaches, oranges, pineapples, seedless grapes and unsweetened strawberries.

FRESH FRUIT SALAD WITH POPPY SEED AND YOGURT DRESSING

SERVES 6
½ CUP PER SERVING

3 cups assorted fresh fruit, cut into bite-size pieces
1 cup lowfat lemon yogurt
¼ teaspoon poppy seeds

Let your imagination run wild: use dramatically different combinations of fresh fruit. The dressing will only enhance the flavor—guaranteed!

Place fruit in individual serving bowls. In a small bowl, mix yogurt and poppy seeds with a whisk, then pour over fruit, using 2 to 3 tablespoons per serving.

NUTRIENT ANALYSIS

Calories	92.15kcal
Protein	2.52gm
Carbohydrate	20.47gm
Total Fat	0.73gm
Saturated	0.35gm
Polyunsaturated	0.09gm
Monounsaturated	0.14gm
Cholesterol	1.60mg
Sodium	27.62mg

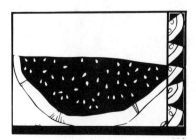

HERBED CHICKEN SALAD

2 cups cooked chicken, cut into bite-size pieces
¼ cup plain nonfat yogurt
¼ cup reduced-calorie mayonnaise
2 green onions with tops, thinly sliced
1 small carrot, grated
2 radishes, grated
3 tablespoons chopped celery
2 tablespoons chopped green pepper
2 tablespoons chopped fresh parsley
1 teaspoon Worcestershire sauce
1 teaspoon Herb Seasoning (see page 27)
¼ teaspoon freshly ground black pepper, or to taste
1½ tablespoons tarragon vinegar

GARNISH
Lettuce leaves, rinsed and dried
1 8-ounce can mandarin oranges packed in fruit
    juice, drained, or 3 small tomatoes, sliced

Combine all salad ingredients except garnish. Mix well, cover and refrigerate at least 1 hour. To serve, place a scoop of salad on a lettuce leaf and garnish with orange segments or tomato slices.

SERVES 6
**½ CUP PER
SERVING**

This salad is excellent used as stuffing for tomatoes, peppers or zucchini. It is also good in pita pockets, in sandwiches or on whole wheat crackers.

**NUTRIENT
ANALYSIS**

Calories	145.94kcal
Protein	14.70gm
Carbohydrate	11.70gm
Total Fat	4.59gm
Saturated	1.10gm
Polyunsaturated	1.68gm
Monounsaturated	1.26gm
Cholesterol	40.24mg
Sodium	111.80mg

HAM AND RICE SALAD

SERVES 8
1¼ CUPS PER SERVING

This makes a terrific one-dish entree. Team it with fresh fruit salad and crusty bread.

NUTRIENT ANALYSIS

Calories	221.02kcal
Protein	10.96gm
Carbohydrate	27.04gm
Total Fat	8.23gm
Saturated	1.62gm
Polyunsaturated	3.54gm
Monounsaturated	2.43gm
Cholesterol	21.69mg
Sodium	290.16mg

1 cup long-grain or brown rice
2 to 2½ cups homemade Chicken Stock (see page 263)
8 ounces lean ham, visible fat removed, cut into ¼-inch cubes
1 cup fresh or frozen corn kernels, defrosted
1 cup frozen green peas, defrosted
4 green onions with tops, thinly sliced
1 medium red, yellow or green bell pepper, finely chopped
4 to 5 radishes, finely chopped
¼ cup minced fresh parsley
1 tablespoon fresh dill weed or 1 teaspoon dried dill weed

DRESSING

3 tablespoons acceptable vegetable oil
¼ cup herbed or wine vinegar
½ teaspoon Dijon mustard
¼ teaspoon salt (optional)
Freshly ground black pepper to taste

GARNISH

1 small head lettuce, preferably red leaf, rinsed and dried
Few sprigs fresh mint or parsley

Cook rice according to package instructions, substituting stock for liquid and omitting salt. Allow to cool.

In a large bowl, combine rice, ham, corn, peas, green onions, pepper, radishes, parsley and dill weed. In a small bowl, mix together oil, vinegar, mustard, salt and pepper to make the dressing.

Combine dressing and rice mixture, tossing lightly. Store refrigerated. Serve at room temperature or chilled. Place a scoop on a bed of lettuce and garnish with mint or parsley sprigs.

SALMON AND PASTA SALAD

1 cup uncooked elbow macaroni, 4 ounces
2 teaspoons acceptable vegetable oil
1 7⅔-ounce can salmon, drained, skin removed
1 tablespoon Worcestershire sauce
½ medium white onion, minced
1 10-ounce package frozen green peas, slightly
   defrosted
1 large red bell pepper, diced

DRESSING
1 cup lowfat cottage cheese
2 tablespoons fresh lemon juice
2 to 3 dashes hot pepper sauce
1 to 2 tablespoons chopped fresh dill weed or 1 to 2
   teaspoons dried dill weed

SERVES 8
1½ CUPS PER
SERVING

This easy-to-fix main dish
or appetizer salad is great
for hot summer days.
Mash the bones of the
salmon to get full benefit
of the calcium they
contain. To get all the fiber
from the bell pepper, leave
in the pith (white inner
ribs).

Cook macaroni according to package directions, omitting salt. Drain and rinse under cold running water until noodles are cool. Drain, place in bowl and add oil; mix to coat evenly. Set aside.

In a bowl, mash salmon, including bones. Add Worcestershire, onion, peas, bell pepper and cooked macaroni. Mix well.

In a blender, process cottage cheese, lemon juice and hot pepper sauce until creamy. Mix in dill. Pour over the salmon-noodle mixture and stir. Refrigerate. Serve chilled.

NUTRIENT ANALYSIS

Calories	164.68kcal
Protein	13.40gm
Carbohydrate	18.31gm
Total Fat	4.27gm
Saturated	1.12gm
Polyunsaturated	1.37gm
Monounsaturated	1.34gm
Cholesterol	11.78mg
Sodium	314.81mg

SEAFOOD PASTA SALAD

SERVES 6
1⅓ CUPS PER SERVING

This versatile, one-dish meal is quick to prepare and elegant to serve. For an interesting look, select pasta shapes such as shells, corkscrews or twists. Prepare a few hours before serving to heighten flavors.

NUTRIENT ANALYSIS

Calories	303.60kcal
Protein	12.54gm
Carbohydrate	46.27gm
Total Fat	7.89gm
Saturated	1.08gm
Polyunsaturated	0.94gm
Monounsaturated	5.08gm
Cholesterol	11.23mg
Sodium	144.31mg

1 10-ounce package dry pasta
2 cups cooked seafood, skin and bones removed (see recipe for Poached Fish and Fish Stock, page 93)
1 small red onion, finely chopped
1 medium red, green or yellow bell pepper, chopped
4 to 5 radishes, finely chopped
1 cup frozen green peas, defrosted
¼ cup minced fresh basil or 2 tablespoons dried basil
¼ cup minced fresh parsley

DRESSING
3 tablespoons olive oil
¼ cup herbed wine or white vinegar
½ teaspoon Dijon mustard
¼ teaspoon salt (optional)
Freshly ground black pepper to taste

GARNISH
1 small head romaine lettuce, rinsed and dried
2 small tomatoes, cut into wedges

Cook pasta according to package directions, omitting salt. Drain and rinse under cold running water until pasta is cool.

In a large bowl, combine pasta, seafood, onion, pepper, radishes, peas, basil and parsley. In a small bowl, mix together oil, vinegar, mustard, salt and pepper. Add to the pasta mixture; toss lightly to combine. Store refrigerated. Serve at room temperature or chilled.

For an attractive presentation, line a serving bowl or a platter with lettuce, fill with pasta and top with tomato wedges.

Salad Dressings

Creamy Vinaigrette
Creamy Herb Dressing
Oil and Vinegar Dressing
Low-Calorie Dressing
Tofu Mayonnaise
Herbed or Fruit Vinegar

CREAMY VINAIGRETTE

2 cloves garlic, minced
½ cup olive oil
2 tablespoons fresh lemon juice
½ teaspoon Dijon mustard
¼ teaspoon freshly ground black pepper
½ 14-ounce can artichoke hearts, drained

S E R V E S   1 2
1   T A B L E S P O O N
P E R   S E R V I N G

In a blender or the workbowl of a food processor fitted with a metal blade, process all ingredients until silky smooth. Chill and serve over salad greens.

Pureeing the artichoke hearts makes this a wonderfully smooth dressing. After making the dressing, you will still have half a can of artichoke hearts left. Just toss them in with your salad!

N U T R I E N T
A N A L Y S I S

Calories	83.98kcal
Protein	0.38gm
Carbohydrate	1.49gm
Total Fat	9.04gm
Saturated	1.22gm
Polyunsaturated	0.76gm
Monounsaturated	6.63gm
Cholesterol	0.00mg
Sodium	6.68mg

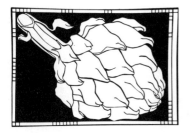

CREAMY HERB DRESSING

SERVES 20
1 TABLESPOON
PER SERVING

Serve this dressing hot or cold! It can be used as a dip or a dressing for salads, poultry, baked potatoes or cold seafood.

NUTRIENT ANALYSIS

Calories	25.00kcal
Protein	1.54gm
Carbohydrate	2.97gm
Total Fat	0.83gm
Saturated	0.52gm
Polyunsaturated	0.03gm
Monounsaturated	0.24gm
Cholesterol	3.04mg
Sodium	22.00mg

½ cup nonfat yogurt
½ cup lowfat sour cream
2 tablespoons minced fresh parsley or cilantro
½ teaspoon Lemon Herb Seasoning (see page 27)
1 green onion with top, minced
½ teaspoon honey or sugar
¼ teaspoon Italian seasoning (optional)

Using a hand beater, whip together yogurt and sour cream. Stir in remaining ingredients. Keeps well when refrigerated.

To serve hot, gently warm over medium heat, stirring until heated throughout. Do not boil.

OIL AND VINEGAR DRESSING

3 tablespoons olive oil
3 tablespoons cider or wine vinegar
2 tablespoons water
1 to 2 teaspoons stone-ground mustard
1 tablespoon finely chopped fresh or ½ teaspoon
   dried parsley, sweet basil, oregano, chives or
   tarragon

In a jar with a tight-fitting lid, combine ingredients. Shake well to blend.

SERVES 6
1⅓ TABLESPOONS PER SERVING

Make this dressing several hours ahead and refrigerate to allow the flavors to blend.

NUTRIENT ANALYSIS

Calories	62.62kcal
Protein	0.17gm
Carbohydrate	0.15gm
Total Fat	6.94gm
Saturated	0.92gm
Polyunsaturated	0.61gm
Monounsaturated	4.99gm
Cholesterol	0.00mg
Sodium	0.12mg

LOW-CALORIE DRESSING

SERVES 6
2 TABLESPOONS
PER SERVING

Substituting other herbs such as mint, oregano, tarragon or herb seasoning for the parsley will give a range of flavored salad dressings.

NUTRIENT ANALYSIS

Calories	10.95kcal
Protein	0.39gm
Carbohydrate	2.54gm
Total Fat	0.05gm
Saturated	0.00gm
Polyunsaturated	0.00gm
Monounsaturated	0.00gm
Cholesterol	0.00mg
Sodium	114.36mg

1 6-ounce can vegetable or tomato juice
1 tablespoon very finely chopped onion
1 tablespoon very finely chopped celery
1 tablespoon very finely chopped bell pepper
1 tablespoon grated carrot
1 teaspoon fresh lemon juice
½ teaspoon sugar
1 tablespoon finely chopped fresh parsley or
    cilantro or ½ teaspoon dried parsley or cilantro
¼ teaspoon hot pepper sauce (optional) or ½
    teaspoon Worcestershire sauce (optional)
Freshly ground black pepper to taste

In a jar with a tight-fitting lid, combine all ingredients. Shake well and refrigerate for at least 2 hours, allowing flavors to blend.

TOFU MAYONNAISE

½ pound firm tofu
½ teaspoon dry mustard or ¼ teaspoon prepared
  mustard
⅛ teaspoon cayenne pepper, or to taste (optional)
½ teaspoon salt
2 tablespoons fresh lemon juice
3 tablespoons corn oil
2 tablespoons water

In a food processor or blender, process tofu, mustard, cayenne pepper, salt and lemon juice until mixed. With machine still running, add oil *very* slowly and then add water. Blend until smooth. Stop the machine a few times during processing and scrape the sides.

Keeps for up to three months when refrigerated in an airtight container.

SERVES 12
1 TABLESPOON
PER SERVING

This recipe makes a delightful lowfat substitute for the typical mayonnaise found on your grocer's shelf.

NUTRIENT ANALYSIS

Calories	45.00kcal
Protein	1.55gm
Carbohydrate	0.54gm
Total Fat	4.33gm
Saturated	0.56gm
Polyunsaturated	2.51gm
Monounsaturated	1.03gm
Cholesterol	0.00mg
Sodium	93.00mg

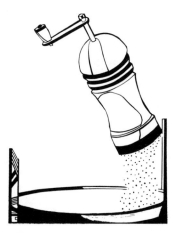

HERBED OR FRUIT VINEGAR

MAKES APPROXIMATELY 1½ QUARTS

Herbed vinegars are simple to make. They are delicious substitutes for salt and for high-fat salad dressings: They taste wonderful on salads and vegetables. Use them as marinades or as a base for mayonnaise. Invent your own flavors and make several bottles! Here are some ideas to get you started.

NUTRIENT ANALYSIS*

Calories	46.15kcal
Protein	2.15gm
Carbohydrate	10.12gm
Total Fat	0.70gm
Saturated	0.06gm
Polyunsaturated	0.07gm
Monounsaturated	0.06gm
Cholesterol	0.00mg
Sodium	7.13mg

* For entire recipe.

1 quart red or white vinegar
2 tablespoons black, white or green peppercorns, crushed
2 cups fresh herbs such as oregano, rosemary, tarragon, thyme, sage or chopped shallots; or berries such as blueberries, blackberries or raspberries
2 to 4 cloves garlic (optional)
2 tablespoons juniper berries (optional)

In a nonaluminum saucepan, bring vinegar and pepper to a boil, remove from heat and allow to cool to 120° to 125° F., or until still very warm.

Wash and dry two quart-size bottles or several smaller jars. Use inexpensive corked bottles, which are available in most cookware stores, or use your own clean wine bottles and corks.

Divide the fresh herbs or berries among the bottles and add garlic and juniper berries. Pour in vinegar to about 2 inches from the top, allowing room for the flavors to mellow. Cork the bottles and allow to mature for at least 2 weeks before using.

Some other good ingredient combinations include:
- White wine vinegar or white distilled vinegar, black pepper, tarragon and shallots
- Red wine vinegar, white pepper, rosemary and blueberries
- Red wine vinegar, black pepper, thyme and juniper berries
- Cider vinegar, black pepper, tarragon and garlic
- Balsamic vinegar, sage and blackberries

Fish

Poached Fish and Fish Stock
Stuffed Fillet of Fish
Poached Fish in Oriental Broth
Broiled Fish Steaks
Halibut Kabobs
Fish in a Package
Fish with Mustard Sauce over Steamed Spinach
Crispy Fish with Fennel Seeds
Fish Stew
Seafood Cioppino
Baked Crabmeat
Tuna-Noodle Casserole
Creamed Tuna and Peas over English Muffins
Tuna Salad Pita Sandwiches

POACHED FISH AND FISH STOCK

1 small carrot, coarsely chopped
1 stalk celery, coarsely chopped
1 small onion, coarsely chopped
2 tablespoons white wine vinegar or rice vinegar
8 whole black peppercorns
1 bay leaf
1 pound fish fillets, fresh or frozen and defrosted

**SERVES 3
APPROXIMATELY 4
OUNCES PER
SERVING**

Poaching is an excellent way to prepare fish. It's easy and requires little cleanup. Try poached fish with the Caper Sauce for Fish (page 187) or the sauce used in the Chilled Stuffed Artichoke recipe (page 151).

To judge the cooking time, measure the fish at its thickest point and allow 10 minutes poaching time for each inch of thickness.

In a large skillet, place vegetables, vinegar, peppercorns and bay leaf. Lay fish on top and add cool tap water just to cover. Heat, uncovered, over medium heat until water begins to simmer; make sure the water does not boil. Simmer for about 10 minutes per inch of thickness at the thickest point, until flesh is firm and no longer translucent.

Remove fish to a serving platter by carefully lifting with two large, slotted spatulas. Let sit for a few minutes, then drain off any excess liquid. To serve cold, allow fish that has been refrigerated to stand at room temperature for 10 to 15 minutes; this enhances its flavor.

Strain the poaching liquid to make fish stock for use in soups, sauces or for poaching other fish.

The poaching liquid may be stored in the refrigerator for up to 2 days or frozen for up to 3 months.

**NUTRIENT
ANALYSIS**

Calories	120.05kcal
Protein	21.86gm
Carbohydrate	6.06gm
Total Fat	1.15gm
Saturated	0.19gm
Polyunsaturated	0.39gm
Monounsaturated	0.11gm
Cholesterol	67.36mg
Sodium	149.53mg

STUFFED FILLET OF FISH

SERVES 6

This dish can be prepared ahead: Fillets can be stuffed, covered with plastic wrap and refrigerated for several hours before baking.

NUTRIENT ANALYSIS

Calories	177.26kcal
Protein	22.25gm
Carbohydrate	6.49gm
Total Fat	7.31gm
Saturated	0.88gm
Polyunsaturated	2.95gm
Monounsaturated	2.77gm
Cholesterol	63.98mg
Sodium	143.69mg

Vegetable oil spray
6 fish fillets, such as sole or flounder, about 5
    ounces each
½ teaspoon white pepper
½ teaspoon paprika
1 tablespoon acceptable vegetable oil
6 ounces fresh mushrooms, finely chopped
4 green onions with tops, finely chopped
¼ cup chopped almonds
¼ cup unseasoned bread crumbs
¼ cup minced fresh parsley
½ tablespoon acceptable vegetable oil

GARNISH
2 tablespoons minced fresh parsley

Preheat oven to 375° F. Lightly grease six oven-proof 6-ounce custard cups or one muffin pan with six 2½ × 1¼-inch cups with vegetable oil spray. Curl each fillet inside a custard or muffin cup. Sprinkle with pepper and paprika.

In a nonstick skillet, heat 1 tablespoon oil over medium-high heat. Add mushrooms and onions and sauté until tender, about 2 minutes. Remove skillet from heat. Stir in almonds, bread crumbs and parsley. Spoon mixture equally into center of each fillet.

Brush tops with remaining oil. Bake 15 minutes, or until fish is no longer translucent. Carefully remove each stuffed fillet from cup, spoon juice over top and garnish with parsley.

POACHED FISH IN ORIENTAL BROTH

2 tablespoons dry sherry
3 cups homemade Chicken Stock (see page 263)
2 tablespoons low-sodium soy sauce
2 slices fresh lemon
3 thin slices fresh ginger
⅛ teaspoon cayenne pepper
1¼ pounds orange roughy or other thick, mild fish
    fillets
5 to 6 green onions, tops only, cut into 1-inch pieces
1 medium red bell pepper, cut into ¼ × 1-inch
    pieces
1 stalk celery, cut into ¼ × 1-inch pieces
½ teaspoon sesame oil
1 carrot, grated
Freshly ground black pepper to taste

**SERVES 4
APPROXIMATELY 4
OUNCES PER
SERVING**

*Packed with spices and
seasonings, this broth
gives the fish a delicate
flavor. Carrot as the final
touch makes the dish
pretty enough for
company.*

**NUTRIENT
ANALYSIS**

Calories	159.86kcal
Protein	24.10gm
Carbohydrate	12.05gm
Total Fat	2.21gm
Saturated	0.39gm
Polyunsaturated	0.76gm
Monounsaturated	0.45gm
Cholesterol	68.89mg
Sodium	496.22mg

In a nonaluminum fish poacher, a wok or a large skillet bring sherry, chicken stock, soy sauce, lemon, ginger and cayenne pepper to a boil. Reduce heat and add fish and a little water, if needed, to just cover fish. Simmer in stock for 10 minutes per inch of thickness at the thickest point, or just until fish is no longer translucent. Do not overcook.

Remove fish with slotted spatulas and place equal portions in four soup bowls. Return liquid to a boil. Add green onions, bell pepper and celery. Cook 2 to 3 minutes, or until tender-crisp. Remove and discard ginger and lemon. Using a slotted spoon, remove vegetables and place over fish. Stir sesame oil into poaching liquid. Evenly pour liquid over fish and vegetables in bowls.

Scatter grated carrot and grind fresh pepper over each serving. Serve immediately.

BROILED FISH STEAKS

SERVES 6
APPROXIMATELY 4
OUNCES PER
SERVING

This elegant entree, accompanied by wild rice and sautéed mixed vegetables or a tossed salad, is quick and easy to prepare. Salmon steaks are particularly delicious prepared this way.

NUTRIENT ANALYSIS

Calories	229.38kcal
Protein	21.81gm
Carbohydrate	2.79gm
Total Fat	14.93gm
Saturated	3.62gm
Polyunsaturated	4.06gm
Monounsaturated	5.55gm
Cholesterol	86.34mg
Sodium	142.67mg

6 fish steaks, approximately ½ inch thick, about 5 ounces each
2 tablespoons reduced-calorie mayonnaise
1 tablespoon Lemon Herb Seasoning (see page 27)
Paprika to taste

GARNISH
1 lemon, sliced thin
6 sprigs fresh parsley

Preheat broiler.

Rinse fish and pat dry. Lightly coat both sides of each fish piece with mayonnaise. Place in a shallow baking dish. Sprinkle with half of the lemon herb seasoning and paprika. Broil 3 to 4 minutes. Turn fish and sprinkle with remaining seasonings. Broil for another 3 to 4 minutes, or until fish flakes when tested with a fork or is no longer translucent. Garnish with lemon slices and a sprig of fresh parsley. Serve immediately.

HALIBUT KABOBS

1 pound halibut steak, 1 inch thick
¼ cup fresh lemon juice, juice of 1 lemon
¼ cup olive oil
3 shallots, thinly sliced
1 teaspoon Italian herb seasoning
½ teaspoon dried thyme, crushed
½ large red onion, cut lengthwise into thirds

GARNISH
1 lemon, cut into wedges

Preheat broiler.

Cut fish into 1-inch cubes and set aside. In a bowl, mix lemon juice, oil, shallots, herb seasoning and thyme. Add fish and toss to coat. Marinate in refrigerator for at least 5 minutes, but no more than 1 hour.

Pry onion apart into single layers. Thread each skewer, alternating onion and fish, using four pieces of fish and five pieces of onion.

Place skewers on a broiler pan and broil four inches from heat 2 to 2½ minutes on each side, or until fish is no longer translucent. Garnish with lemon wedges.

**SERVES 4
1 KABOB PER
SERVING**

This skewered main dish is elegant and easy to prepare. It looks especially pretty when served on a bed of Spaghetti Squash (see page 178). If you use wooden skewers, soak them in water for at least 30 minutes to keep the wood from charring while broiling.

**NUTRIENT
ANALYSIS**

Calories	149.36kcal
Protein	16.45gm
Carbohydrate	5.03gm
Total Fat	7.65gm
Saturated	1.06gm
Polyunsaturated	0.89gm
Monounsaturated	5.06gm
Cholesterol	51.03mg
Sodium	91.08mg

FISH IN A PACKAGE

SERVES 10
APPROXIMATELY
5 OUNCES PER
SERVING

The fish used in this recipe can be bass, red snapper, large mackerel, bluefish or haddock. To make the preparation easy, use fish fillets. Presenting the fish in foil makes quite a dramatic entree. Serve it with a crisp green salad, wild rice, carrots and a fresh fruit dessert.

NUTRIENT ANALYSIS

Calories	178.91kcal
Protein	31.34gm
Carbohydrate	6.70gm
Total Fat	3.18gm
Saturated	0.51gm
Polyunsaturated	1.45gm
Monounsaturated	0.56gm
Cholesterol	95.94mg
Sodium	309.89mg

1 6- to 7-pound fish, scaled, cleaned and head removed, if desired, or 10 fish fillets, 5 ounces each

STUFFING

1 tablespoon acceptable vegetable oil
1 small onion, chopped
½ pound fresh mushrooms, sliced
¼ cup minced fresh parsley
2 tablespoons fresh dill weed or 2 teaspoons dried dill weed
½ cup unseasoned bread crumbs
½ teaspoon salt (optional)
Freshly ground black pepper to taste
½ fresh lemon
½ cup white wine or homemade Chicken Stock (see page 263)

GARNISH

1 lemon, sliced
Fresh parsley sprigs

Preheat oven to 350° F.

Rinse fish and pat dry. Slit fish along the belly to make a cavity for the stuffing. If using fish fillets, place the stuffing between two fillets, skin-side out.

To prepare the stuffing, heat oil in a heavy, non-stick skillet over medium-high heat. Sauté onion lightly 2 to 3 minutes, or until translucent. Add mushrooms and continue to sauté for another 5 minutes. Remove from heat. Stir in parsley, dill weed, bread crumbs, salt and pepper. Squeeze lemon juice over stuffing and set aside to cool and to allow bread crumbs to absorb the lemon juice.

Line a baking sheet with a sheet of heavy-duty foil long enough to wrap and seal the foil package around the fish. Place fish in center of foil and spoon stuffing into cavity just before baking. Use toothpicks to secure fish. Drizzle with wine or stock. Wrap foil over fish and seal tightly to prevent steam and flavor from escaping. Bake whole fish 1 to 1¼ hours. If using fillets, bake about 45 minutes, or until fish flakes very easily with fork.

Use caution when opening foil package, to prevent steam burn. Fish is done when no longer translucent. Carefully slide fish onto serving platter and garnish with lemon slices and parsley.

FISH WITH MUSTARD SAUCE OVER STEAMED SPINACH

4 fish fillets, sole or flounder, about 5 ounces each
¼ cup prepared reduced-calorie ranch dressing
1½ tablespoons prepared yellow mustard
3 tablespoons plain nonfat yogurt
½ pound fresh spinach

Preheat oven to 400° F.

Rinse fish and pat dry. Arrange in ovenproof glass baking dish.

Mix the dressing, mustard and yogurt. Spoon evenly over fish. Bake until done or until fish is no longer translucent, about 10 minutes per inch of thickness at the thickest point.

While fish is baking, remove tough stems from spinach and rinse. Heat a nonstick skillet over medium-high heat. When skillet is hot, add spinach and stir-fry just to wilt the leaves, about 30 seconds. Arrange spinach in single layer on serving plates. Top with baked fish. Serve immediately.

SERVES 4
APPROXIMATELY 4
OUNCES PER
SERVING

The golden mustard sauce, white fish and dark green spinach make for a picture-perfect plate.

NUTRIENT ANALYSIS

Calories	128.71kcal
Protein	22.53gm
Carbohydrate	6.15gm
Total Fat	2.09gm
Saturated	0.31gm
Polyunsaturated	0.92gm
Monounsaturated	0.31gm
Cholesterol	63.98mg
Sodium	353.09mg

CRISPY FISH WITH FENNEL SEEDS

**SERVES 4
APPROXIMATELY
4 OUNCES PER
SERVING**

Here is a low-cholesterol recipe for people who like their fish breaded and fried. For a different taste, try your favorite herb seasoning instead of fennel seeds.

**NUTRIENT
ANALYSIS**

Calories	308.27kcal
Protein	27.85gm
Carbohydrate	47.49gm
Total Fat	2.69gm
Saturated	0.22gm
Polyunsaturated	0.51gm
Monounsaturated	0.27gm
Cholesterol	63.97mg
Sodium	271.11mg

1 cup all-purpose flour
2 large egg whites, lightly beaten
1¼ cups whole-grain wheat and barley nugget cereal
1 tablespoon fennel seeds or 2 tablespoons Lemon Herb Seasoning (see page 27)
4 fish fillets, orange roughy or any other white fish, about 5 ounces each, about ½-inch thick

GARNISH
1 lemon, cut into wedges

Preheat oven to 400° F.

Select three pie plates or similar dishes with shallow sides. In the first dish, place flour. In the second, place egg whites. In the third, place cereal mixed with fennel seeds or herb seasoning.

Rinse fish and pat dry. Dredge a fillet in flour, turning to coat both sides. Shake off excess. Then place it in the egg whites, again coating both sides. Finally, put it in the cereal-seasoning mixture, turning to coat both sides. Repeat for each fillet.

Lay fillets on ungreased baking sheet. Bake until fish is no longer translucent, allowing about 10 minutes per inch thickness at the thickest point. Serve with lemon wedges.

FISH STEW

¼ cup fresh lemon juice
1½ pounds fish fillets, at least ¾-inch thick,
    skinned, boned and cut into 2-inch squares
8 green onions with tops, thinly sliced
1 cup chopped tomatoes
3 cloves garlic, minced
½ tablespoon minced fresh ginger or ½ teaspoon
    ground ginger
1½ cups water
¼ cup ketchup
½ cup chopped fresh parsley

Sprinkle lemon juice over fish, mix well and set aside.

In a 2½- to 3-quart saucepan over medium-high heat, cook green onions 1 minute, or until wilted. Add tomatoes and cook an additional 2 to 3 minutes, or until tomatoes are almost reduced to a pulp. Add garlic, ginger, water, ketchup and parsley. Reduce heat, cover pan and allow to simmer 10 minutes.

Add fish and continue to simmer, covered, another 10 to 15 mintues, or until fish is almost cooked. Remove cover and simmer another 4 to 5 minutes to thicken sauce. Serve hot.

SERVES 6
1 CUP PER SERVING

A delicacy from the West Indies, this fragrant stew is not only simple to make, it also tastes wonderful and is a refreshing change from the usual baked fish. Serve it with a loaf of crusty bread or on a bed of hot rice.

NUTRIENT ANALYSIS

Calories	102.50kcal
Protein	16.77gm
Carbohydrate	7.29gm
Total Fat	0.96gm
Saturated	0.15gm
Polyunsaturated	0.31gm
Monounsaturated	0.08gm
Cholesterol	50.83mg
Sodium	208.45mg

SEAFOOD CIOPPINO

SERVES 5
2 CUPS PER
SERVING

Cioppino, a meal in a bowl, is great for entertaining because there is no last-minute cooking to worry about. Serve with crusty bread, salad and fresh fruit for dessert. This dish freezes well, though afterward the fish will be darker than when fresh; the flavor, however will be just as good or even better.

NUTRIENT ANALYSIS

Calories	245.56kcal
Protein	31.94gm
Carbohydrate	17.20gm
Total Fat	5.52gm
Saturated	0.82gm
Polyunsaturated	2.41gm
Monounsaturated	1.10gm
Cholesterol	111.96mg
Sodium	256.59mg

1 tablespoon acceptable vegetable oil
½ cup coarsely chopped celery
1 large carrot, thinly sliced
1 medium green pepper, coarsely chopped
½ large yellow onion, coarsely chopped
1 6-ounce can no-salt-added tomato puree
3 8-ounce bottles clam juice
1½ cups dry white wine
1 bay leaf
1 8-ounce can baby clams
1 pound halibut or shark steaks, skin removed, cut
   into 1-inch pieces
1 tablespoon chopped fresh basil or 1 teaspoon
   dried basil
1 teaspoon chopped fresh oregano or ¼ teaspoon
   dried oregano
1 teaspoon chopped fresh thyme or ¼ teaspoon
   dried thyme
¼ cup finely chopped fresh parsley
5 crab claws

In a large nonstick skillet over medium-high heat, heat oil. Add celery, carrots, pepper and onion and sauté until tender, about 5 to 7 minutes. Set aside.

In a 4-quart saucepan, bring tomato puree, clam juice, white wine and bay leaf to a boil, covered. Add clams (including juice), shark or halibut, basil, oregano, thyme and parsley. Return mixture to a boil, reduce heat and allow to simmer 15 minutes, partially covered. Add crab and heat for 2 minutes more. Remove bay leaf and serve immediately.

BAKED CRABMEAT

Vegetable oil spray
1 tablespoon acceptable margarine
¼ cup finely chopped onion
1 pound crabmeat, all cartilage removed
2 tablespoons Dijon mustard
1 teaspoon Worcestershire sauce
4 large egg whites, stiffly beaten
2 tablespoons Parmesan cheese

**SERVES 6 AS AN
ENTREE
2 OUNCES
PER SERVING
SERVES 12 AS AN
APPETIZER
1 OUNCE PER
SERVING**

*This dish is a real treat—
light, festive and healthful.*

Preheat oven to 350° F. Spray a 9 × 9-inch oven-proof casserole dish with vegetable oil spray.

In a small pan over medium-high heat, melt margarine. Add onions and sauté 2 to 3 minutes, or until soft. In a medium bowl, combine onion, crabmeat, mustard and Worcestershire sauce. Gently fold in beaten egg whites. Pour mixture into casserole dish and sprinkle with cheese.

Bake 25 minutes, or until puffed and lightly browned. Remove from oven and cut into squares. Serve immediately.

**NUTRIENT
ANALYSIS***

Calories	121.45kcal
Protein	16.70gm
Carbohydrate	2.29gm
Total Fat	4.01gm
Saturated	0.97gm
Polyunsaturated	1.17gm
Monounsaturated	1.37gm
Cholesterol	77.42mg
Sodium	333.27mg

* Based on entree-size serving.

TUNA-NOODLE CASSEROLE

SERVES 6
1 3×5-INCH
PORTION PER
SERVING

This lowfat version of an old standby will please everyone in your family. Be prepared in case they ask for seconds!

NUTRIENT ANALYSIS

Calories	342.36kcal
Protein	30.25gm
Carbohydrate	40.17gm
Total Fat	5.58gm
Saturated	2.53gm
Polyunsaturated	1.06gm
Monounsaturated	1.43gm
Cholesterol	50.21mg
Sodium	479.39mg

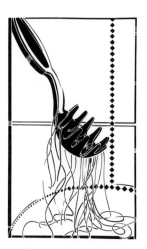

1 8-ounce package linguine, vermicelli, spaghetti or other thin noodles
1 teaspoon acceptable vegetable oil
1 small onion, chopped
1 clove garlic, minced
2 6½-ounce cans tuna, in spring water, drained and rinsed
⅓ cup finely chopped green bell pepper
½ cup finely chopped carrots
¼ cup finely chopped fresh parsley
¼ teaspoon paprika, or to taste
½ cup lowfat sour cream
1 cup lowfat cottage cheese
½ cup plain nonfat yogurt
½ cup bread crumbs, toasted
¼ cup grated Parmesan cheese

Cook noodles according to directions on package, omitting salt. Rinse and drain.

Preheat oven to 350° F.

In nonstick skillet, heat oil over medium-high heat; sauté onion and garlic until onion is transparent, 2 to 3 minutes, stirring frequently.

In a large bowl, combine sautéed onion and garlic with tuna, green pepper, carrots, parsley and paprika; set aside.

In a small bowl, blend together sour cream, cottage cheese and yogurt; add to tuna mixture along with noodles. Pour into a 9 × 11 × 2-inch casserole. Combine bread crumbs and Parmesan cheese and sprinkle over top of casserole. Bake 30 to 45 minutes, or until top is lightly browned.

CREAMED TUNA AND PEAS OVER ENGLISH MUFFINS

2 tablespoons acceptable vegetable oil
3 tablespoons all-purpose flour
⅛ teaspoon salt, optional
White pepper to taste
1 bay leaf
2 cups skim milk
1 teaspoon dry sherry, optional
1 10-ounce package frozen green peas
1 12½-ounce can tuna, packed in water, drained
   and rinsed
4 whole-grain English muffins, split and lightly
   toasted

SERVES 4
¾ CUP SAUCE
OVER 2 MUFFIN
HALVES PER
SERVING

This is one of those homey foods that we seem never to grow tired of. The sherry gives it a flavorful twist.

In a small saucepan, heat oil over medium heat. Add flour, salt, pepper and bay leaf, stirring constantly, 1 minute. Gradually add milk and sherry, stirring constantly, until mixture thickens, 2 to 3 minutes. Remove from heat and discard bay leaf.

Meanwhile, cook peas half as long as stated on the package; drain. Flake tuna with a fork. Add peas and tuna to sauce and mix well. Heat thoroughly. Place ¾ cup mixture over each split English muffin and serve immediately.

NUTRIENT ANALYSIS

Calories	410.05kcal
Protein	35.33gm
Carbohydrate	43.01gm
Total Fat	11.33gm
Saturated	1.82gm
Polyunsaturated	5.61gm
Monounsaturated	3.16gm
Cholesterol	58.42mg
Sodium	357.93mg

TUNA SALAD PITA SANDWICHES

SERVES 6
½ PITA SANDWICH
PER SERVING

Here is an old favorite
served in a new-fangled
way.

NUTRIENT
ANALYSIS

Calories	178.12kcal
Protein	12.56gm
Carbohydrate	26.80gm
Total Fat	2.36gm
Saturated	0.39gm
Polyunsaturated	1.10gm
Monounsaturated	0.42gm
Cholesterol	19.58mg
Sodium	325.80mg

1 6½-ounce can tuna in spring water, drained and
    rinsed
3 green onions with tops, finely chopped
2 tablespoons finely chopped celery
2 tablespoons finely chopped fresh parsley
1 medium carrot, shredded
1 small tomato, finely chopped
2 tablespoons finely chopped green pepper
3 tablespoons reduced-calorie mayonnaise
2 tablespoons Salsa (see page 191) or picante sauce
Freshly ground black pepper to taste
3 whole-wheat pitas, approximately 7 inches in
    diameter

ACCOMPANIMENTS
6 lettuce leaves, rinsed and dried
1 medium tomato, sliced
6 fresh mushrooms, sliced
½ cup alfalfa or bean sprouts (optional)
6 sprigs parsley

Combine all ingredients except pitas and the accompaniments. Mix well. Refrigerate for at least 1
hour.

Cut each pita in half. Line each half with a leaf
of lettuce, a slice of tomato, mushroom slices and
sprouts. Add tuna salad and garnish with a sprig of
parsley.

Poultry

Cheese/Herb Chicken Medallions
Garlic Chicken Fillets in Balsamic Vinegar
Chinese Chicken Vegetable Stir-Fry
Chicken with Mustard and Herbs
Oriental Grilled Chicken
Chicken Ragout
Chicken in White Sauce
Chicken Fajitas
Chickenwich
Crispy Oven-Fried Chicken
Hearty Chicken Stew
Brunswick Stew
Tandoori Cornish Hens
Roast Cornish Hens
Roast Turkey
Turkey Tetrazzini

CHEESE/HERB CHICKEN MEDALLIONS

6 boneless chicken breasts, about 5 ounces each, all
  visible fat removed
1 tablespoon finely chopped fresh chives, or 1
  teaspoon dried chives
1 tablespoon finely chopped fresh basil, or 1
  teaspoon dried basil
Freshly ground black pepper to taste
¼ teaspoon paprika
3 ounces part-skim mozzarella cheese, shredded

GARNISH
2 carrots
2 tablespoons Pesto (see page 190)

Preheat oven to 400° F.

Place chicken breasts on a flat surface; pat dry. Evenly sprinkle each breast with herbs, pepper and paprika.

Form cheese into six loose balls and place one in the center of each breast. Roll chicken around cheese and tie with string to keep together, making sure that the ends are tucked in and tied to prevent the cheese from oozing out. Place in an ungreased baking dish. Bake 15 to 20 minutes, or until meat has turned white throughout.

While chicken is baking, prepare carrot curls for garnish. Using a potato parer, pare carrots lengthwise into long, fine strips and soak in ice water for at least 10 minutes. Drain and pat dry. Allow chicken to cool for about 10 minutes. To serve, cut each breast into ½-inch medallions and arrange on a bed of carrot curls. Top each medallion with a little Pesto Sauce.

SERVES 6 AS AN ENTREE APPROXIMATELY 4 OUNCES PER SERVING SERVES 12 AS AN APPETIZER APPROXIMATELY 2 OUNCES PER SERVING

Top this family favorite with dabs of zesty Pesto Sauce and carrot curls. Although any fresh vegetable can be used for garnish, carrots add a wonderful splash of color. The medallions can be served hot or at room temperature.

Chilling the mozzarella beforehand keeps it from oozing when baking.

NUTRIENT ANALYSIS*

Calories	217.25kcal
Protein	34.39gm
Carbohydrate	3.55gm
Total Fat	6.43gm
Saturated	2.41gm
Polyunsaturated	0.91gm
Monounsaturated	2.41gm
Cholesterol	83.21mg
Sodium	142.26mg

* Based on entree-size serving.

GARLIC CHICKEN FILLETS IN BALSAMIC VINEGAR

**SERVES 6
5 OUNCES PER
SERVING**

This flavorful, tender chicken dish is quick and easy to prepare. The balsamic vinegar, available in some supermarkets and most gourmet shops, makes the sauce smooth and balanced. This entree can be the center of an elegant meal that you can throw together for unexpected company. Team it with Savory Brown Rice or Golden Rice (see pages 176, 177), add a steamed vegetable or a tossed salad and sit back and feast on the raves.

**NUTRIENT
ANALYSIS**

Calories	255.04kcal
Protein	34.17gm
Carbohydrate	10.35gm
Total Fat	7.66gm
Saturated	1.48gm
Polyunsaturated	1.16gm
Monounsaturated	4.31gm
Cholesterol	80.76mg
Sodium	67.40mg

2 pounds boneless chicken breasts, skinned, all
    visible fat removed
½ cup all-purpose flour
2 tablespoons olive oil
6 to 8 cloves garlic, minced
1 cup homemade Chicken Stock (see page 263)
⅓ cup balsamic vinegar
Freshly ground black pepper to taste
1 tablespoon cornstarch
2 tablespoons water

Split chicken breasts in half lengthwise and dredge in flour; remove excess.

In a large, heavy nonstick skillet, heat oil over medium-high heat. Cook chicken breasts on one side about 2 to 3 minutes, or until golden. Add garlic. Turn chicken and continue cooking about 2 to 3 minutes, or until golden. Add stock, balsamic vinegar and pepper. Reduce heat to medium-low, cover skillet and cook 5 to 10 minutes, or until chicken is tender. (The timing depends on the thickness of the chicken breasts.) Remove chicken from skillet. Keep warm.

In a small bowl, dissolve cornstarch in water, stirring until smooth. Add to skillet and cook 1 to 2 minutes, or until thick and smooth. Pour sauce over chicken and serve immediately.

CHINESE CHICKEN VEGETABLE STIR-FRY

1 pound boneless chicken breasts, skinned, all
   visible fat removed and cut into 1-inch cubes
1½ tablespoons low-sodium soy sauce
1 tablespoon grated fresh ginger or 1 teaspoon
   ground ginger
2 tablespoons acceptable vegetable oil
2 medium green, red or yellow bell peppers, cut
   into 1-inch strips
4 ounces fresh mushrooms, thinly sliced
4 green onions with tops, cut into 1-inch strips
¾ cup pineapple chunks, fresh or canned in juice
1½ tablespoons cornstarch
⅔ cup homemade Chicken Stock (see page 263)
¼ cup pineapple juice, or reserved juice from
   canned pineapple

GARNISH
1 tablespoon sesame seeds, toasted

SERVES 6
1 CUP PER SERVING

Serve this dish on a bed of hot rice or noodles.

NUTRIENT ANALYSIS

Calories	182.86kcal
Protein	18.80gm
Carbohydrate	11.42gm
Total Fat	7.09gm
Saturated	0.94gm
Polyunsaturated	1.59gm
Monounsaturated	3.96gm
Cholesterol	40.57mg
Sodium	207.05mg

Marinate chicken in soy sauce and ginger 30 to 45 minutes, stirring occasionally. In nonstick wok or skillet, heat oil over high heat. Add marinated chicken and stir-fry for 2 minutes. Using a slotted spoon, remove chicken, leaving juices in the pan. Add peppers, mushrooms and onions and stir-fry for 1 minute. Add pineapple and chicken and stir-fry another 2 to 3 minutes. Vegetables should be tender-crisp.

Blend cornstarch with stock and pineapple juice. Stir into the chicken mixture and cook about 1 minute, or until thickened. Remove from heat and garnish with sesame seeds.

CHICKEN WITH MUSTARD AND HERBS

SERVES 4 APPROXIMATELY 3 OUNCES PER SERVING

This recipe makes an elegant entree for dinner. Cold, it also can be used for special chicken sandwiches. Herb seasonings are handy for adding a dash of flavor. Try them in your cooking and at the table, too.

4 boneless chicken breasts, about 4 ounces each, skinned, all visible fat removed
1 tablespoon Herb Seasoning for salads (see page 27)
1 teaspoon lemon pepper seasoning
1 tablespoon acceptable vegetable oil
¼ cup spicy brown mustard

Preheat oven to 350° F.

Place chicken breasts in a baking pan. Mix remaining ingredients together to make a paste. Thickly and evenly spread it over top of each chicken breast. Bake 20 minutes, or just until meat has turned white throughout.

NUTRIENT ANALYSIS

Calories	173.64kcal
Protein	25.39gm
Carbohydrate	2.53gm
Total Fat	6.53gm
Saturated	1.14gm
Polyunsaturated	2.70gm
Monounsaturated	1.72gm
Cholesterol	59.96mg
Sodium	234.58mg

ORIENTAL GRILLED CHICKEN

MARINADE
2 tablespoons acceptable vegetable oil
¼ cup honey
3 tablespoons red wine vinegar
¼ cup low-sodium soy sauce
1 clove garlic, minced
2 tablespoons finely chopped fresh parsley
2 teaspoons grated fresh ginger or 1 teaspoon
     ginger powder
½ teaspoon freshly ground black pepper

12 pieces chicken, about 3½ to 4 pounds, skinned,
     all visible fat removed

S E R V E S   6
2   P I E C E S   C H I C K E N
P E R   S E R V I N G

The marinade makes this chicken delicious. Grilling gives it a slight barbecue taste. The optional method of broiling works well also.

N U T R I E N T
A N A L Y S I S

Calories	286.15kcal
Protein	33.27gm
Carbohydrate	13.04gm
Total Fat	10.82gm
Saturated	2.42gm
Polyunsaturated	4.25gm
Monounsaturated	3.05gm
Cholesterol	90.24mg
Sodium	507.26mg

In a bowl, combine all marinade ingredients and mix well. Add chicken and turn to coat all pieces. Cover and refrigerate for at least 2 hours, turning occasionally.

Grilling Method: Grill chicken pieces 6 inches away from white-hot coals. Grill 30 to 45 minutes, brushing pieces with marinade and turning pieces frequently, until chicken is tender but not dry.

Broiler Method: Preheat broiler. Arrange chicken pieces on baking sheet and place 5 inches away from the heat. Broil 25 to 30 minutes, brushing pieces with marinade and turning frequently, until chicken is tender but not dry.

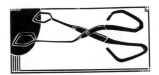

CHICKEN RAGOUT

SERVES 6
2 PIECES CHICKEN
PER SERVING

This easy French stew is delicately flavored with thyme and tarragon. Using fresh instead of dried herbs will make it extra special. Served in your prettiest casserole, it will be a favorite with guests. Have plenty of crusty French bread on hand to sop up the juices!

**NUTRIENT
ANALYSIS**

Calories	291.54kcal
Protein	34.89gm
Carbohydrate	21.80gm
Total Fat	6.89gm
Saturated	1.85gm
Polyunsaturated	1.63gm
Monounsaturated	2.34gm
Cholesterol	80.09mg
Sodium	205.66mg

⅓ cup plus 2 tablespoons all-purpose flour
½ teaspoon freshly ground black pepper, or to taste
12 pieces chicken, about 3½ pounds, skinned, all
*   visible fat removed*
Vegetable oil spray
1 teaspoon olive oil
1 medium yellow or white onion, sliced
1 pound fresh mushrooms, sliced
2 cloves garlic, minced
¼ cup fresh thyme or 1 tablespoon dried thyme
¼ cup fresh tarragon or 1 tablespoon dried
*   tarragon*
¼ cup finely chopped fresh parsley
¼ teaspoon salt (optional)
1 cup homemade Chicken Stock (see page 263)
1 cup dry white wine or 1 cup additional
*   homemade Chicken Stock*
¼ cup cold water
2 cups green peas, fresh or frozen

Preheat oven to 400° F.

Combine ⅓ cup flour, pepper and chicken pieces in a plastic bag. Shake well to coat pieces.

Spray a nonstick skillet with vegetable oil spray. Heat skillet over medium-high heat, add chicken pieces a few at a time, and brown on all sides. Remove pieces to an ovenproof casserole or Dutch oven. Repeat process with remaining chicken. In skillet, heat oil, add onions and cook 2 to 3 minutes, or until onions are translucent. Add mushrooms, garlic, thyme, tarragon, parsley, salt, stock and wine; mix together. Pour over chicken pieces. Cover chicken and bake 45 minutes.

In a small bowl, blend 2 tablespoons flour and water. Gradually add to the liquid in the casserole, while stirring lightly. Add peas. Cover and continue to bake another 15 to 20 minutes, or until chicken and peas are tender and sauce thickened.

CHICKEN IN WHITE SAUCE

Vegetable oil spray

12 pieces chicken, about 3½ pounds, skinned, all
visible fat removed

¼ cup Madeira or port wine or homemade Chicken
Stock (see page 263)

2 tablespoons minced fresh sage or 1 teaspoon dried
sage

2 tablespoons minced fresh thyme or 1 teaspoon
dried thyme

3 green onions with tops, thinly sliced

¼ cup finely chopped fresh parsley

¼ teaspoon salt (optional)

Freshly ground black pepper to taste

1½ cups White Sauce (see page 188)

SERVES 6
2 PIECES CHICKEN
PER SERVING

This is a great dish for
entertaining. You can even
make it a day ahead of
time.

NUTRIENT
ANALYSIS*

Calories	293.56kcal
Protein	39.99gm
Carbohydrate	6.58gm
Total Fat	10.92gm
Saturated	2.67gm
Polyunsaturated	3.88gm
Monounsaturated	3.13gm
Cholesterol	106.51mg
Sodium	281.38mg

* Using wine.

Preheat oven to 350° F.

Spray a nonstick skillet with vegetable oil spray.
Heat skillet over medium-high heat, add chicken
pieces a few at a time and lightly brown on all sides.
Remove pieces to an ovenproof casserole or Dutch
oven. Repeat process with remaining chicken. Pour
wine or stock over warm chicken pieces, toss to
cover and allow to stand for 10 minutes.

Mix herbs, onions, parsley and seasonings into
White Sauce. Pour over chicken pieces. Cover and
bake 45 to 60 minutes, or until chicken pieces are
tender.

If making ahead, refrigerate; reheat before serving.

CHICKEN FAJITAS

SERVES 4
2 FAJITAS PER
SERVING

This delicious dish is fun to make and good for you, too. Enjoy it with shredded lettuce, sliced tomatoes, Salsa, Guacamole and Refried Beans (see pages 191, 73 and 160).

NUTRIENT ANALYSIS*

Calories	346.19kcal
Protein	34.03gm
Carbohydrate	23.58gm
Total Fat	13.06gm
Saturated	3.48gm
Polyunsaturated	5.23gm
Monounsaturated	3.37gm
Cholesterol	74.95mg
Sodium	315.75mg

* Including garnishes.

1 clove garlic, finely minced
1 tablespoon acceptable vegetable oil
1½ tablespoons fresh lemon or lime juice
3 tablespoons Worcestershire sauce
⅛ teaspoon freshly ground black pepper, or to taste
1¼ pounds boneless chicken breasts, skinned, all
    visible fat removed
1 large onion
1 large green pepper
2 teaspoons acceptable vegetable oil
8 corn tortillas

Preheat broiler.

To make marinade, combine garlic, oil, lemon or lime juice, Worcestershire sauce and pepper in a bowl.

Cut chicken lengthwise into thin ⅜-inch strips. Add to marinade, toss to coat evenly and let chicken marinate in refrigerator 10 to 20 minutes, turning at least once.

Slice the onion and pepper into thin ⅛-inch strips.

In a nonstick skillet, heat 2 teaspoons oil over medium-high heat. Add onion and pepper slices and sauté, stirring constantly, about 5 minutes, or until onion is slightly brown.

Wrap tortillas in foil and place on lower shelf of oven. Heat thoroughly.

Line broiler pan with foil. Place chicken on the foil and broil about 3 inches from heat for 4 minutes.

To serve, place three cooked chicken strips on each tortilla, top with onions, peppers and assorted garnishes as desired. Roll tortilla around chicken strips and eat with fingers.

CHICKENWICH

4 boneless chicken breasts, about 4 ounces each,
    skinned, all visible fat removed
4 slices part-skim mozzarella cheese, about 4
    ounces
4 slices ham, about 4 ounces, visible fat removed
3 tablespoons whole-wheat or all-purpose flour
1 teaspoon dry mustard
½ teaspoon paprika
2 teaspoons olive oil

Place chicken breasts, smooth-side up, between two sheets of plastic wrap. Using a meat mallet or a rolling pin, pound chicken to twice its original diameter and set aside.

Fold each slice of cheese in half and place it on a slice of ham. Fold the ham over the cheese to form a packet that is about half as big as the piece of chicken and place one packet on top of each chicken piece. Fold the chicken in half over the mozzarella ham packet to enclose it.

Mix flour, mustard powder and paprika. Dip chicken into mixture and tap lightly to remove excess.

In a nonstick skillet, heat oil over medium heat. When oil is hot, add chicken to pan, sauté on each side for about 4 or 5 minutes, then sauté each seam side for about 20 seconds to seal. Serve immediately.

SERVES 4
1 PER SERVING

Our Chickenwich is made with ham. Yes, ham! Ham is leaner than you may think. Modern farming methods make it possible to produce pork that is low in fat. Ham is still high in sodium because of the salt and sodium nitrate used in processing, so you may want to balance your diet by having a low-sodium entree at your next meal.

NUTRIENT ANALYSIS

Calories	280.31kcal
Protein	37.41gm
Carbohydrate	3.74gm
Total Fat	11.96gm
Saturated	4.74gm
Polyunsaturated	1.22gm
Monounsaturated	4.97gm
Cholesterol	93.87mg
Sodium	362.80mg

CRISPY OVEN-FRIED CHICKEN

SERVES 6
2 PIECES CHICKEN
PER SERVING

This is a heart-healthy alternative to traditional fried chicken. It's spicy, crispy and easy to make.

NUTRIENT ANALYSIS

Calories	373.49kcal
Protein	39.30gm
Carbohydrate	15.40gm
Total Fat	16.47gm
Saturated	3.31gm
Polyunsaturated	7.23gm
Monounsaturated	4.49gm
Cholesterol	105.28mg
Sodium	413.61mg

12 pieces chicken, about 3½ pounds, skinned, all
 visible fat removed
¼ cup acceptable vegetable oil
¼ teaspoon salt (optional)
Freshly ground black pepper to taste
1 teaspoon ground ginger, or to taste
1 clove garlic, crushed (optional)
1 teaspoon paprika
4 cups wheat-flake cereal, lightly crushed

Preheat oven to 350° F.

Rinse chicken and pat dry.

Combine oil, salt, pepper, ginger, garlic and paprika in a small bowl. Place cereal in a pie plate or on a piece of foil. Brush each piece of chicken on both sides with oil mixture, then dip in cereal crumbs, pressing lightly to get an even coating on all sides. Place on an ungreased baking sheet. Bake 45 to 60 minutes, or until chicken is golden brown and tender. Timing will vary according to the thickness of the chicken pieces.

HEARTY CHICKEN STEW

2 tablespoons acceptable vegetable oil
1 medium onion, finely chopped
1 tablespoon minced fresh ginger or 1 teaspoon
   ground ginger
3 cloves garlic, minced
2 tablespoons all-purpose flour
2 medium tomatoes, diced
8 to 10 peppercorns, or to taste
6 whole cloves
1 cinnamon stick
8 pieces chicken, about 2½ pounds, skinned, all
   visible fat removed
2 cups water
1 tablespoon Worcestershire sauce
¾ pound baby carrots, fresh or frozen
6 ounces green peas, fresh or frozen
8 ounces red or white new potatoes, scrubbed and
   unpeeled

SERVES 8
1½ CUPS PER
SERVING

This is a good recipe to make ahead and refrigerate or freeze until needed. The herbs and spices give this dish a wonderful Oriental flavor.

NUTRIENT ANALYSIS

Calories	215.25kcal
Protein	18.49gm
Carbohydrate	19.97gm
Total Fat	6.68gm
Saturated	1.11gm
Polyunsaturated	1.76gm
Monounsaturated	3.07gm
Cholesterol	42.47mg
Sodium	94.31mg

In a deep skillet or Dutch oven, heat oil over medium-high heat. Sauté onions, ginger and garlic until onions are soft, about 3 minutes. Add flour and cook 1 minute, stirring quickly to prevent sticking. Stir in tomatoes and allow to cook another 2 minutes.

Wrap peppercorns, cloves and cinnamon in a small piece of cheesecloth. Add chicken, cheesecloth package, water and Worcestershire sauce to onion mixture. Reduce heat and simmer, covered, 20 minutes. Add carrots, peas and potatoes. Continue to simmer, covered, until chicken and vegetables are cooked, 20 to 25 minutes. Remove cheesecloth package and serve the stew steaming hot.

BRUNSWICK STEW

SERVES 6

1½ CUPS PER
SERVING

NUTRIENT
ANALYSIS

Calories	255.20kcal
Protein	23.80gm
Carbohydrate	31.40gm
Total Fat	5.29gm
Saturated	0.98gm
Polyunsaturated	1.11gm
Monounsaturated	2.36gm
Cholesterol	43.20mg
Sodium	250.58mg

1 tablespoon olive oil
1 medium onion, chopped
1 pound boneless chicken breasts, skinned, all
    visible fat removed and cut into 1-inch cubes
1½ cups chopped tomatoes
1 6-ounce can no-salt-added tomato paste
10 ounces baby lima beans, fresh or frozen
10 ounces corn kernels, fresh or frozen
3 cups homemade Chicken Stock (see page 263)
1 tablespoon Worcestershire sauce
3 tablespoons fresh lemon juice

In a deep skillet or Dutch oven, heat oil over medium-high heat. Add onion and sauté until soft, about 3 minutes. Add chicken pieces and remaining ingredients. Reduce heat to low, cover and simmer 1 hour.

TANDOORI CORNISH HENS

3 Cornish hens, approximately 1 pound each
1 teaspoon chili powder, or to taste
½ teaspoon salt (optional)
Freshly ground black pepper to taste
3 tablespoons fresh lime juice

MARINADE
1 cup plain nonfat yogurt
3 cloves garlic
1-inch piece fresh ginger, coarsely chopped
1 small onion, coarsely chopped
1 teaspoon cumin seeds
½ teaspoon ground turmeric
½ teaspoon chili powder, or to taste
1 teaspoon sugar

GARNISH
1 lime, cut into wedges
Few sprigs fresh cilantro or parsley

S E R V E S 6
½ H E N P E R
S E R V I N G

One of the most popular Indian dishes, tandoori chicken is spicy but not hot. This easy and attractive lowfat dish is marinated in yogurt and spices. The recipe works equally well with chicken parts, a whole chicken or Cornish hens. Cornish hens are preferable because of their low fat content.

Thaw the hens if frozen. Rinse, remove giblets and necks and pat dry. Make several slits in the skin, then split each hen in half along the breastbone.

Mix together chili powder, salt, pepper and lime juice. Rub mixture all over poultry and set aside for about 15 minutes.

In a blender, puree all marinade ingredients. Place poultry pieces in a bowl and add marinade. Mix well to coat all the pieces. Cover and refrigerate for at least 8 hours, turning occasionally.

Preheat oven to 400° F.

Place hens, skin-side up, on a rack in a roasting pan and spoon marinade over the pieces. Bake, basting frequently with marinade, until thoroughly cooked, 45 to 60 minutes, or until hens are very tender. Test for doneness by pricking the skin of the thigh; the juice should run clear. Serve hot. Remove skin before eating and garnish with lime and cilantro or parsley.

NUTRIENT ANALYSIS

Calories	208.95kcal
Protein	27.23gm
Carbohydrate	8.16gm
Total Fat	7.97gm
Saturated	2.24gm
Polyunsaturated	1.82gm
Monounsaturated	2.93gm
Cholesterol	80.27mg
Sodium	281.32mg

ROAST CORNISH HENS

SERVES 6
½ HEN PER
SERVING

For that special occasion, serve this with Savory Brown Rice (see page 177). Add a dash of color with steamed vegetables.

NUTRIENT ANALYSIS

Calories	228.76kcal
Protein	24.84gm
Carbohydrate	5.58gm
Total Fat	12.31gm
Saturated	2.74gm
Polyunsaturated	4.42gm
Monounsaturated	3.99gm
Cholesterol	79.12mg
Sodium	66.36mg

3 Cornish hens, approximately 1 pound each
1 tablespoon whole peppercorns, coarsely crushed
3 tablespoons chopped fresh tarragon or 1
    tablespoon dried tarragon
1 medium pear, cut into thirds
1 cup fresh parsley sprigs, rinsed
2 tablespoons acceptable vegetable oil
Water

Thaw hens if frozen.

Preheat oven to 425° F.

Remove giblets and discard. Save the necks for making stock. Rinse hens and pat dry. Gently loosen skin from meat on breast and legs by breaking the membrane that holds the skin to the meat and sliding your hand between the two to loosen the skin. Spread pepper and tarragon under the skin and in the cavity. Stuff each cavity with pieces of pear and parsley.

Place the hens on a rack, breast-side up, on the top of a 3-inch-deep roaster pan. Soak a cheesecloth in oil and cover hens with the oiled cloth. This keeps the meat from drying out. Put water in the pan to a depth of 1 to 1½ inches to provide moisture and pan drippings for gravy. Place hens in oven, reduce heat immediately to 325° F. and bake 45 to 60 minutes. Test for doneness by pricking the skin of the thigh; the juice should run clear. Defat the drippings and make Pan Gravy (see page 192). Cut each hen in half before serving.

ROAST TURKEY

1 11- to 12-pound fresh or frozen turkey
2 tablespoons whole black, white or green
   peppercorns, or a mixture, coarsely crushed
1 large apple, quartered
1 cup fresh parsley sprigs, rinsed
¼ cup acceptable vegetable oil (canola oil works
   well)
Water

Thaw turkey if frozen.
   Preheat oven to 425° F.

Remove giblets and discard. Save the neck for making stock. Rinse turkey and pat dry. Gently loosen skin from meat on breast and legs by breaking the membrane that holds the skin to the meat and sliding your hand between the two to loosen the skin.

Spread peppercorns under the skin and in the cavity. Stuff the cavity with apple and parsley.

Place the turkey on a rack, breast-side up, on the top of a 3-inch-deep roaster pan. Soak a cheesecloth in oil and cover turkey with the oiled cloth. This keeps the meat from drying out. Put water in the pan to a depth of 1 to 1½ inches to provide moisture and pan drippings for gravy. Place turkey in oven and reduce heat immediately to 325° F. Bake 2 to 3 hours, or 12 to 15 minutes per pound. Test for doneness by pricking the skin of the thigh; the juice should run clear. Or use a thermometer inserted in the thigh; it should register 185° F. when the turkey is fully cooked.

Let the turkey rest 20 minutes before serving. Defat the drippings and make Pan Gravy (see page 192). Serve turkey on a large heated platter and carve, removing the skin.

**SERVES 12
APPROXIMATELY 4
OUNCES BONELESS
TURKEY PER
SERVING**

Eating healthfully on holidays is made easier with recipes like this. For a traditional meal, serve it with Cornbread Dressing, Green Beans Almondine and Pumpkin Pie (pages 212, 159 and 226).

**NUTRIENT
ANALYSIS**

Calories	355.15kcal
Protein	48.56gm
Carbohydrate	6.04gm
Total Fat	14.13gm
Saturated	3.05gm
Polyunsaturated	3.71gm
Monounsaturated	5.78gm
Cholesterol	135.85mg
Sodium	121.49mg

TURKEY TETRAZZINI

SERVES 8
1½ CUPS PER SERVING

This is a great way to use turkey leftovers.

NUTRIENT ANALYSIS

Calories	204.65kcal
Protein	18.41gm
Carbohydrate	22.32gm
Total Fat	4.38gm
Saturated	1.17gm
Polyunsaturated	1.57gm
Monounsaturated	1.20gm
Cholesterol	33.14mg
Sodium	297.57mg

1 14- to 15-ounce box macaroni and cheese (with powdered cheese-sauce packet)
1 tablespoon acceptable vegetable oil
1 cup coarsely chopped onion
½ cup chopped green bell pepper
2 cloves garlic, finely minced
8 ounces fresh mushrooms, sliced
Vegetable oil spray
12 ounces cooked breast of turkey, cubed, about 2 cups
1½ cups skim milk
2 tablespoons dry sherry

TOPPING (OPTIONAL)
½ cup grated Defatted Cheddar Cheese (see page 261)

Preheat oven to 350° F.

Cook macaroni according to package directions, omitting salt.

While macaroni is cooking, heat oil in a large skillet. Sauté onion, green pepper and garlic over medium-high heat 2 to 3 minutes, or until soft. Add mushrooms and cook 2 more minutes, or until soft.

Spray a 3-quart casserole with vegetable oil spray, if desired. Drain the macaroni and combine with cheese packet, sautéed vegetables, turkey, milk and sherry. Pour into prepared casserole dish. Cover and bake 35 to 40 minutes, or until most of the liquid is absorbed.

Remove from oven and sprinkle with defatted cheddar cheese. Cover and allow casserole to sit for about 5 minutes, or just until cheese melts.

Meats

Marinated Steak
Swedish Meatloaf with Dill Sauce
Shepherd's Pie
Bulgar and Ground Beef Casserole
Beef Ragout
Sloppy Joes
Mexican Beef and Cornbread Pie
Vegetable-Beef Burgers
Chili
Beef or Venison Stroganoff
Lamb and Red Beans
Pork with Savory Sauce
Pork and Tofu Stir-Fry
Scrambled Eggs and Ham in Sweet Potato Boat

MARINATED STEAK

1½ pounds flank steak, 1 inch thick, all visible fat removed
Freshly ground pepper to taste

SERVES 6
APPROXIMATELY
3 OUNCES
PER SERVING

MARINADE

2 tablespoons acceptable vegetable oil
3 tablespoons tarragon or wine vinegar
½ cup dry red wine
3 cloves garlic, crushed
3 tablespoons minced fresh parsley
1 tablespoon chopped fresh oregano or 1 teaspoon dried oregano
1 tablespoon chopped fresh tarragon or 1 teaspoon dried tarragon
1 bay leaf
½ teaspoon freshly ground black pepper

Steak on a cholesterol-lowering diet? Sure. Just select the meat carefully and trim all visible fat. This marinade is a favorite among steak lovers. One taste will convince you, too!

Place steak in a baking dish. In a small bowl, combine ingredients for marinade. Pour over steak and turn to coat. Cover and refrigerate for at least 8 hours, turning occasionally.

Preheat broiler.

Remove steak from marinade, pat dry and sprinkle with additional freshly ground pepper. Broil 4 to 6 inches from heat 4 to 7 minutes on each side for medium-well done, or 3 to 5 minutes on each side for medium-rare. Slice thin diagonally across the grain. Serve warm.

NUTRIENT ANALYSIS

Calories	198.96kcal
Protein	25.19gm
Carbohydrate	1.94gm
Total Fat	9.72gm
Saturated	2.82gm
Polyunsaturated	2.98gm
Monounsaturated	3.31gm
Cholesterol	72.38mg
Sodium	50.08mg

SWEDISH MEATLOAF WITH DILL SAUCE

SERVES 6 APPROXIMATELY 4 OUNCES OF MEATLOAF AND ¼ CUP OF SAUCE PER SERVING

If you like Swedish meatballs, you'll love this moist and flavorful meatloaf.

NUTRIENT ANALYSIS OF SWEDISH MEATLOAF

Calories	209.07kcal
Protein	24.11gm
Carbohydrate	14.22gm
Total Fat	5.25gm
Saturated	1.90gm
Polyunsaturated	0.94gm
Monounsaturated	1.88gm
Cholesterol	58.03mg
Sodium	195.24mg

Vegetable oil spray
1 teaspoon acceptable vegetable oil
½ medium onion, finely minced
2 cloves garlic, finely minced
¾ cup rye bread crumbs, about 4 slices
⅓ cup buttermilk
1 large egg white, lightly beaten
⅛ teaspoon freshly ground black pepper
¼ teaspoon ground nutmeg
¼ teaspoon ground ginger
⅛ teaspoon ground allspice
1 tablespoon chopped fresh dill or 1 teaspoon dried dill
¾ pound very lean ground sirloin
½ pound ground chicken breast (skin and all visible fat removed before grinding)

SAUCE

1 tablespoon acceptable margarine, unsalted
2 tablespoons all-purpose flour
1 cup homemade Beef Stock (see page 264)
3 tablespoons dry sherry
¾ cup evaporated skim milk
⅛ teaspoon freshly ground pepper
¼ teaspoon ground nutmeg
¼ teaspoon ground allspice
¼ teaspoon ground ginger
3 tablespoons chopped fresh dill or 1½ tablespoons dried dill

Preheat oven to 425° F. Spray a 9 × 5-inch oven-proof loaf pan with vegetable oil spray; set aside.

To make the loaf, heat oil in a large, nonstick skillet at medium setting. Add onion and sauté, stirring frequently, about 4 minutes. Add garlic and continue to sauté, stirring constantly, 1 minute more, or until onion is soft.

Mix bread crumbs and buttermilk in a large bowl and let soak 5 minutes. Add sautéed onion and garlic, egg white, pepper, nutmeg, ginger, allspice and dill. Use your hands to lightly mix. Add ground beef and chicken. Mix well to evenly distribute ingredients. Lightly pat into prepared loaf pan. Place in oven and reduce temperature to 350° F. Bake 30 minutes.

While meatloaf is cooking, make the sauce. In heavy saucepan, melt margarine over medium heat. Remove pan from heat and blend in flour. Return to heat and gradually add beef stock, sherry and milk. Stir constantly with a wire whisk until fully blended and mixture thickens, about 6 to 8 minutes. Remove from heat and blend in remaining ingredients.

Remove meatloaf from oven and pour off fat. Pour sauce over meatloaf, cover with foil and return to oven. Continue to cook 15 minutes more or until done. Serve hot.

NUTRIENT ANALYSIS OF DILL SAUCE

Calories	47.97kcal
Protein	1.79gm
Carbohydrate	5.81gm
Total Fat	2.31gm
Saturated	0.43gm
Polyunsaturated	0.69gm
Monounsaturated	0.95gm
Cholesterol	1.65mg
Sodium	15.41mg

SHEPHERD'S PIE

SERVES 6
1 3 × 5-INCH
PORTION
PER SERVING

Assemble this easy entree
ahead of time and bake it
just before serving.

**NUTRIENT
ANALYSIS**

Calories	256.67kcal
Protein	21.38gm
Carbohydrate	30.53gm
Total Fat	4.55gm
Saturated	1.84gm
Polyunsaturated	0.39gm
Monounsaturated	1.77gm
Cholesterol	49.01mg
Sodium	314.96mg

1½ pounds potatoes, peeled
¼ cup skim milk
Freshly ground pepper to taste
1 pound very lean ground sirloin
1 large onion, finely chopped
1 large bell pepper, chopped
3 medium carrots, chopped
½ cup green peas, fresh or frozen
1 medium tomato, chopped
¼ cup chopped fresh parsley
¾ cup homemade Chicken Stock (see page 263)
½ teaspoon salt
Freshly ground black pepper to taste
2 tablespoons Worcestershire sauce
1 tablespoon cornstarch
2 tablespoons cold water

Boil potatoes until tender. Mash together with skim milk and pepper until smooth; keep warm.

Preheat oven to 350° F.

Heat a heavy, nonstick skillet, at least 10 inches in diameter, over medium-high heat. Add ground beef and sauté, stirring occasionally, 4 to 5 minutes, or until meat is no longer pink. Pour contents of pan into a strainer or colander lined with paper towels. Allow fat to drain out. Return meat to pan, add onion and cook until onions are translucent, 4 to 5 minutes. Add bell pepper, carrots, peas, tomato, parsley, chicken stock, salt, pepper and Worchestershire sauce. Simmer, uncovered, 15 minutes.

Dissolve cornstarch in water and stir into meat mixture. Spoon into an ungreased 10 × 10 × 2-inch or 9 × 11 × 2-inch baking dish. Spread mashed potatoes over the surface, using a fork for texture. Bake 30 to 35 minutes, or until lightly browned.

BULGUR AND GROUND BEEF CASSEROLE

1 cup bulgur
1½ cups cold water
1 pound very lean ground sirloin
2 medium onions, chopped
¼ teaspoon salt
Freshly ground black pepper to taste
½ cup finely chopped fresh cilantro or parsley
1 tablespoon chopped fresh dill weed or ½ teaspoon
    dried dill weed
4 medium tomatoes, chopped
2 tablespoons fresh lemon juice
½ cup canned low-sodium vegetable juice

GARNISH
2 tomatoes, cut into wedges
1 lemon, sliced thin

SERVES 6
1 3 × 5-INCH
PORTION
PER SERVING

Bulgur or cracked wheat is available in most supermarkets and health food stores. It has a delicious, nutty flavor and is an excellent substitute for rice.

NUTRIENT ANALYSIS

Calories	267.52kcal
Protein	21.83gm
Carbohydrate	32.32gm
Total Fat	4.91gm
Saturated	1.84gm
Polyunsaturated	0.43gm
Monounsaturated	1.79gm
Cholesterol	48.25mg
Sodium	138.27mg

Preheat oven to 350° F.

In a medium bowl, soak bulgur in cold water 15 to 30 minutes, or until soft. Set aside.

Heat a heavy, nonstick skillet, at least 10 inches in diameter, over medium-high heat. Add ground beef and sauté, stirring occasionally, 4 to 5 minutes, or until meat is no longer pink. Pour contents of pan into a strainer or colander lined with paper towels. Allow fat to drain out. Return meat to pan, add onions, and cook until onions are translucent, 3 to 4 minutes. Add salt, pepper and herbs. Drain bulgur and add to meat. Add tomatoes, lemon juice and vegetable juice. Stir lightly.

Place mixture in a 10 × 10 × 2-inch or 9 × 11 × 2-inch baking dish or ovenproof casserole. Bake, uncovered, 15 to 20 minutes, or until heated thoroughly. Garnish with tomato and lemon.

BEEF RAGOUT

SERVES 6
1⅓ CUPS PER
SERVING

This hearty ground beef dish is quick and easy to prepare. Instead of buying ground beef in a package, have your butcher grind a sirloin steak for you. Ask him to remove all visible fat beforehand and to clean the grinder to remove any fat from previous grindings.

NUTRIENT ANALYSIS

Calories	394.25kcal
Protein	37.76gm
Carbohydrate	41.81gm
Total Fat	8.63gm
Saturated	3.13gm
Polyunsaturated	1.33gm
Monounsaturated	2.81gm
Cholesterol	72.38mg
Sodium	262.03mg

1½ pounds very lean ground sirloin
1 large onion, chopped
½ cup water
¾ cup dry red wine or ¾ cup additional water
1 red chili pepper, seeded and chopped (optional)
3 cloves garlic, minced
2 large tomatoes, chopped
1 8-ounce can no-salt-added tomato sauce
1 teaspoon chili powder, or to taste
1 teaspoon ground cumin
1 tablespoon fresh oregano or 1 teaspoon dried oregano
½ teaspoon salt (optional)
Freshly ground black pepper to taste
2 15-ounce cans kidney beans, rinsed and drained

GARNISH
¼ cup chopped fresh parsley

Heat a heavy, nonstick skillet, at least 10 inches in diameter, over medium-high heat. Add ground beef and sauté, stirring occasionally, 4 to 5 minutes, or until meat is no longer pink. Pour contents of pan into a strainer or colander lined with paper towels. Allow fat to drain out. Return meat to the pan, add onions and sauté 4 to 5 minutes, or until onions are translucent. Stir in water, wine, hot pepper, garlic, tomatoes, tomato sauce, chili powder, cumin, oregano, salt and pepper. Bring mixture to a boil, reduce heat and simmer, partially covered, about 45 minutes, stirring occasionally. Add kidney beans and simmer 10 to 15 minutes, or until beans are heated thoroughly. Sprinkle with parsley before serving.

SLOPPY JOES

SAUCE

1 8-ounce can no-salt-added tomato sauce
½ cup ketchup
1½ tablespoons Worcestershire sauce
1 teaspoon prepared yellow mustard
½ teaspoon dry mustard
1 teaspoon molasses
1 clove garlic, finely minced
¼ teaspoon freshly grated orange peel
Pinch ground cloves
Hot pepper sauce to taste

1 pound very lean ground sirloin
½ small onion, finely chopped
6 whole-wheat hamburger buns, toasted if desired

SERVES 6
½ CUP PER
SERVING

You can eat to lower your blood cholesterol and still enjoy some old favorites. Here's a pared-down version of Sloppy Joes with perked-up flavor.

NUTRIENT ANALYSIS

Calories	260.28kcal
Protein	21.89gm
Carbohydrate	30.19gm
Total Fat	5.61gm
Saturated	2.05gm
Polyunsaturated	0.73gm
Monounsaturated	2.05gm
Cholesterol	48.82mg
Sodium	549.99mg

In a saucepan over low heat, combine sauce ingredients. Mix well and simmer while preparing meat.

Next, heat a heavy, nonstick skillet, at least 10 inches in diameter, over medium-high heat. Add ground beef and sauté, stirring occasionally, 4 to 5 minutes, or until meat is no longer pink. Pour contents of pan into a strainer or colander lined with paper towels. Allow fat to drain out.

Add onion to pan and sauté, stirring frequently, about 5 minutes, or until translucent. Return meat to pan and add sauce. Heat 3 minutes, stirring occasionally. Add additional hot pepper sauce, if desired. Spoon ½ cup mixture over each bun. Serve immediately.

The sauce and meat mixture freezes well.

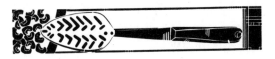

MEXICAN BEEF AND CORNBREAD PIE

SERVES 6
1 3 × 5-INCH
PORTION
PER SERVING

A blend of the Old South and South-of-the-Border makes this a real winner. Serve with your favorite green salad for a hearty family meal.

NUTRIENT ANALYSIS*

Calories	370.70kcal
Protein	25.28gm
Carbohydrate	49.16gm
Total Fat	8.66gm
Saturated	2.09gm
Polyunsaturated	1.30gm
Monounsaturated	3.36gm
Cholesterol	49.98mg
Sodium	478.57mg

* Based on canola oil.

MEAT MIXTURE

1 pound very lean ground sirloin
1 large onion, chopped, about 1 cup
2 large tomatoes, chopped, about 2 cups
1 10-ounce package frozen whole kernel corn
1 large green bell pepper, chopped, about 1 to 1½ cups
1 teaspoon cumin powder
1 teaspoon chili powder, or to taste
½ teaspoon salt (optional)
1 tablespoon Worcestershire sauce
1 cup homemade Chicken or Beef Stock (see pages 263, 264)

CORNBREAD MIXTURE

1 ½ cups yellow cornmeal
¼ cup all-purpose flour
1 teaspoon sugar (optional)
¼ teaspoon salt (optional)
2 teaspoons baking powder
3 large egg whites, lightly beaten
½ cup skim milk
1 tablespoon acceptable vegetable oil

Preheat oven to 400° F.

Heat a heavy, nonstick skillet, at least 10 inches in diameter, over medium-high heat. Add ground beef and sauté, stirring occasionally, 4 to 5 minutes, or until meat is no longer pink. Pour contents of pan into a strainer or colander lined with paper towels. Allow fat to drain out. Return meat to the pan, add onions and cook until onions are translucent, about 3 minutes. Add tomatoes, corn, bell pepper, cumin, chili powder, salt, Worcestershire sauce and stock. Simmer, uncovered, 20 to 25 minutes.

In a bowl, mix together cornmeal, flour, sugar,

salt and baking powder. In another bowl, combine egg whites, milk and oil; add to cornmeal mixture. Mix lightly.

Place meat mixture in a 10 × 10 × 2-inch baking dish. Spoon cornbread mixture over meat and spread lightly to cover surface. Bake, uncovered, 30 to 40 minutes, or until cornbread is golden brown.

VEGETABLE-BEEF BURGERS

MEAT MIXTURE
1 pound very lean ground sirloin
1 small tomato, finely chopped
1 medium onion, finely chopped
1 small green bell pepper, finely chopped
½ teaspoon freshly ground black pepper, or to taste
1 teaspoon Worcestershire sauce
Vegetable oil spray

ACCOMPANIMENTS
6 whole-wheat hamburger buns
1 large tomato, sliced
6 lettuce leaves
Mustard to taste
Ketchup to taste

SERVES 6

If you thought your lowfat diet meant never eating another hamburger, think again. This recipe is low in fat and will be high on your list of favorites.

NUTRIENT ANALYSIS*

Calories	238.40kcal
Protein	21.54gm
Carbohydrate	24.77gm
Total Fat	5.46gm
Saturated	2.04gm
Polyunsaturated	0.71gm
Monounsaturated	2.02gm
Cholesterol	48.52mg
Sodium	278.33mg

* For burger with lettuce, tomato slice, mustard and ketchup on whole-wheat bun.

Combine ground beef, tomato, onion, green pepper, freshly ground pepper and Worcestershire sauce. Mix well. Divide mixture into six portions and shape each into a patty about ½ inch thick.

Spray a heavy, nonstick skillet with vegetable oil spray and heat over medium-high heat. Add beef patties and cook 5 to 7 minutes on each side, or until done as desired. Handle meat patties very carefully to prevent breaking.

Place cooked patties on paper towels and blot to absorb fat. Serve on buns with tomato, lettuce, mustard and ketchup.

CHILI

SERVES 6
1¼ CUPS PER
SERVING

For that four-alarm taste, add a jalapeño pepper or two! This recipes tastes best when made the day before, allowing the flavors to mingle.

NUTRIENT ANALYSIS

Calories	374.46kcal
Protein	30.02gm
Carbohydrate	46.07gm
Total Fat	9.38gm
Saturated	2.68gm
Polyunsaturated	2.34gm
Monounsaturated	2.99gm
Cholesterol	47.96mg
Sodium	286.83mg

1 pound very lean ground sirloin
2 large onions, chopped
2 to 4 cloves garlic, minced
2 8-ounce cans no-salt-added tomato sauce
1½ cups water
3 tablespoons chili powder
⅛ teaspoon cayenne pepper, or to taste
1 teaspoon ground cumin
1 tablespoon fresh oregano or 1 teaspoon dried oregano
Freshly ground black pepper to taste
½ teaspoon salt (optional)
2 15-ounce cans pinto beans, rinsed and drained
2 tablespoons cornstarch
¼ cup cold water

GARNISH
Corn Crisps (see page 213)

Heat a heavy, nonstick skillet over medium-high heat. Add ground beef and sauté, stirring occasionally, 4 to 5 minutes, or until meat is no longer pink. Pour contents of pan into a strainer or colander lined with paper towels. Allow fat to drain out.

In a large, heavy saucepan or Dutch oven, heat oil over medium-high heat. Add onions and sauté 2 to 3 minutes, or until translucent. Add meat, garlic, tomato sauce and 1½ cups water. Simmer 20 minutes. Stir in chili powder, cayenne pepper, cumin, oregano, pepper, salt and pinto beans. Allow to simmer an additional 30 to 40 minutes. Combine cornstarch and cold water. Stir into chili mixture to thicken, and cook an additional 3 to 4 minutes. Serve hot, garnished with Corn Crisps.

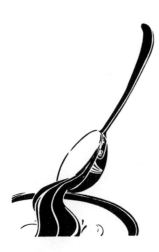

BEEF OR VENISON STROGANOFF

½ cup all-purpose flour
½ teaspoon freshly ground black pepper
2 pounds boneless beef round steak or venison, all
     visible fat removed, cut into bite-size pieces
2 tablespoons acceptable vegetable oil
1 large onion, sliced ¼-inch thick
1¾ cups homemade Beef Stock (see page 264)
¼ cup dry sherry
1 pound fresh mushrooms, thickly sliced
1 12-ounce package macaroni
1 cup Double-Thick Yogurt (see page 262)
2 tablespoons ketchup
1 tablespoon Worcestershire sauce
¼ teaspoon salt

In a large bowl, mix flour and pepper. Add meat and toss to coat evenly.

In a large, nonstick skillet or Dutch oven, heat oil over medium-high heat. Add meat and onions and sauté, stirring frequently, until meat is nearly browned on all sides, about 5 minutes. Add stock and sherry; stir well. Partially cover and simmer over low heat, stirring occasionally, 1½ hours, or until meat is tender.

While meat simmers, sauté mushrooms in a nonstick skillet over medium heat, stirring occasionally. Cook 20 minutes. Add mushrooms to the meat.

Cook macaroni according to package directions, omitting salt; drain.

Place Double-Thick Yogurt, ketchup, Worcestershire sauce and salt in a medium bowl. Whisk together to mix well and set aside.

When meat is fully cooked, add yogurt mixture. Stir and heat about 5 minutes. Serve over macaroni.

The meat mixture freezes well. Just omit the Double-Thick Yogurt, and add it after reheating.

SERVES 10
¾ CUP STROGANOFF AND ¾ CUP MACARONI PER SERVING

The long, slow cooking tenderizes the meat and gives the stroganoff a chance to develop its full flavor. Use beef or venison in this recipe.

NUTRIENT ANALYSIS OF BEEF STROGANOFF

Calories	340.01kcal
Protein	29.31gm
Carbohydrate	37.50gm
Total Fat	7.64gm
Saturated	2.33gm
Polyunsaturated	2.10gm
Monounsaturated	2.54gm
Cholesterol	60.28mg
Sodium	292.67mg

NUTRIENT ANALYSIS OF VENISON STROGANOFF

Calories	345.73kcal
Protein	31.66gm
Carbohydrate	37.50gm
Total Fat	7.64gm
Saturated	2.21gm
Polyunsaturated	3.16gm
Monounsaturated	1.58gm
Cholesterol	43.77mg
Sodium	309.18mg

LAMB AND RED BEANS

SERVES 8
1½ CUPS
PER SERVING

Make a double batch and freeze some for later.

NUTRIENT ANALYSIS

Calories	361.92kcal
Protein	31.82gm
Carbohydrate	30.02gm
Total Fat	12.72gm
Saturated	4.04gm
Polyunsaturated	1.37gm
Monounsaturated	5.59gm
Cholesterol	80.27mg
Sodium	84.04mg

2 tablespoons olive oil
2 medium onions, chopped
3 cloves garlic, finely chopped
2 pounds lean lamb, all visible fat removed, cut into
   bite-size pieces
6 medium tomatoes, chopped
2 15-ounce cans red kidney beans, rinsed and
   drained
1 teaspoon turmeric
1 teaspoon freshly ground black pepper, or to taste
1 tablespoon fresh lemon juice
¼ cup finely chopped fresh parsley
1 tablespoon finely chopped fresh mint or 1
   teaspoon dried mint
¾ cup homemade Chicken Stock (see page 263)
½ cup plain nonfat yogurt, lightly beaten

GARNISH
2 tablespoons fresh parsley, chopped

Preheat oven to 350° F.

In Dutch oven or ovenproof casserole, heat oil over medium-high heat. Add onions and garlic, and sauté until onions are soft. Stir in lamb pieces and allow to brown on all sides, about 5 to 7 minutes. Add tomatoes, kidney beans, turmeric, pepper, lemon juice, parsley, mint and chicken stock. Bring to a boil, cover and transfer to oven. Bake 1 to 1½ hours, or until lamb pieces are tender. Remove from oven. Stir in yogurt, and garnish with parsley.

This dish freezes well for up to two months. If freezing, omit yogurt and garnish. Reheat in a preheated 350° F. oven until heated thoroughly, 30 to 35 minutes, then add yogurt and garnish.

PORK WITH SAVORY SAUCE

¾ *cup homemade Chicken Stock (see page 263)*
¼ *cup raspberry or balsamic vinegar*
4 teaspoons olive oil
2 tablespoons port wine
½ teaspoon coarsely ground black pepper
½ teaspoon dried oregano
1 garlic clove, minced
1 teaspoon cornstarch
2 tablespoons cold water
1¼ pounds pork tenderloin, all visible fat removed,
    cut into ¼-inch medallions

**SERVES 4
APPROXIMATELY
4 OUNCES
PER SERVING**

The raspberry or balsamic vinegar gives this dish a dash of elegance.

NUTRIENT ANALYSIS

Calories	215.39kcal
Protein	29.22gm
Carbohydrate	1.89gm
Total Fat	9.42gm
Saturated	2.29gm
Polyunsaturated	0.99gm
Monounsaturated	5.49gm
Cholesterol	93.55mg
Sodium	73.03mg

In a small saucepan, combine stock, vinegar, 2 teaspoons oil, wine, pepper, oregano and garlic. Cook, uncovered, over medium-high heat about 20 minutes, or until liquid is reduced to ½ cup.

Mix cornstarch and water and stir to fully dissolve. Add to the pan, stirring to mix well. Heat over medium heat, stirring until mixture thickens, about 1 minute. Cover, remove from heat and set aside.

Heat 2 teaspoons oil in a nonstick skillet over medium-high heat. Add pork and sauté 3 to 4 minutes on each side, or until pork is no longer pink. Pour 2 tablespoons of sauce over each piece. Serve hot.

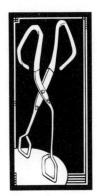

PORK AND TOFU STIR-FRY

SERVES 6
1½ CUPS
PER SERVING

This dish is wonderful served on a Pasta Pancake (see page 167). It can also be served with ordinary noodles or rice. If you marinate the pork and slice the vegetables in advance, the meal can be put together quickly.

Tofu is an excellent high-protein, lowfat food made from soy milk. It is extremely versatile and can be used creatively in several ways—salads, dips, sandwiches, casseroles, burgers and even desserts like ice cream. Over the years, tofu has gained great popularity and is now considered an important protein source in a lowfat diet. It is available in health food stores and most supermarkets.

1 pound lean, boneless pork, all visible fat removed

MARINADE
1 tablespoon homemade Chicken Stock (see page 263)
1 tablespoon dry sherry (optional)
1 tablespoon low-sodium soy sauce
2 tablespoons minced fresh ginger or 1 teaspoon ginger powder
2 cloves garlic, minced

SAUCE
½ cup water
2 teaspoons low-sodium soy sauce
1 tablespoon honey
1 tablespoon Worcestershire sauce
1 tablespoon cornstarch

VEGETABLES
3 teaspoons acceptable vegetable oil, to be used 1 teaspoon at a time
1 small green bell pepper, cut into 1-inch strips
1 small red or yellow bell pepper, cut into 1-inch strips
1 small onion, cut into wedges
6 green onions with tops, sliced diagonally
2 stalks celery, sliced diagonally
20 snow peas, trimmed
1 cup finely sliced red cabbage

8 ounces firm tofu, drained and cut into ½-inch cubes
10 to 12 cherry tomatoes, halved

Slice pork into thin 1-inch strips.

In a small bowl, combine all ingredients for marinade; add sliced pork and toss to coat. In another bowl, combine all ingredients for sauce; stir to blend and set aside.

Heat 1 teaspoon of the oil in a large, nonstick

skillet or wok over high heat. Add vegetables and stir-fry 2 minutes. Remove vegetables from pan; set aside.

Heat another teaspoon of oil and stir-fry tofu 1 to 2 minutes, or until light golden brown. Remove and set aside with vegetables.

Heat remaining teaspoon of oil, add pork and marinade. Stir-fry until meat loses its pink color. Stir in tomatoes and reserved sauce. Cook until sauce starts to bubble and thicken. Add reserved vegetables and heat thoroughly, 1 to 2 minutes.

NUTRIENT ANALYSIS

Calories	196.95kcal
Protein	20.72gm
Carbohydrate	14.96gm
Total Fat	6.64gm
Saturated	1.45gm
Polyunsaturated	2.60gm
Monounsaturated	2.08gm
Cholesterol	49.09mg
Sodium	281.18mg

SCRAMBLED EGGS AND HAM IN SWEET POTATO BOAT

SERVES 2
1 BOAT
PER SERVING

This dish is great for a light meal, including breakfast. The ham or Canadian bacon offers lots of flavor with very little fat.

NUTRIENT ANALYSIS

Calories	201.16kcal
Protein	15.42gm
Carbohydrate	27.89gm
Total Fat	2.82gm
Saturated	0.95gm
Polyunsaturated	0.36gm
Monounsaturated	1.17gm
Cholesterol	16.54mg
Sodium	551.34mg

4 large egg whites
2 teaspoons skim milk
2 ounces Canadian bacon or ham, visible fat removed, diced
Vegetable oil spray
2 medium sweet potatoes, baked

GARNISH (optional)
1 tablespoon grated Defatted Cheddar Cheese (see page 261)
Freshly ground black pepper to taste

In a small bowl, whisk together egg whites and milk. Add Canadian bacon or ham.

Spray a small, nonstick frying pan with vegetable oil spray and place over medium heat. Add egg mixture and stir. Cook until semi-firm.

Cut each potato in half, lengthwise. Top potato halves with scrambled eggs. Garnish with cheese and pepper. Serve hot.

Vegetarian Dishes

Vegetarian Sauce with Whole-Wheat Pasta
Pasta Primavera
Macaroni and Cheese
Spinach-Stuffed Pizza
Spicy Lentil Curry
Chilled Stuffed Artichokes
Eggplant Parmigiana
Tofu Salad Sandwiches
Tofu Quiche
Spanish-Style Scrambled Eggs
Shredded Wheat with Banana-Milk Topping

VEGETARIAN SAUCE WITH WHOLE-WHEAT PASTA

2 tablespoons olive oil
6 green onions, with tops, chopped
1 large red or white onion, chopped
4 cloves garlic, minced
8 ounces mushrooms, sliced
2 ribs celery with leaves, chopped
2 medium red, green or yellow bell peppers,
    chopped
1 16-ounce can vegetarian beans or 1 16-ounce can
    kidney beans
1 16-ounce can no-salt-added tomatoes
1 cup water
½ cup dry red wine (optional)
¼ cup minced fresh parsley
1 bay leaf
1 tablespoon chopped fresh oregano or 1 teaspoon
    dried oregano
1 tablespoon chopped fresh basil or ½ teaspoon
    dried basil
Freshly ground black pepper to taste
12 ounces whole-wheat pasta
4 ounces part-skim mozzarella cheese, shredded

SERVES 6
1½ CUPS
PER SERVING

The whole-wheat pasta used in this recipe gives this dish a wonderful, nutty flavor. The sauce can be made in advance and reheated at serving time. The flavors improve with age. Leftovers or the whole recipe can be frozen.

NUTRIENT ANALYSIS

Calories	449.00kcal
Protein	24.09gm
Carbohydrate	73.74gm
Total Fat	9.32gm
Saturated	2.94gm
Polyunsaturated	1.16gm
Monounsaturated	4.40gm
Cholesterol	10.21mg
Sodium	142.08mg

In a large saucepan or Dutch oven, heat oil over medium-high heat. Add onions and garlic and sauté until onions are soft, 2 to 3 minutes. Add remaining ingredients, except pasta and cheese, and bring to a boil. Reduce heat and simmer, covered, about 1 hour, stirring frequently. Remove bay leaf before serving.

Cook noodles according to package directions, omitting salt. Rinse and drain. Serve sauce over hot pasta. Sprinkle with 1 to 2 tablespoons shredded cheese per serving.

PASTA PRIMAVERA

SERVES 4
2 CUPS
PER SERVING

This is a wonderful and simple one-dish meal. Make the sauce a day ahead of time and prepare the vegetables a few hours before serving. The pasta is best when prepared ''al dente,'' cooked until tender, yet still firm. Try using freshly grated Parmesan cheese, which releases the cheese's full flavor.

NUTRIENT ANALYSIS

Calories	383.96kcal
Protein	18.51gm
Carbohydrate	61.14gm
Total Fat	8.08gm
Saturated	2.67gm
Polyunsaturated	0.75gm
Monounsaturated	3.52gm
Cholesterol	9.81mg
Sodium	418.48mg

3 cups broccoli florets, cut into bite-size pieces
½ pound fresh mushrooms, quartered
2 small zucchini, sliced into ¼-inch rounds
1 tablespoon olive oil
3 cloves garlic, minced
1 pint cherry tomatoes, stemmed and cut in half
8 ounces fettuccine

SAUCE
¾ cup skim milk
3 tablespoons nonfat "butter" granules
⅔ cup part-skim ricotta cheese
¼ cup grated Parmesan cheese
2 tablespoons chopped fresh basil or 1 tablespoon
    dried basil
2 teaspoons dry sherry

GARNISH
2 tablespoons grated Parmesan cheese
Freshly ground black pepper to taste

In a large saucepan fitted with a steamer basket, layer broccoli, mushrooms and zucchini. Steam for about 3 minutes, or until just tender-crisp. Set aside.

In a large, nonstick skillet or nonstick wok, heat olive oil over medium-high heat. Add garlic and sauté for 1 minute, stirring frequently. Add tomatoes and sauté for 2 minutes, stirring frequently, until tomatoes are slightly cooked, but not wilted. Set aside.

Cook fettuccine according to package directions, omitting salt. Drain well.

Combine milk, "butter" granules, ricotta cheese, Parmesan cheese, basil and sherry in a blender. Process until smooth. In a small saucepan, heat sauce over low heat, stirring occasionally, until warm.

In a large serving dish, toss the drained pasta, vegetables and sauce to coat well. Garnish each portion with Parmesan cheese and pepper. Serve immediately.

MACARONI AND CHEESE

1 7-ounce package macaroni and cheese (with
    powdered cheese-sauce packet)
2 tablespoons skim milk
⅓ cup lowfat sour cream

**SERVES 3
1 CUP PER
SERVING**

Cook the noodles according to package directions, omitting salt. Drain, then add milk and sour cream instead of the butter or margarine called for on the package. Mix well to coat evenly. Add contents of the cheese-sauce packet; mix well. Serve hot.

This recipe starts with a favorite packaged food. The great cheese flavor and very little fat will surprise you. That's because lowfat sour cream is used instead of butter or margarine. Try it as a main dish for a light meal.

**NUTRIENT
ANALYSIS**

Calories	283.85kcal
Protein	9.99gm
Carbohydrate	45.39gm
Total Fat	5.42gm
Saturated	2.64gm
Polyunsaturated	0.79gm
Monounsaturated	1.59gm
Cholesterol	12.39mg
Sodium	680.03mg

SPINACH-STUFFED PIZZA

SERVES 6
⅙ OF 9-INCH DOUBLE-CRUST PIE

The fresh spinach gives this pizza a delightful taste. Don't expect leftovers!

NUTRIENT ANALYSIS

Calories	304.43kcal
Protein	16.71gm
Carbohydrate	39.98gm
Total Fat	9.90gm
Saturated	4.30gm
Polyunsaturated	1.37gm
Monounsaturated	3.62gm
Cholesterol	20.10mg
Sodium	514.38mg

DOUGH
¾ cup very warm water (105° to 115° F.)
1 teaspoon sugar
1 package rapid-rise yeast
1½ cups whole-wheat flour
¾ cup all-purpose flour
Vegetable oil spray

FILLING
6 ounces fresh spinach
1½ cups shredded part-skim mozzarella cheese, about 6 ounces
⅓ cup grated Parmesan cheese, about 1 ounce

TOPPING
4 ounces fresh mushrooms, thinly sliced
2 teaspoons olive oil
1 cup prepared pizza or spaghetti sauce

To make the dough, combine sugar and water. Add yeast and stir to dissolve. Let sit for about 5 minutes. The yeast will bubble and develop a frothy head.

In a large bowl, mix the flours. Make a well in the center and slowly pour in the yeast mixture, while mixing. Knead the dough 6 to 8 minutes, or until a ball of smooth-yet-elastic dough forms. If dough is sticky, add more all-purpose flour as you knead. Lighly dust the ball of dough with all-purpose flour, put into the bowl and cover with plastic wrap and a towel. Place in a warm, draft-free place and allow to rise until doubled in bulk, about 30 minutes.

Preheat oven to 475° F.

Punch down and divide dough into two balls. Keep one in the bowl, covered with plastic wrap, and place the other on a lightly floured surface. Use a lightly floured rolling pin to roll the ball into an

11-inch circle. Spray the bottom and sides of a 9-inch glass pie plate with vegetable oil spray. Place the rolled dough in the plate so that it covers the bottom and sides. With a fork, generously prick the dough on the bottom. Bake 4 minutes, remove to a rack and let cool.

To prepare the filling, rinse, stem, dry and chop the spinach. Mix with cheeses and spread in the prebaked crust.

Roll the second dough ball into an 11-inch circle, place over the filling and tuck the edges of dough around the bottom crust layer. Compress the filling by applying light pressure to the dough with the palms of your hands. Cut a 1-inch slit in the center of the top crust.

To make the topping, heat oil in a small nonstick skillet over medium-high heat. Add mushrooms and sauté 3 to 4 minutes, or until soft, stirring occasionally. Evenly spread the topping over the top crust and top with pizza sauce. Place on middle rack of oven, reduce temperature to 450° F. and bake 15 minutes. Reduce temperature to 400° F. and bake another 5 to 10 minutes, or until edges are deep golden brown.

SPICY LENTIL CURRY

SERVES 6
1 CUP PER
SERVING

This makes a good vegetarian meal when served with rice and yogurt. Leftovers are delicious with pita bread. You'll want to make extra to freeze.

NUTRIENT ANALYSIS

Calories	218.05kcal
Protein	13.23gm
Carbohydrate	36.35gm
Total Fat	4.27gm
Saturated	0.54gm
Polyunsaturated	2.16gm
Monounsaturated	0.85gm
Cholesterol	0.00mg
Sodium	201.93mg

1½ cups lentils, washed and drained
6 cups water
1 tablespoon acceptable vegetable oil
1 teaspoon cumin seeds
1 large onion, chopped
1 medium tomato, chopped
1 red hot chili pepper (optional)
1 tablespoon grated fresh ginger or 1 teaspoon
    powdered ginger
1 clove garlic, minced
½ teaspoon ground turmeric
½ teaspoon salt

GARNISH
2 tablespoons chopped fresh cilantro or parsley

In a heavy saucepan, heat lentils and water over medium-high heat. Bring to a boil, then reduce heat. Simmer, partially covered, 45 to 50 minutes, or until lentils are tender, occasionally skimming off the foam. Stir to prevent sticking.

In a nonstick skillet, heat oil over medium-high heat. Sauté cumin seeds for just a minute, taking care not to burn them. Add onions and cook until light brown, 4 to 5 minutes. Add tomato and hot pepper and continue to cook until tomato is reduced to a pulp, about 5 minutes, stirring frequently. Remove hot pepper.

When lentils are tender, stir in onion mixture, ginger, garlic, turmeric and salt and cook another 10 to 15 minutes. Serve hot, garnished with cilantro or parsley.

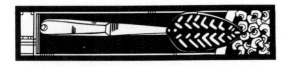

CHILLED STUFFED ARTICHOKES

4 artichokes
1 tablespoon fresh lemon juice
3 cups Steamed Vegetables with Ginger (see page 184)

SAUCE
5 ounces tofu, drained
½ cup tomato puree
¼ cup prepared horseradish
2 teaspoons fresh lemon juice
2 teaspoons white vinegar
½ teaspoon Lemon Herb Seasoning (see page 27)
½ teaspoon onion powder
½ teaspoon sugar
A few drops hot pepper sauce
Freshly ground white pepper to taste

SERVES 4

This elegant and different main dish is fun to eat. The combination of artichokes and assorted vegetables with a smooth, creamy sauce is delightful.

NUTRIENT ANALYSIS

Calories	77.87kcal
Protein	6.55gm
Carbohydrate	17.20gm
Total Fat	1.81gm
Saturated	0.24gm
Polyunsaturated	0.87gm
Monounsaturated	0.35gm
Cholesterol	0.00mg
Sodium	57.58mg

Remove stem and tough leaves from the base of each artichoke. Cut off top third of leaves. Place the prepared artichokes and lemon juice in a deep saucepan. Add boiling water to cover. Cover and cook 30 minutes, or until one of the lower artichoke leaves pulls off easily. Remove from water, turn upside down to drain, then refrigerate to cool.

Remove the center, fuzzy portion of each artichoke and fill with ¾ cup chilled Steamed Vegetables with Ginger.

In a blender or the workbowl of a food processor fitted with a metal blade, process sauce ingredients until fully blended. Pour ⅓ cup of sauce over each serving.

EGGPLANT PARMIGIANA

SERVES 6
1 4×4-INCH
PORTION PER
SERVING

We've lifted the fat—but kept the flavor—of this Italian favorite. To complete the meal, add garden salad and Whole-Wheat French Bread (see page 201).

NUTRIENT ANALYSIS

Calories	235.21kcal
Protein	16.46gm
Carbohydrate	28.05gm
Total Fat	9.50gm
Saturated	3.47gm
Polyunsaturated	1.50gm
Monounsaturated	3.45gm
Cholesterol	14.72mg
Sodium	284.07mg

SAUCE
1 14-ounce can artichoke hearts, drained
2 8-ounce cans no-salt-added tomato sauce
1 6-ounce can no-salt-added tomato paste
1 tablespoon olive oil
¼ teaspoon fennel seeds, crushed (optional)
1 tablespoon Italian herb seasoning
2 cloves garlic, finely minced
⅛ teaspoon freshly ground black pepper
Dash hot pepper sauce

EGGPLANT-CHEESE LAYERS
1 eggplant, about 1 pound, sliced into ⅜-inch rounds
10 ounces tofu, drained
1 large egg white
1 cup part-skim mozzarella cheese, shredded, about 4 ounces
1 tablespoon all-purpose flour (if needed)
⅓ cup grated Parmesan cheese, about 1 ounce
⅓ cup bread crumbs from French or sourdough bread

In a blender or the workbowl of a food processor fitted with a metal blade, blend sauce ingredients for about 30 seconds, or until no lumps remain. Set aside.

Preheat broiler. Place eggplant slices on baking sheet; do not overlap. Broil 4 inches from heat, 3 to 4 minutes per side, being careful not to burn the eggplant. Remove from oven and let cool.

Preheat oven to 350° F.

Place tofu between two thick layers of paper towels. Place between two plates and press down on the top plate. Pour off the liquid. In a blender, process tofu and egg white until smooth; set aside.

To keep mozzarella from sticking together, it may be necessary to mix it with flour.

In a 2-quart ovenproof glass $8 \times 11\frac{1}{2} \times 2$-inch pan, assemble the layers in order from bottom to top: a third sauce, half eggplant slices, a third sauce, mozzarella, tofu-egg mixture, remaining eggplant slices, remaining sauce, Parmesan cheese and bread crumbs.

Bake, uncovered, 35 minutes. Let sit 5 minutes before serving.

TOFU SALAD SANDWICHES

20 ounces tofu, drained
2 small stalks celery, finely chopped
½ small red onion, minced
½ medium green bell pepper, finely chopped
½ medium red bell pepper, finely chopped
3 tablespoons low-calorie Italian dressing
1 tablespoon soy sauce or tamari
1 teaspoon fresh lemon juice
Pinch cayenne pepper
Garlic powder to taste
5 whole-wheat pitas, approximately 7 inches in
    diameter
10 leaves Boston lettuce, rinsed and dried
20 fresh mushrooms, sliced

**SERVES 5
1 WHOLE PITA
AND ⅔ CUP
FILLING PER
SERVING**

This dish tastes like egg salad but is cholesterol-free. The tofu absorbs the flavor of seasonings well.

Place tofu between two thick layers of paper towels. Place between two plates and press down on the top plate. Pour off the liquid. Place pressed tofu and remaining ingredients except pitas, lettuce and mushrooms in a medium bowl. Mix well, breaking up any large pieces of tofu. Refrigerate for a few hours to allow flavors to blend.

Cut each pita in half to form pockets and line with lettuce and mushrooms. Add about ⅓ cup of tofu salad to each half of pita. Serve immediately.

**NUTRIENT
ANALYSIS**

Calories	164.07kcal
Protein	9.45gm
Carbohydrate	24.65gm
Total Fat	3.54gm
Saturated	0.52gm
Polyunsaturated	1.95gm
Monounsaturated	0.70gm
Cholesterol	0.27mg
Sodium	364.42mg

TOFU QUICHE

SERVES 8
⅛ PIE PER
SERVING

Do you love quiche but
realize that all the cream
and butter in it aren't for
you? Here's a creamy, yet
cream-free, quiche. Enjoy!

NUTRIENT
ANALYSIS

Calories	127.90kcal
Protein	11.77gm
Carbohydrate	11.56gm
Total Fat	4.46gm
Saturated	1.07gm
Polyunsaturated	1.28gm
Monounsaturated	1.74gm
Cholesterol	18.26mg
Sodium	242.96mg

CRUST
Vegetable oil spray
2 shredded wheat biscuits, crushed

FILLING
1 teaspoon olive oil
1 medium onion, finely chopped
2 cups frozen chopped vegetables (a good mixture is
* broccoli, corn and red bell peppers)*
4 large egg whites
10 ounces firm tofu, drained
1 tablespoon fresh lemon juice
1 tablespoon nonfat "butter" granules (optional)
Pinch ground nutmeg
Pinch freshly ground black pepper
8 ounces lean ham, visible fat removed

GARNISH
Ground nutmeg

Preheat oven to 350° F.

Spray a 9-inch pie pan with vegetable oil spray
and add crushed shredded wheat biscuits evenly to
bottom of pan.

In a large, nonstick skillet, heat oil at medium
setting. Add onion and sauté, stirring frequently,
until onion is soft. Add vegetables, mix thoroughly,
remove from heat and set aside.

In a blender or the workbowl of a food processor
fitted with a metal blade, process egg whites, tofu,
lemon juice, "butter" granules, nutmeg and pepper
until smooth and creamy. Cut ham into eight
pieces and add to tofu mixture. Process just until
ham is diced.

Evenly place the onion-vegetable mixture over
the biscuit crust. Pour tofu-ham mixture over vegetables, spreading evenly with a spatula. Bake 40 to
45 minutes, or until a knife inserted in the center
comes out clean. Top with a light dusting of nutmeg. Serve hot or at room temperature.

SPANISH-STYLE SCRAMBLED EGGS

1 teaspoon acceptable vegetable oil
1 green onion, finely chopped
1 small ripe tomato, finely chopped
6 large egg whites
1 tablespoon Salsa (see page 191) or picante sauce
Freshly ground black pepper to taste
1 tablespoon minced fresh cilantro or parsley

GARNISH

Cilantro or parsley sprigs
1 tomato, cut into wedges

In nonstick skillet, heat oil over medium-high heat. Add onions and tomato; sauté until onions are soft, 1 to 2 minutes. Reduce heat to low.

In a bowl, combine egg whites, Salsa or picante sauce and pepper; beat until frothy. Add to the skillet. Cook over low heat, stirring occasionally, until almost set. Add cilantro or parsley and stir until eggs are fully set. Garnish with cilantro or parsley and tomato.

SERVES 3
⅓ CUP PER SERVING

NUTRIENT ANALYSIS

Calories	68.07kcal
Protein	7.63gm
Carbohydrate	5.31gm
Total Fat	1.70gm
Saturated	0.20gm
Polyunsaturated	0.89gm
Monounsaturated	0.37gm
Cholesterol	0.00mg
Sodium	155.34mg

SHREDDED WHEAT WITH BANANA-MILK TOPPING

SERVES 2
APPROXIMATELY 1
CUP PER SERVING

This makes a quick, nutritious breakfast.

NUTRIENT ANALYSIS

Calories	350.77kcal
Protein	14.91gm
Carbohydrate	67.21gm
Total Fat	5.95gm
Saturated	0.86gm
Polyunsaturated	1.56gm
Monounsaturated	2.98gm
Cholesterol	3.68mg
Sodium	102.10mg

1 ripe banana
2 cups bite-size shredded wheat biscuits
¼ cup wheat bran (unprocessed miller's bran)
2 tablespoons sliced almonds
1½ cups skim milk
1 or 2 drops vanilla extract

Peel banana and place in a heavy plastic bag. Freeze at least 6 hours. Remove from freezer and cut into eighths.

Divide shredded wheat biscuits into two serving bowls. Top with wheat bran and almonds. In blender, process banana slices, milk and vanilla until slightly frothy. Pour over cereal. Serve immediately.

Vegetables

Green Beans Almondine
Refried Beans
Beets in Orange Sauce
Stir-Fried Broccoli
Honey Carrots
Sautéed Carrots
Corn on the Cob
Sautéed Greens
Pasta Pancake
Southern-Style Black-eyed Peas
Green Peas with Lettuce
Baked Potatoes with Vegetable Topping
Herbed Baby Potatoes
Home-Fried Potatoes
Favorite Mashed Potatoes
Scalloped Potatoes
Steamed New Potatoes with Garlic Sauce
Golden Rice
Savory Brown Rice
Spaghetti Squash
Spinach Cheese Strudel
Sautéed Cherry Tomatoes
Sautéed Zucchini
Ratatouille
Chinese Vegetable Stir-Fry
Steamed Vegetables with Ginger

GREEN BEANS ALMONDINE

1 pound fresh green beans
1 teaspoon acceptable margarine
1 tablespoon chopped fresh oregano or 1 teaspoon
    dried oregano
Freshly ground black pepper to taste
3 tablespoons sliced almonds

Trim and slice green beans into 2-inch sections. In nonstick skillet, heat margarine over medium-high heat. Add green beans and sauté 2 to 3 minutes, stirring constantly so beans cook evenly. Add oregano and pepper; sauté 20 to 30 seconds. Beans should be tender-crisp. Sprinkle with almonds and serve immediately.

SERVES 6
**½ CUP PER
SERVING**

**NUTRIENT
ANALYSIS**

Calories	47.03kcal
Protein	1.92gm
Carbohydrate	5.24gm
Total Fat	2.69gm
Saturated	0.28gm
Polyunsaturated	0.63gm
Monounsaturated	1.62gm
Cholesterol	0.00mg
Sodium	9.44mg

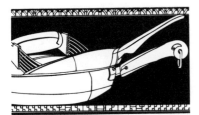

REFRIED BEANS

SERVES 5
½ CUP PER
SERVING

Many canned refried beans contain lard. This recipe has only a small amount of vegetable oil, so it fits right into a healthful diet.

NUTRIENT ANALYSIS

Calories	192.91kcal
Protein	11.61gm
Carbohydrate	34.08gm
Total Fat	2.99gm
Saturated	0.56gm
Polyunsaturated	1.47gm
Monounsaturated	0.41gm
Cholesterol	0.00mg
Sodium	13.67mg

1 teaspoon acceptable vegetable oil
2 tablespoons finely chopped onion
2 cloves garlic, minced
2 15-ounce cans no-salt-added pinto beans
1 tablespoon reduced-sodium ketchup
2 tablespoons canned, diced green chili peppers

In large, nonstick skillet, heat oil over medium heat. Add onion and sauté about 5 minutes, or until soft. Add garlic and sauté another 2 to 3 minutes. Set aside. Drain beans well, reserving liquid. Put beans in shallow bowl and mash with a potato masher or fork. Add ½ cup of reserved bean liquid and ketchup, and mash again. Add bean mixture and chili peppers to the sautéed garlic and onion. Mix well.

Heat over medium heat, stirring constantly, until beans are thoroughly heated.

BEETS IN ORANGE SAUCE

2 pounds fresh beets
1 tablespoon sugar
1 tablespoon cornstarch
1/4 teaspoon salt (optional)
2/3 cup fresh orange juice
2 teaspoons grated orange rind, or to taste
1 teaspoon acceptable margarine

GARNISH
1 orange, peeled and divided into sections

SERVES 6
3/4 CUP PER
SERVING

The smooth orange sauce adds zest and flair to brightly colored beets. To prevent the color of beets from "bleeding" during cooking and also to preserve nutrients, leave about 2 inches of stem on the beets. Peel beets only after they have been cooked.

Cook beets until tender. Drain, peel and slice.

To prepare sauce, combine sugar, cornstarch and salt. Slowly add orange juice and orange rind, stirring until smooth. Cook over medium heat, stirring constantly, until thickened, 5 to 8 minutes. Add margarine and stir until melted.

Pour sauce over warm beets, garnish with orange sections and serve.

NUTRIENT ANALYSIS

Calories	92.00kcal
Protein	2.05gm
Carbohydrate	20.30gm
Total Fat	0.85gm
Saturated	0.12gm
Polyunsaturated	0.23gm
Monounsaturated	0.30gm
Cholesterol	0.00mg
Sodium	159.91mg

STIR-FRIED BROCCOLI

SERVES 6
½ CUP PER
SERVING

This recipe uses only the broccoli florets. Use the stems in soups, or cook and serve them as a vegetable side dish.

NUTRIENT ANALYSIS

Calories	61.60kcal
Protein	4.65gm
Carbohydrate	8.13gm
Total Fat	2.41gm
Saturated	0.32gm
Polyunsaturated	0.65gm
Monounsaturated	0.87gm
Cholesterol	0.00mg
Sodium	49.15mg

1½ pounds broccoli
4 green onions with tops, cut into 1-inch strips
1 tablespoon acceptable margarine
1 teaspoon Lemon Herb Seasoning (see page 27)

Trim broccoli, reserving stems for use in another recipe. Rinse and break broccoli florets into bite-size pieces. In a nonstick skillet, stir-fry broccoli and onions 2 to 3 minutes over medium-high heat. Add margarine, sprinkle with seasoning and toss to coat evenly. Broccoli should be tender-crisp. Serve immediately.

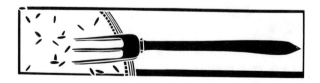

HONEY CARROTS

1½ pounds baby carrots, fresh or frozen
½ cup water
1 tablespoon acceptable margarine
½ tablespoon brown sugar
2 tablespoons honey
2 to 3 tablespoons minced fresh parsley

Rinse and trim carrots, if fresh. Bring water to a boil in a medium saucepan. Add carrots, reduce heat, cover and simmer about 10 minutes, or until carrots are tender-crisp. Drain.

If using frozen carrots, follow package directions for cooking.

In a nonstick skillet, melt margarine over medium-high heat. Add sugar, honey and carrots. Reduce heat and turn carrots frequently until well glazed, 1 to 2 minutes. Sprinkle with parsley before serving.

SERVES 6
½ CUP PER SERVING

Carrots fixed this way will be a favorite—even among the young ones in your family.

NUTRIENT ANALYSIS

Calories	88.27kcal
Protein	1.41gm
Carbohydrate	17.36gm
Total Fat	2.19gm
Saturated	0.31gm
Polyunsaturated	0.64gm
Monounsaturated	0.86gm
Cholesterol	0.00mg
Sodium	74.81mg

SAUTÉED CARROTS

SERVES 6
½ CUP PER
SERVING

Tired of plain carrots? Try these for a distinctive change of pace. The apple and lemon juices make the difference.

NUTRIENT
ANALYSIS

Calories	43.77kcal
Protein	0.93gm
Carbohydrate	7.90gm
Total Fat	1.00gm
Saturated	0.13gm
Polyunsaturated	0.36gm
Monounsaturated	0.31gm
Cholesterol	0.00mg
Sodium	44.56mg

1 pound carrots, peeled and grated
1 tablespoon fresh lemon juice
2 tablespoons frozen apple juice concentrate, defrosted
1 teaspoon margarine or 1½ teaspoons nonfat "butter" granules

GARNISH
1 teaspoon poppy seeds

In a nonstick skillet, combine carrots, lemon juice and apple juice concentrate. Place over medium-high heat and sauté about 3 minutes, stirring constantly. Add margarine or "butter" granules and stir to coat evenly. Garnish with poppy seeds and serve hot.

CORN ON THE COB

4 ears fresh corn, husked
4 teaspoons nonfat "butter" granules
¼ teaspoon curry powder

In a large saucepan, bring 5 quarts of water to a boil. Add corn and return to a boil. Boil uncovered 2 minutes; remove from heat. Let stand uncovered 10 minutes. Remove corn from water.

While corn cooks, follow directions on the package to reconstitute the nonfat "butter" granules with water. Mix with curry powder. Drizzle over corn and serve immediately.

SERVES 4

How can anyone improve on plain, fresh corn? Try just a little curry powder, and see for yourself.

NUTRIENT ANALYSIS

Calories	76.48kcal
Protein	2.58gm
Carbohydrate	17.69gm
Total Fat	0.86gm
Saturated	0.10gm
Polyunsaturated	0.45gm
Monounsaturated	0.18gm
Cholesterol	0.02mg
Sodium	88.15mg

SAUTÉED GREENS

SERVES 6
½ CUP PER SERVING

Good nutrition and good taste—all in one dish. This cooking method leaves the greens tender-crisp, and the spices add a dash of flavor.

NUTRIENT ANALYSIS

Calories	68.34kcal
Protein	2.12gm
Carbohydrate	5.57gm
Total Fat	4.88gm
Saturated	0.61gm
Polyunsaturated	0.38gm
Monounsaturated	3.32gm
Cholesterol	0.00mg
Sodium	18.94mg

1 bunch collard greens, about ¾ pound, rinsed,
    stems removed and coarsely shredded
⅓ medium head cabbage, coarsely shredded
2 tablespoons olive oil
1 clove garlic, minced
1 medium onion, cut into quarters and sliced
1 to 2 teaspoons rice vinegar (optional)

In a large saucepan, boil 3 quarts of water. Add collard greens, return to a boil and cook 3 to 4 minutes, or until greens are tender-crisp. With a slotted spoon, remove greens, leaving the water in the pan. Place greens in a colander and set aside.

Return water to a boil, add cabbage and cook 1 minute. Pour into the colander and let drain. Set aside.

In a large skillet, heat olive oil over medium-low setting. Sauté garlic and onions 3 to 4 minutes, or until tender-crisp. Add greens and cabbage, and sauté 2 to 3 minutes, stirring occasionally. Add vinegar. Toss and serve immediately.

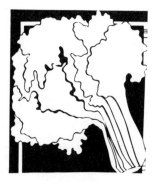

PASTA PANCAKE

16 ounces fine linguine, vermicelli or thin spaghetti
2 tablespoons acceptable vegetable oil, divided
Vegetable oil spray
1 teaspoon sesame seeds, toasted

Preheat oven to 400° F.

Cook noodles according to package directions, omitting salt. Drain, add 1 tablespoon oil and toss to coat.

Grease a large 12-inch pizza or round baking pan with vegetable oil spray. Heat pan in preheated oven 3 to 4 minutes. Arrange noodles on heated pan and press down lightly. Drizzle the remaining tablespoon of oil on top. Bake 15 to 20 minutes, or until the edges are crisp and lightly browned. Sprinkle with sesame seeds. Cut into eight wedges and serve.

**SERVES 8
1 WEDGE PER
SERVING**

Try this for a tasty alternative to plain noodles. The recipe can be made from freshly cooked or leftover noodles.

NUTRIENT ANALYSIS

Calories	224.42kcal
Protein	6.59gm
Carbohydrate	39.16gm
Total Fat	4.23gm
Saturated	0.56gm
Polyunsaturated	2.36gm
Monounsaturated	0.97gm
Cholesterol	0.00mg
Sodium	166.60mg

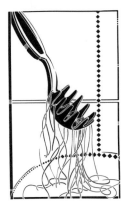

SOUTHERN-STYLE BLACK-EYED PEAS

SERVES 4 (AS A MAIN DISH)
1½ CUPS PER SERVING
SERVES 12 (AS A SIDE DISH)
½ CUP PER SERVING

1 pound dried black-eyed peas
½ medium onion, diced
1 medium carrot, thinly sliced
1 serrano pepper, seeded and thinly sliced
    (optional)
4 ounces smoke-flavored lean ham, visible fat
    removed, diced
5 cups water

Make this mainstay of Southern cuisine in a crockpot or on top of the stove. Black-eyed peas are rich in protein and contain a soluble fiber that may help lower blood cholesterol slightly. Seasoning the peas with ham instead of the traditional salt pork lowers the fat content considerably.

Crockpot directions: Rinse peas under cold running water. Place all ingredients in crockpot. Cook on low setting 8 to 10 hours, or until peas are tender.

Stove-top directions: Rinse peas under cold running water. Place all ingredients in a large saucepan or Dutch oven. Add two additional cups of water. Bring to a boil and skim off any foam. Reduce heat to medium-low. Cover and simmer 2 hours, or until peas are tender.

NUTRIENT ANALYSIS*

Calories	665.79kcal
Protein	39.46gm
Carbohydrate	107.56gm
Total Fat	10.31gm
Saturated	1.57gm
Polyunsaturated	3.98gm
Monounsaturated	2.71gm
Cholesterol	18.26mg
Sodium	219.81mg

* For a main-dish serving.

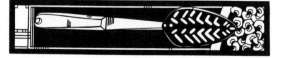

GREEN PEAS WITH LETTUCE

2 pounds fresh or 1 pound frozen green peas
1 tablespoon acceptable margarine
1 small onion, finely chopped
¼ teaspoon salt (optional)
½ teaspoon freshly ground black pepper, or to taste
1 to 2 tablespoons homemade Chicken Stock (see
   page 263)
½ head lettuce, iceberg or romaine, rinsed, dried
   and finely shredded
½ tablespoon chopped fresh thyme or ½ teaspoon
   dried thyme
1 tablespoon minced fresh parsley

Shell peas if fresh, defrost if frozen.

In a nonstick skillet, heat margarine over medium-high heat. Sauté onion until transparent, 2 to 3 minutes. Add peas, salt, pepper and stock. Cover and cook 1 minute. Top peas with lettuce. Cover tightly and cook over low heat 4 to 8 minutes, or until peas are tender. Sprinkle with herbs; toss and serve hot.

SERVES 6
½ CUP PER SERVING

This classic French vegetable dish goes well with meat, fish or poultry dishes.

NUTRIENT ANALYSIS

Calories	81.61kcal
Protein	4.62gm
Carbohydrate	11.77gm
Total Fat	2.25gm
Saturated	0.41gm
Polyunsaturated	0.68gm
Monounsaturated	0.95gm
Cholesterol	0.14mg
Sodium	159.39mg

BAKED POTATOES WITH VEGETABLE TOPPING

SERVES 6
1 POTATO PER SERVING

NUTRIENT ANALYSIS

Calories	199.19kcal
Protein	7.82gm
Carbohydrate	39.49gm
Total Fat	1.58gm
Saturated	0.85gm
Polyunsaturated	0.19gm
Monounsaturated	0.38gm
Cholesterol	3.84mg
Sodium	124.55mg

6 medium baking potatoes, about 2 pounds
1 small onion, finely chopped
2 green onions with tops, finely chopped
1 small carrot, shredded
2 radishes, shredded
¼ cup cucumber, peeled, finely chopped
2 tablespoons cider vinegar
1 tablespoon chopped fresh basil or ½ teaspoon
  dried basil
½ cup plain nonfat yogurt
¼ cup grated Parmesan cheese
¼ cup skim milk
1 teaspoon nonfat "butter" granules
Freshly ground black pepper to taste

Preheat oven to 400° F.

Bake potatoes for 50 to 60 minutes, or until tender.

Combine onion, green onions, carrot, radishes, cucumber, vinegar and basil. Toss to mix well; set aside.

Cut a 1-inch-thick slice off the top of each potato, carefully scoop out the pulp and reserve the shells. Mash potato pulp with yogurt, Parmesan cheese, skim milk, "butter" granules and pepper. Mix until smooth. Stuff potato mixture into reserved shells. Place on baking sheet and bake at 350° F. for 25 to 30 minutes. Serve hot, topped with vegetable mixture.

HERBED BABY POTATOES

1½ *pounds small red or new potatoes, scrubbed,*
  unpeeled and quartered
2 *tablespoons olive oil*
2 *tablespoons minced fresh parsley*
1 *tablespoon chopped fresh oregano or 1 teaspoon*
  dried oregano
½ *teaspoon paprika*
½ *teaspoon garlic powder*
Freshly ground black pepper to taste

GARNISH
2 *tablespoons minced fresh parsley*

Preheat oven to 350° F.

In a 2-quart casserole, toss potatoes in oil to coat each piece. Add remaining ingredients, except parsley for garnish. Toss to coat evenly. Bake 30 to 40 minutes, or until lightly browned. Garnish with parsley.

SERVES 6
½ CUP PER
SERVING

Take simple kitchen staples, add to new potatoes, and you have a tasty side dish that goes well with almost anything.

NUTRIENT ANALYSIS

Calories	129.97kcal
Protein	2.59gm
Carbohydrate	20.22gm
Total Fat	4.70gm
Saturated	0.63gm
Polyunsaturated	0.50gm
Monounsaturated	3.33gm
Cholesterol	0.00mg
Sodium	4.68mg

HOME-FRIED POTATOES

SERVES 6
¾ CUP PER
SERVING

These potatoes are a family favorite and are delicious with Chicken with Mustard and Herbs or Crispy Oven-Fried Chicken (see pages 112 and 118).

NUTRIENT ANALYSIS

Calories	107.13kcal
Protein	2.44gm
Carbohydrate	19.58gm
Total Fat	2.43gm
Saturated	0.31gm
Polyunsaturated	1.45gm
Monounsaturated	0.55gm
Cholesterol	0.00mg
Sodium	92.01mg

1 tablespoon acceptable vegetable oil
1½ pounds small red or new potatoes, scrubbed, unpeeled, cooked and quartered
1 teaspoon paprika
Freshly ground black pepper to taste
¼ teaspoon salt (optional)

In a heavy, nonstick skillet, heat oil over medium-high heat. Sauté potatoes until golden brown, 5 to 8 minutes. Stir and shake pan frequently to prevent potatoes from sticking. Add paprika, pepper and salt. Toss to mix. Serve immediately.

FAVORITE MASHED POTATOES

10 medium potatoes, unpeeled, about 3 pounds
1 cup skim milk
6 tablespoons nonfat "butter" granules
Freshly ground black pepper to taste

**SERVES 10
APPROXIMATELY
¾ CUP PER
SERVING**

Steam potatoes until they can easily be pierced with a fork.

In a small saucepan, heat milk until warm and set aside. Peel potatoes. Place potatoes, milk and "butter" granules in a large bowl and mash with a potato masher until smooth. Add pepper to taste. Serve warm.

Here's a recipe for creamy and buttery-tasting mashed potatoes.

**NUTRIENT
ANALYSIS**

Calories	133.51kcal
Protein	4.02gm
Carbohydrate	29.49gm
Total Fat	0.33gm
Saturated	0.05gm
Polyunsaturated	0.12gm
Monounsaturated	0.01gm
Cholesterol	0.52mg
Sodium	170.27mg

SCALLOPED POTATOES

SERVES 6
1 4 × 4-INCH
PORTION PER
SERVING

How can you make lowfat scalloped potatoes? Use lowfat ingredients and ''butter'' granules. Your heart—and your taste buds—will love you for it.

NUTRIENT ANALYSIS

Calories	190.77kcal
Protein	6.10gm
Carbohydrate	31.65gm
Total Fat	3.08gm
Saturated	1.77gm
Polyunsaturated	0.23gm
Monounsaturated	0.80gm
Cholesterol	10.76mg
Sodium	207.97mg

Vegetable oil spray
1 cup lowfat sour cream
1¾ cups skim milk
3 tablespoons nonfat "butter" granules
1 tablespoon cornstarch
⅛ teaspoon freshly ground black pepper
4 medium potatoes, about 1½ pounds, scrubbed,
    unpeeled, and cut into ⅛- to ¼-inch-thick slices
½ medium onion, diced
Paprika to taste

Preheat oven to 350° F. Spray an 8 × 11½ × 2-inch baking pan with vegetable oil spray.

In a medium bowl, whisk together sour cream, skim milk, "butter" granules, cornstarch and pepper. Set aside.

Line pan with a third of the potatoes. Pour a third of the sour cream mixture over the potatoes. Sprinkle half of the onion over the sour cream mixture. Repeat the layers in order: a third of the potatoes, a third of the sour cream mixture and the remaining onions. Place the rest of the potatoes on top and pour the remaining sour cream mixture over the contents of the pan. Cover with aluminum foil and bake 1 hour. Uncover and bake an additional 20 minutes. Sprinkle with paprika. Let stand 5 minutes before serving.

STEAMED NEW POTATOES WITH GARLIC SAUCE

8 small or 4 large new potatoes, about 1¼ pounds,
unpeeled, scrubbed and, if large, cut in half
2 heads garlic
2 teaspoons skim milk
1 teaspoon acceptable vegetable oil
1 teaspoon nonfat "butter" granules
2 teaspoons chopped fresh parsley
Freshly ground black pepper to taste

SERVES 4
1 LARGE OR 2
SMALL POTATOES
PER SERVING

The steamed garlic used in this sauce has a surprisingly mild flavor. The dish is easy to fix and offers a nice change of pace.

In a medium saucepan, place a steamer basket and add water to a depth of 1 to 2 inches. Be sure the water does not reach the bottom of the basket. Cover saucepan and bring to a boil over medium-high heat. Place potatoes in steamer basket. Separate cloves of garlic, but do not peel the paper-thin skins surrounding each clove. Scatter cloves around potatoes. Cover and steam about 20 minutes, or until a fork can be easily inserted into potatoes.

Remove garlic from pan. Remove skins from garlic cloves by peeling them off with your hands or by pushing the garlic pulp out of the cloves. Discard skins and mash garlic pulp with milk, oil and "butter" granules.

Remove potatoes from pan and cut them in half. Serve with a dollop of garlic sauce, parsley and pepper.

NUTRIENT ANALYSIS

Calories	146.38kcal
Protein	3.84gm
Carbohydrate	30.62gm
Total Fat	1.34gm
Saturated	0.17gm
Polyunsaturated	0.81gm
Monounsaturated	0.28gm
Cholesterol	0.05mg
Sodium	28.33mg

GOLDEN RICE

SERVES 6
½ CUP PER SERVING

This dish is known as "pilau" in Indian cuisine and as "pilaf" in Middle Eastern and Greek cuisine. It can be made from long-grain rice or, for an exotic flavor, from basmati rice. Basmati is an aromatic, long-grain rice from India and Pakistan.

NUTRIENT ANALYSIS

Calories	129.01kcal
Protein	3.02gm
Carbohydrate	26.22gm
Total Fat	1.49gm
Saturated	0.16gm
Polyunsaturated	0.30gm
Monounsaturated	0.91gm
Cholesterol	1.14mg
Sodium	274.17mg

1 cup long-grain basmati rice
1 cup homemade Chicken Stock (see page 263)
1 cup water
1 cinnamon stick
1 bay leaf
¼ teaspoon salt (optional)
¼ teaspoon ground turmeric or ½ teaspoon saffron
2 tablespoons slivered almonds

Rinse rice in several changes of water before cooking.

In a 2-quart saucepan over medium-high heat, bring chicken stock and water to a boil. Add rice, cinnamon, bay leaf and salt; stir. Reduce heat and simmer, covered, 20 minutes. Add turmeric or saffron and stir lightly with a fork. Continue to cook, covered, over low heat, another 10 minutes, or until rice is tender and liquid is absorbed. Remove cinnamon stick and bay leaf. Sprinkle with almonds and serve hot.

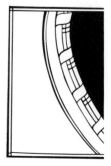

SAVORY BROWN RICE

1 cup brown rice
1 tablespoon acceptable vegetable oil
2 green onions with tops, thinly sliced
1 teaspoon caraway seeds
1 cinnamon stick
1 cup homemade Chicken Stock (see page 263)
1½ cups water

Rinse rice in several changes of water.

In 2- or 3-quart saucepan, heat oil over medium-high heat. Add onions, caraway and cinnamon. Sauté, stirring frequently, until onions are soft, about 3 minutes. Stir in the rice and sauté for an additional minute. Add stock and water, bring mixture to a boil. Reduce heat and simmer, covered, 30 to 40 minutes, or until rice is tender and liquid is absorbed.

Fluff rice with fork, remove cinnamon stick and serve immediately.

SERVES 6
½ CUP PER SERVING

Try this in place of the usual white rice for a nutritious side dish that is a tasty accompaniment to almost any entree.

NUTRIENT ANALYSIS

Calories	116.30kcal
Protein	2.48gm
Carbohydrate	20.51gm
Total Fat	4.00gm
Saturated	0.28gm
Polyunsaturated	0.82gm
Monounsaturated	1.57gm
Cholesterol	1.13mg
Sodium	5.69mg

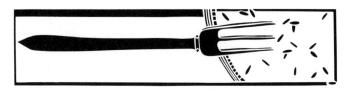

SPAGHETTI SQUASH

SERVES 6
½ CUP PER SERVING

Is it spaghetti or is it squash? Whatever, you'll love the taste and texture of one of nature's surprise packages.

NUTRIENT ANALYSIS

Calories	43.03kcal
Protein	1.14gm
Carbohydrate	10.42gm
Total Fat	0.36gm
Saturated	0.00gm
Polyunsaturated	0.00gm
Monounsaturated	0.00gm
Cholesterol	0.01mg
Sodium	57.70mg

3 pounds spaghetti squash
2 teaspoons nonfat "butter" granules

Preheat oven to 350° F.

Cut squash lengthwise and scrape with a spoon to remove seeds. Place water in a shallow baking dish to a depth of ½ inch. Place squash, cut-side down, in the dish. Bake 35 to 40 minutes, or until squash gives under slight pressure. While still warm, remove squash pulp and place it in a serving bowl. Using a fork, separate squash into strands. Sprinkle on "butter" granules, mix well and serve immediately.

SPINACH CHEESE STRUDEL

SERVES 6
2 1½-INCH SLICES PER SERVING

8 ounces fresh spinach
1 tablespoon acceptable margarine
6 green onions with tops, chopped
8 sheets phyllo dough
3 tablespoons acceptable margarine, melted
1½ ounces feta cheese
½ teaspoon caraway seeds
¼ teaspoon freshly ground black pepper, or to taste
1 tablespoon honey

Preheat oven to 350° F.

Rinse, stem, hand-tear spinach and put in a bowl.

In a nonstick skillet, heat 1 tablespoon margarine over medium-high heat. Add green onions and sauté until soft, about 1 to 2 minutes. Pour cooked onions over spinach and mix while still hot enough to wilt spinach.

Lightly brush every other sheet of phyllo with melted margarine and stack the sheets on top of each other. Spread spinach-onion mixture over the phyllo, leaving a 1-inch border on all sides.

Crumble the feta cheese. Sprinkle cheese, caraway and pepper over spinach mixture. Drizzle honey over the top.

Roll lengthwise, jelly-roll fashion, and place on a nonstick baking sheet, making sure that the ends of the roll are tucked under and seam-side faces down. Brush the top lightly with remaining margarine. Cut through the pastry to the spinach, at 1½-inch intervals, to provide vents for steam to escape. Bake 20 to 30 minutes, or until a light golden brown. Slice, using vent lines as guides.

This recipe freezes well. Prepare as above but omit the final brushing with margarine, and the baking. Freeze overnight on a baking sheet, then wrap well in freezer paper or foil. To prevent the pastry from getting soggy, do not defrost before baking. Place on a baking sheet, brush with margarine and bake 35 to 45 minutes, or until golden brown.

Phyllo is a paper-thin dough, available frozen in 1-pound packages of about 24 sheets in most large supermarkets and specialty groceries. Phyllo should be defrosted in the refrigerator. Unopened, the defrosted dough will keep for a month, if refrigerated. Refreezing can make the dough crumbly. When working with the dough, keep it covered with a damp cloth to prevent drying.

Feta cheese is made from sheep's milk and is lower in fat than most cow's milk cheese. Soaking the cheese in cold water and then draining it removes some of the salt.

NUTRIENT ANALYSIS

Calories	205.58kcal
Protein	6.01gm
Carbohydrate	23.60gm
Total Fat	10.29gm
Saturated	2.76gm
Polyunsaturated	2.68gm
Monounsaturated	4.12gm
Cholesterol	7.44mg
Sodium	172.73mg

SAUTÉED CHERRY TOMATOES

SERVES 5
½ CUP PER SERVING

Don't put all the cherry tomatoes in your salad— save some for this creative side dish. It adds color and variety to any meal.

NUTRIENT ANALYSIS

Calories	43.82kcal
Protein	0.79gm
Carbohydrate	4.10gm
Total Fat	2.85gm
Saturated	0.37gm
Polyunsaturated	0.26gm
Monounsaturated	2.00gm
Cholesterol	0.00mg
Sodium	2.43mg

1 pint cherry tomatoes
1 tablespoon olive oil
1 clove garlic, finely minced
3 tablespoons finely chopped fresh parsley
½ shredded wheat biscuit, crushed
⅛ teaspoon freshly ground black pepper, or to taste

Rinse, stem and halve the tomatoes. In a nonstick skillet, heat oil over medium-high heat. Add garlic and sauté 30 seconds. Add tomatoes and parsley and sauté 20 to 30 seconds, or until tomato skins just begin to wilt. Stir constantly so all surfaces of tomatoes cook evenly. Toss with biscuit crumbs and pepper. Serve immediately.

SAUTÉED ZUCCHINI

1 tablespoon acceptable vegetable oil
2 pounds zucchini, sliced into ½-inch-thick rounds
½ cup whole-wheat bread crumbs, toasted
2 tablespoons minced almonds
1 tablespoon grated Parmesan cheese
¼ cup fresh parsley, finely chopped
1 tablespoon chopped fresh oregano or ½ teaspoon
  dried oregano
1 clove garlic, minced (optional)
Freshly ground black pepper to taste

SERVES 6
¾ CUP PER
SERVING

*Add a touch of Italy to
your menu. The herbs and
spices blend for a unique-
tasting side dish.*

In a nonstick skillet, heat oil over medium-high
heat. Add zucchini and sauté until just tender and
lightly browned, 5 to 8 minutes. Combine remaining ingredients and add to zucchini. Remove from
heat, toss gently and serve immediately.

**NUTRIENT
ANALYSIS**

Calories	107.95kcal
Protein	4.60gm
Carbohydrate	14.45gm
Total Fat	4.57gm
Saturated	0.54gm
Polyunsaturated	1.08gm
Monounsaturated	2.52gm
Cholesterol	1.06mg
Sodium	110.23mg

RATATOUILLE

SERVES 6
1 CUP PER
SERVING

This recipe for French stew uses a simple, lowfat method that results in a delicious blend of textures and flavors. Ratatouille is an excellent accompaniment to chicken or fish. It also tastes wonderful served hot on a baked potato or cold with chunks of crusty French bread.

**NUTRIENT
ANALYSIS**

Calories	119.80kcal
Protein	4.15gm
Carbohydrate	17.04gm
Total Fat	5.11gm
Saturated	0.65gm
Polyunsaturated	0.47gm
Monounsaturated	3.31gm
Cholesterol	0.00mg
Sodium	370.36mg

1 large eggplant, cut into 1-inch cubes
4 medium zucchini, sliced ½ inch thick
1 teaspoon salt
2 tablespoons olive oil
2 medium onions, sliced
2 medium red, green or yellow bell peppers, chopped
2 large tomatoes, chopped
2 cloves garlic, minced
Freshly ground black pepper to taste
1 tablespoon chopped fresh thyme or 1 teaspoon dried thyme
1 tablespoon chopped fresh oregano or 1 teaspoon dried oregano
1 tablespoon chopped fresh basil or 1 teaspoon dried basil

Put eggplant and zucchini in a colander, sprinkle with salt and toss lightly. Allow to drain for at least 30 minutes. Rinse and pat dry with paper towels.

In a heavy, nonstick skillet, heat oil over medium-high heat. Sauté onions until translucent, 2 to 3 minutes. Stir in peppers, tomatoes, eggplant, zucchini, garlic, salt, pepper, thyme, oregano and basil. Reduce heat, cover and simmer 30 to 45 minutes, or until vegetables are thoroughly cooked. Stir occasionally to prevent sticking. Uncover and cook another 5 minutes to reduce liquid.

Ratatouille is best made a day ahead to allow flavors to blend. Serve warm or cold.

CHINESE VEGETABLE STIR-FRY

1½ tablespoons low-sodium soy sauce
2 tablespoons acceptable vegetable oil
¼ cup homemade Chicken Stock (see page 263)
2 cups finely shredded red cabbage
1 large carrot, finely sliced on the diagonal and
   then cut into very thin strips
1 cup snow peas, stems and strings removed
2 medium green, red or yellow bell peppers, cut
   into 1-inch strips
4 ounces fresh mushrooms, thinly sliced
4 green onions with tops, cut into fine 1-inch strips
1 tablespoon grated fresh ginger or 1 teaspoon
   powdered ginger

GARNISH

1 tablespoon sesame seeds, toasted

SERVES 6
1 CUP PER SERVING

This is a wonderful side dish. The secret is to prepare all the vegetables ahead of time and stir-fry them just before serving. This keeps the texture crisp and crunchy. The combinations can be changed to accommodate seasonal vegetables.

Combine soy sauce, oil and chicken stock.

Heat a nonstick wok or skillet over high heat and add soy sauce mixture. Over high heat, stir-fry cabbage, carrots, snow peas, bell peppers, mushrooms and onions, stirring constantly, 2 minutes. Add ginger, stir to mix well and remove from heat. Vegetables should be tender-crisp.

Garnish with toasted sesame seeds and serve immediately.

NUTRIENT ANALYSIS

Calories	100.52kcal
Protein	3.51gm
Carbohydrate	11.02gm
Total Fat	5.61gm
Saturated	0.74gm
Polyunsaturated	3.06gm
Monounsaturated	1.41gm
Cholesterol	0.28mg
Sodium	187.49mg

STEAMED VEGETABLES WITH GINGER

**SERVES 8
APPROXIMATELY ¾
CUP PER SERVING**

*This vegetable combo
bears little resemblance to
mixed vegetables of old.
The ginger makes the
difference.*

**NUTRIENT
ANALYSIS**

Calories	21.11kcal
Protein	1.29gm
Carbohydrate	4.34gm
Total Fat	0.14gm
Saturated	0.00gm
Polyunsaturated	0.00gm
Monounsaturated	0.00gm
Cholesterol	0.00mg
Sodium	13.43mg

*2 medium carrots, sliced into ¼-inch-thick rounds
1 cup cauliflower florets
1 cup broccoli florets
2 small zucchini, sliced into ½-inch-thick rounds
1½-inch piece fresh ginger root, julienned*

In the bottom of a medium saucepan, place steamer basket and water to a depth of 1 inch. Bring to a boil. Layer steamer basket, in order, with carrots, cauliflower, broccoli, zucchini and ginger. Cover and steam 5 to 7 minutes, or until barely tender. Remove steamer basket from saucepan. Remove ginger. Pour vegetables into serving dish and serve immediately.

Sauces

Caper Sauce for Fish
White Sauce (Béchamel)
Cucumber Raita
Tomato Mint Raita
Pesto
Salsa
Pan Gravy
Creamy Dessert Topping
Cheesecake Sauce
Berry Sauce
Blueberry Sauce
Apple-Raisin Sauce

CAPER SAUCE FOR FISH

1 cup tofu, about 7 ounces, drained and crumbled
2 tablespoons reduced-calorie mayonnaise
2 tablespoons fresh lemon juice
2 tablespoons capers, drained
2 tablespoons chopped fresh dill or 2 teaspoons
   dried dill
2 tablespoons chopped fresh parsley

In a blender or the workbowl of a food processor fitted with a metal blade, process all ingredients until smooth. Serve hot or cold.

**MAKES 1 CUP
SERVES 8
2 TABLESPOONS
PER SERVING**

This recipe uses reduced-calorie mayonnaise, which has about half the fat of regular mayonnaise.

**NUTRIENT
ANALYSIS**

Calories	32.54kcal
Protein	2.05gm
Carbohydrate	1.38gm
Total Fat	2.33gm
Saturated	0.41gm
Polyunsaturated	1.11gm
Monounsaturated	0.75gm
Cholesterol	2.50mg
Sodium	79.86mg

WHITE SAUCE (BÉCHAMEL)

MAKES 2 CUPS
SERVES 4
½ CUP PER
SERVING

This basic French sauce can be used with poultry, meat or vegetables.

NUTRIENT
ANALYSIS

Calories	61.79kcal
Protein	2.38gm
Carbohydrate	5.15gm
Total Fat	3.55gm
Saturated	0.51gm
Polyunsaturated	2.02gm
Monounsaturated	0.85gm
Cholesterol	1.22mg
Sodium	98.55mg

2 tablespoons acceptable vegetable oil
3 tablespoons all-purpose flour
2 cups skim milk
¼ teaspoon salt (optional)
Freshly ground black pepper to taste
1 bay leaf (optional)

In a 1-quart saucepan, heat oil over medium-high heat. Blend in flour. Cook, stirring constantly, 1 minute, or until mixture becomes foamy. Gradually add milk. Stir in seasonings and bay leaf. Stir vigorously with a wooden spoon until mixture thickens, 5 to 8 minutes. Remove bay leaf before serving.

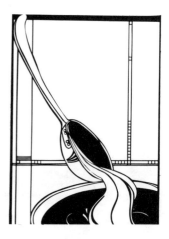

CUCUMBER RAITA

8 ounces plain nonfat yogurt
1 small cucumber, peeled, seeded and finely diced
¼ cup finely diced green bell pepper
2 tablespoons finely chopped fresh parsley or
  cilantro
¼ teaspoon ground cumin
Freshly ground black pepper to taste

**MAKES 1½ TO 2
CUPS
SERVES 6 – 8
¼ CUP PER
SERVING**

In a bowl, whisk the yogurt until smooth. Add remaining ingredients except pepper. Stir well, cover and chill until ready to serve. Can be made up to 1 hour in advance. Sprinkle with pepper before serving.

Raita (rah-eé-ta) is an Indian yogurt sauce. It makes a cool and refreshing accompaniment to any spicy dish.

TOMATO MINT RAITA

8 ounces plain nonfat yogurt
2 medium tomatoes, peeled and finely chopped
4 green onions with tops, finely chopped
1 red chili pepper, seeded and finely chopped
  (optional)
¼ cup finely chopped fresh mint
¼ teaspoon ground cumin
¼ teaspoon salt (optional)
Paprika to taste

GARNISH
Sprig mint

Place yogurt in a bowl and whisk until smooth. Add remaining ingredients except paprika. Stir well, cover and chill until ready to serve. Can be made up to 1 hour in advance. Sprinkle with paprika before serving. Garnish with mint.

**MAKES 1½ TO
2 CUPS
SERVES 6 – 8
¼ CUP PER
SERVING**

**NUTRIENT
ANALYSIS***

Calories	155.18kcal
Protein	14.55gm
Carbohydrate	23.70gm
Total Fat	0.79gm
Saturated	0.29gm
Polyunsaturated	0.10gm
Monounsaturated	0.09gm
Cholesterol	4.00mg
Sodium	189.92mg

* For entire recipe of Cucumber Raita or Tomato Mint Raita.

PESTO

MAKES 2 CUPS
SERVES 32
1 TABLESPOON
PER SERVING

This versatile sauce is excellent as a topping for pasta or baked potatoes, or as a dip or salad dressing. Because of the fat content, limit a serving to 1 to 2 tablespoons. For a change of flavor, try using cilantro leaves instead of basil.

2 cups fresh basil leaves, loosely packed
⅓ cup olive oil
1 clove garlic
⅓ cup freshly grated Parmesan cheese
½ cup pecans or pine nuts
¼ to ½ cup homemade Chicken Stock (see page 263)

In a blender or the workbowl of a food processor fitted with a metal blade, combine basil, oil, garlic, Parmesan and nuts. Process until smooth, occasionally scraping down the sides of the container. If mixture does not move during processing, slowly drizzle chicken stock to loosen it.

Pesto can be made well in advance, covered with plastic wrap and refrigerated. It can also be frozen.

NUTRIENT ANALYSIS

Calories	39.13kcal
Protein	0.55gm
Carbohydrate	0.49gm
Total Fat	3.95gm
Saturated	0.64gm
Polyunsaturated	0.54gm
Monounsaturated	2.57gm
Cholesterol	1.10mg
Sodium	18.69mg

SALSA

6 small ripe tomatoes, chopped
1 to 2 jalapeño peppers, seeded and minced, or to
    taste *
2 tablespoons finely chopped red onion
2 tablespoons finely chopped fresh cilantro or
    parsley
⅓ cup fresh lime juice
2 teaspoons red wine vinegar
⅛ teaspoon salt (optional)
Freshly ground black pepper to taste

For a smooth sauce, thoroughly process all ingredients in blender or food processor. If you prefer a chunky sauce, simply combine the ingredients. Cover and refrigerate.

* Note: Wear rubber gloves when handling hot peppers or wash hands thoroughly after handling. Skin, especially around the eyes, is very sensitive to oil from peppers.

**MAKES 1 TO
1½ CUPS
SERVES 4 – 6
¼ CUP PER
SERVING**

This spicy Mexican sauce is excellent as a topping or a dip. It can also be used to perk up dishes from scrambled eggs to grilled chicken. Make it several hours in advance to allow flavors to blend.

**NUTRIENT
ANALYSIS***

Calories	179.71kcal
Protein	7.56gm
Carbohydrate	36.31gm
Total Fat	1.55gm
Saturated	0.04gm
Polyunsaturated	0.08gm
Monounsaturated	0.02gm
Cholesterol	0.00mg
Sodium	307.11mg

* For entire recipe.

PAN GRAVY

MAKES 2 CUPS
SERVES 11
APPROXIMATELY 3
TABLESPOONS PER
SERVING

1 tablespoon cornstarch
2 tablespoons cold water
2 cups pan juices, defatted*
Freshly ground black pepper to taste
½ teaspoon dried thyme (optional)

**NUTRIENT
ANALYSIS**

Calories	7.58kcal
Protein	0.60gm
Carbohydrate	0.85gm
Total Fat	0.18gm
Saturated	0.05gm
Polyunsaturated	0.04gm
Monounsaturated	0.08gm
Cholesterol	0.00mg
Sodium	10.54mg

In a small bowl, mix cornstarch with water. Heat pan juices over medium-high heat. Add mixture to pan juices while stirring constantly to prevent lumps from forming. Cook until smooth and thickened, about 3 minutes. Add pepper and thyme. Strain if a smooth consistency is desired. Serve hot.

* See page 23.

CREAMY DESSERT TOPPING

½ cup plain nonfat yogurt
½ cup part-skim ricotta cheese
2 tablespoons honey

**SERVES 8
2 TABLESPOONS
PER SERVING**

Combine ingredients and stir until light and creamy. Refrigerate. Serve chilled.

This topping is luscious when drizzled over a bowl of fruit, spread on muffins or poured over a slice of angel food cake. It has a fraction of the calories and fat of whipped cream or butter.

**NUTRIENT
ANALYSIS**

Calories	41.84kcal
Protein	2.40gm
Carbohydrate	6.13gm
Total Fat	1.15gm
Saturated	0.71gm
Polyunsaturated	0.04gm
Monounsaturated	0.33gm
Cholesterol	4.64mg
Sodium	28.61mg

CHEESECAKE SAUCE

SERVES 6
2 TABLESPOONS
PER SERVING

*This sauce is delicious
when poured over a fruit
salad or sorbet.*

**NUTRIENT
ANALYSIS**

Calories	41.21kcal
Protein	2.91gm
Carbohydrate	7.26gm
Total Fat	0.21gm
Saturated	0.13gm
Polyunsaturated	0.01gm
Monounsaturated	0.05gm
Cholesterol	0.93mg
Sodium	84.49mg

¼ *cup nonfat plain yogurt*
½ *cup lowfat cottage cheese*
2 *tablespoons honey*
½ *teaspoon vanilla extract*

In a blender, process all ingredients about 1 minute, or until smooth and creamy. Refrigerate. Serve chilled.

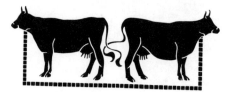

BERRY SAUCE

1 16-ounce bag unsweetened frozen strawberries,
    raspberries or other berries
1 teaspoon cornstarch

SERVES 6
¼ CUP PER
SERVING

Defrost berries and puree in a blender. Mix berry puree and cornstarch in a saucepan. Place over medium-high heat and bring to a boil, stirring frequently until mixture thickens. Refrigerate. Serve chilled.

Pour Berry Sauce over Cheesecake Sauce (see page 194) for a colorful and flavorful topping for fruit salads, yogurt, sorbet or even cottage cheese.

NUTRIENT
ANALYSIS*

Calories	177.15kcal
Protein	3.18gm
Carbohydrate	40.36gm
Total Fat	2.28gm
Saturated	0.00gm
Polyunsaturated	0.01gm
Monounsaturated	0.00gm
Cholesterol	0.00mg
Sodium	4.53mg

* For entire recipe.

BLUEBERRY SAUCE

SERVES 6
⅓ CUP PER
SERVING

This sauce can be served hot or cold. It's great over vanilla ice milk, pancakes or Vanilla Cheesecake (a variation of Mocha Cheesecake, see page 232).

NUTRIENT
ANALYSIS

Calories	64.40kcal
Protein	0.35gm
Carbohydrate	16.14gm
Total Fat	0.20gm
Saturated	0.00gm
Polyunsaturated	0.01gm
Monounsaturated	0.00gm
Cholesterol	0.00mg
Sodium	3.52mg

1 pint fresh blueberries or 2 cups frozen no-sugar-added blueberries
½ cup water
¼ cup sugar
1 tablespoon fresh lemon juice
1 tablespoon cornstarch
2 tablespoons cold water

In a medium saucepan over medium-high heat, bring blueberries, water, sugar and lemon juice to a boil. If using fresh blueberries, reduce heat and simmer 1 to 2 minutes, or until berries soften. If using frozen berries, there's no need to simmer.

In a small bowl, combine cornstarch and water. Add to blueberry mixture and cook over low heat 1 to 2 minutes more, stirring until thick and smooth. Serve hot or cold.

APPLE-RAISIN SAUCE

3 medium apples
2 cups apple juice
¼ cup raisins
1 teaspoon ground cinnamon
1 tablespoon cornstarch
2 tablespoons cold water

SERVES 6
½ CUP PER
SERVING

*Try this deliciously
refreshing sauce over
Whole-Grain Oatmeal
Pancakes (page 209).*

Peel apples, if desired; core and coarsely chop. In a large saucepan, combine apples, juice, raisins and cinnamon over medium-high heat. Bring to a boil, reduce heat and simmer 15 minutes, or until apples are tender.

Meanwhile, combine cornstarch and water in a small bowl. Add to apple-raisin mixture and cook an additional 1 to 2 minutes, stirring until thick and smooth. Serve warm.

**NUTRIENT
ANALYSIS**

Calories	93.48kcal
Protein	0.37gm
Carbohydrate	23.71gm
Total Fat	0.30gm
Saturated	0.06gm
Polyunsaturated	0.09gm
Monounsaturated	0.02gm
Cholesterol	0.00mg
Sodium	4.52mg

Breads

Whole-Wheat French Bread
Honey-Nut Bread
Southern-Style Cornbread
Potato Bread
Zucchini Bread
Oat Bran Muffins
Cardamom Lemon-Peel Muffins
Whole-Grain Oatmeal Pancakes
French Toast
Breakfast Toast
Cheese Danish
Cornbread Dressing
Corn Crisps
Pita Crisps
Croutons
Seasoned Bread Crumbs

WHOLE-WHEAT FRENCH BREAD

Vegetable oil spray
1½ teaspoons active dry yeast, ½ envelope
2 tablespoons honey
1 teaspoon salt
2 cups very warm water (110° to 115° F.)
4 cups whole-wheat flour
3 cups all-purpose flour
1 large egg white, lightly beaten

TOPPING
1 teaspoon sesame seeds (optional)

**MAKES 4 LOAVES
12 SLICES PER
LOAF
2 SLICES PER
SERVING**

This dense bread has a
wonderful texture. Make
up an extra batch and
freeze it. These loaves
disappear fast!

Grease two large baking sheets and one large bowl with vegetable oil spray. Set aside.

In a large bowl, mix together yeast, honey, salt and water. In another bowl, combine whole-wheat and all-purpose flours; mix well. Add 2 cups flour to the yeast mixture and stir well. Stir in 3 more cups of flour. Turn the dough onto a floured board. Knead in as much of the remaining 2 cups of flour as necessary to make a soft, but not sticky, dough. Knead the dough for 8 to 10 minutes or until smooth and elastic. Shape into a ball, and place in the greased bowl, turning to coat all sides. Cover the bowl with a clean towel and set in a warm, draft-free place to rise, 1½ hours or until doubled in bulk.

Turn dough onto a lightly floured surface, punch down and knead out large air bubbles. Divide dough into four equal pieces. Shape each piece into a skinny loaf, about 12 inches long. Arrange on the greased baking sheets and cover with a clean towel. Allow to rise again in a warm, draft-free place for 45 minutes, or until doubled in bulk.

Preheat oven to 350° F.

Brush each loaf with egg white and bake 40 to

**NUTRIENT
ANALYSIS**

Calories	126.85kcal
Protein	4.45gm
Carbohydrate	26.58gm
Total Fat	0.72gm
Saturated	0.12gm
Polyunsaturated	0.36gm
Monounsaturated	0.15gm
Cholesterol	0.00mg
Sodium	92.15mg

continued

WHOLE-WHEAT FRENCH BREAD *(continued)*

50 minutes, or until loaves are golden brown and sound hollow when tapped.

During the last 5 minutes, loaves can be reglazed with egg white and sprinkled with sesame seeds. For a crisp, flaky crust, put a pan of boiling water on the lowest oven shelf during baking.

HONEY-NUT BREAD

**MAKES 2 LOAVES
10 SLICES PER
LOAF
1 SLICE PER
SERVING**

Freeze single slices of this delicious bread for a nutritious lunch-box addition. When packed frozen, a slice will thaw in less than an hour.

**NUTRIENT
ANALYSIS**

Calories	152.08kcal
Protein	3.32gm
Carbohydrate	25.90gm
Total Fat	4.69gm
Saturated	0.72gm
Polyunsaturated	2.17gm
Monounsaturated	1.47gm
Cholesterol	13.95mg
Sodium	91.59mg

*1 cup skim milk
1 cup honey
1¼ cups whole-wheat flour
1¼ cups all-purpose flour
1 tablespoon baking powder
½ teaspoon salt
¼ cup acceptable margarine (½ stick)
1 whole egg plus 2 egg whites, lightly beaten
½ cup chopped walnuts
Vegetable oil spray*

Preheat oven to 325° F.

In a small saucepan, heat milk and honey over medium-high heat until very warm, 120° to 130° F.

In a large bowl, combine whole-wheat and all-purpose flours, baking powder and salt. Add liquid mixture and beat. Add margarine and eggs, and continue beating until well blended. Fold in nuts.

Lightly grease two 9 × 5 × 3-inch loaf pans with vegetable oil spray. Pour in bread mixture and bake 45 to 60 minutes, or until a cake tester inserted into the center of the loaf comes out moist, but not wet. Cool on a rack.

To store, wrap each loaf in foil to preserve moisture. The loaves can be frozen for later use.

SOUTHERN-STYLE CORNBREAD

¼ cup acceptable vegetable oil
1½ cups yellow cornmeal, whole-grain if possible
1½ cups whole-wheat flour
⅓ cup instant powdered nonfat milk
½ teaspoon salt
1½ tablespoons baking powder
3 tablespoons sugar (optional)
3 large egg whites
1½ cups skim milk

SERVES 12
1 WEDGE OR
SQUARE PER
SERVING

This cornbread has a crispy crust and a flavorful, moist center. For a simple yet satisfying meal, serve with Southern-Style Black-Eyed Peas and Sautéed Greens (see pages 168, 166).

Preheat oven to 450° F.

Pour 1 tablespoon of oil into a 10½-inch cast-iron skillet or into a 9 × 11-inch ovenproof glass casserole dish. Set aside.

In a bowl, mix cornmeal, flour, powdered milk, salt, baking powder and sugar. Set aside. In another bowl, beat egg whites with a whisk until slightly frothy. Add milk and remaining oil and whisk again.

Pour liquid ingredients into dry ingredients and mix, but do not overmix (some lumps will remain).

Place skillet or dish in oven 3 or 4 minutes to heat the oil. **Be careful not to let it burn!** Watch the time carefully.

Pour batter into hot skillet or dish. Bake 20 minutes. Immediately remove from pan by turning onto a cutting board.

Cut into twelve wedges or squares. Serve immediately.

NUTRIENT ANALYSIS

Calories	185.36kcal
Protein	5.87gm
Carbohydrate	29.90gm
Total Fat	5.10gm
Saturated	0.69gm
Polyunsaturated	2.93gm
Monounsaturated	1.20gm
Cholesterol	0.95mg
Sodium	236.14mg

POTATO BREAD

**MAKES 4 LOAVES
12 SLICES PER
LOAF
2 SLICES PER
SERVING**

This bread freezes well.

**NUTRIENT
ANALYSIS**

Calories	172.71kcal
Protein	6.11gm
Carbohydrate	31.58gm
Total Fat	2.84gm
Saturated	0.54gm
Polyunsaturated	1.02gm
Monounsaturated	1.07gm
Cholesterol	0.84mg
Sodium	293.19mg

Vegetable oil spray
4 cups whole-wheat flour
4 cups all-purpose flour
2 tablespoons active dry yeast, 2 envelopes
2 tablespoons honey
2½ teaspoons salt
1½ cups mashed potatoes (leftovers are perfect)
1½ cups skim milk
¼ cup acceptable margarine (½ stick)
½ cup water
4 large egg whites

GLAZE
¼ cup skim milk

Grease two large baking sheets and one large bowl with vegetable oil spray. Set aside.

In another large bowl, combine whole-wheat and all-purpose flours. In another large bowl, mix together yeast, honey, salt and 1½ cups of combined flour. In a 2-quart saucepan, combine mashed potatoes, milk, margarine and water. Heat over medium-high heat until very warm, 120° to 130° F., stirring frequently. The margarine does not need to melt completely.

With electric mixer at low speed, beat liquid ingredients into dry ingredients. Add egg whites, increase mixer speed to medium and beat 2 minutes, scraping bowl occasionally. Beat in 1 cup flour to make a thick batter; beat 2 minutes longer. Stir in 3 more cups of flour. Turn the dough onto a well-floured board. Knead in as much of the remaining 2½ cups of flour as necessary to make a soft, but not sticky, dough. Knead the dough for about 10 minutes, or until smooth and elastic. Shape into a ball and place in the greased bowl, turning to coat all sides. Cover the bowl with a clean towel and set in a warm, draft-free place to rise, about 1½ hours, or until doubled in bulk.

Turn the dough onto a lightly floured surface, punch down and knead out the large air bubbles. Divide the dough into four equal pieces. Shape each piece into an oval, about 10 inches long. Cut two parallel slashes on top of each loaf, place on the greased baking sheet (two loaves per sheet) and cover with a clean towel. Allow to rise in a warm, draft-free place for 1 hour, or until doubled in bulk.

Preheat oven to 350° F.

Brush each loaf with skim milk. Bake 35 to 45 minutes, or until loaves are golden brown and sound hollow when tapped. Serve warm or at room temperature.

ZUCCHINI BREAD

**MAKES 1 LOAF
12 SLICES PER
LOAF
1 SLICE PER
SERVING**

A perfect luncheon bread is hard to find, but this comes close. Good nutrition and great taste rolled into one!

**NUTRIENT
ANALYSIS**

Calories	318.04kcal
Protein	6.80gm
Carbohydrate	53.85gm
Total Fat	9.88gm
Saturated	0.93gm
Polyunsaturated	4.67gm
Monounsaturated	3.64gm
Cholesterol	0.61mg
Sodium	151.59mg

Vegetable oil spray
1½ cups whole-wheat flour
1½ cups all-purpose flour
1 cup brown sugar, lightly packed
1 tablespoon baking powder
¼ teaspoon salt (optional)
1 teaspoon ground cinnamon
2 cups shredded, unpeeled zucchini (about 2 small)
1 cup raisins
¼ cup finely chopped walnuts
2 large egg whites
1½ cups skim milk
¼ cup acceptable vegetable oil
1 teaspoon vanilla extract

Preheat oven to 350° F. Grease a 9 × 5 × 3-inch loaf pan with vegetable oil spray.

In a large bowl, combine whole-wheat and all-purpose flours, sugar, baking powder, salt and cinnamon. Stir in zucchini, raisins and nuts; set aside.

In a smaller bowl, beat together egg whites, milk, oil and vanilla. Add liquid ingredients to flour mixture and stir lightly to moisten.

Pour into greased pan and bake 1 hour, or until a cake tester inserted into the center of the loaf comes out moist, but not wet. Remove from pan and allow to cool.

To store, wrap loaf in foil to preserve moisture. Loaf can be frozen for later use.

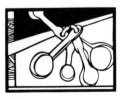

OAT BRAN MUFFINS

2½ cups oat bran, uncooked
¼ cup brown sugar, firmly packed
¼ cup chopped nuts
¼ cup currants
1 tablespoon baking powder
¼ teaspoon salt (optional)
4 large egg whites, lightly beaten
¾ cup skim milk
¼ cup honey
2 tablespoons acceptable vegetable oil
1 teaspoon almond extract
1 teaspoon vanilla extract
Vegetable oil spray

**SERVES 18
1 2½-INCH
MUFFIN PER
SERVING**

You've heard about the healthfulness of oat bran —now taste how good it can be. These delicious, moist muffins are welcome at breakfast, lunch or snack time. Make up an extra batch to freeze. Oat bran is available in some supermarkets and most health food stores. The almond extract gives the muffins a slightly sweet, nutty flavor.

Preheat oven to 350° F.

In a bowl, combine oat bran, sugar, nuts, currants, baking powder and salt. Mix well.

In a small bowl, combine egg whites, milk, honey, oil, almond and vanilla extracts. Add to dry ingredients and mix to blend.

Spray two muffin tins lightly with vegetable oil spray or use paper muffin cups. Spoon mixture evenly into muffin cups. Bake 20 to 25 minutes, or until light brown. Serve warm or at room temperature.

NUTRIENT ANALYSIS

Calories	107.07kcal
Protein	4.45gm
Carbohydrate	14.92gm
Total Fat	3.72gm
Saturated	0.45gm
Polyunsaturated	1.45gm
Monounsaturated	1.60gm
Cholesterol	0.22mg
Sodium	104.08mg

CARDAMOM LEMON-PEEL MUFFINS

SERVES 12
2 2½-INCH
MUFFINS PER
SERVING

The spices in these muffins make them smell and taste wonderful. The cardamom adds a distinctive flavor and enhances the sweetness. Instead of using a lot of fat, applesauce is used to help keep the muffins moist. Oat bran is sometimes called oat bran cereal and is available in some supermarkets and most health food stores. It contains soluble fibers that may help to lower blood cholesterol slightly.

NUTRIENT ANALYSIS

Calories	271.44kcal
Protein	8.32gm
Carbohydrate	37.67gm
Total Fat	11.02gm
Saturated	1.51gm
Polyunsaturated	6.16gm
Monounsaturated	2.80gm
Cholesterol	0.00mg
Sodium	169.47mg

Vegetable oil spray
2½ cups oat bran, uncooked
2 cups whole-wheat flour
1 teaspoon ground cardamom
2 teaspoons baking powder
1½ teaspoons baking soda
2 cups unsweetened applesauce
½ cup acceptable vegetable oil
½ cup honey
4 large egg whites
¼ teaspoon almond extract
Grated rind of 1 lemon

Preheat oven to 400° F.

Spray two muffin tins with vegetable oil spray or use paper muffin cups. In a medium bowl, combine bran, flour, cardamom, baking powder and baking soda. Mix well. In a large bowl, combine applesauce, oil, honey, egg whites, almond extract and lemon peel. Mix well.

Stir dry ingredients into wet ingredients. Mix well, but do not overmix. Fill prepared muffin cups almost full. Place in oven and reduce heat to 375° F. Bake 18 to 20 minutes, or until golden brown. Serve warm or at room temperature.

If you prefer lighter muffins, use 1 cup of white flour to replace 1 cup of the whole-wheat flour.

WHOLE-GRAIN OATMEAL PANCAKES

1¾ *cups skim milk*
1 *tablespoon honey*
1½ *cups rolled oats (not instant oatmeal)*
1 *cup whole-wheat flour*
2 *teaspoons baking powder*
4 *large egg whites*
¼ *cup acceptable vegetable oil*

In a small bowl, mix milk and honey until honey is dissolved. Add oatmeal and stir to coat evenly; set aside. In another bowl, stir together flour and baking powder. Add oat mixture, egg whites and 3 tablespoons oil. Stir just until mixed.

In a large, nonstick skillet, heat remaining tablespoon of oil over medium-high heat. Pour batter, in ¼-cup portions, into skillet. When pancakes have a bubbly surface and have just begun to dry around the edges, turn to cook the other side. Serve immediately.

SERVES 4
3 4-INCH PANCAKES PER SERVING

Short stack or tall—these hearty pancakes are sure to please. The high-fiber goodness of whole grains and oatmeal is a great way to start the day. Serve them with Apple-Raisin Sauce or Blueberry Sauce (pages 197 and 196).

NUTRIENT ANALYSIS

Calories	408.46kcal
Protein	15.25gm
Carbohydrate	52.09gm
Total Fat	16.63gm
Saturated	2.31gm
Polyunsaturated	9.10gm
Monounsaturated	4.10gm
Cholesterol	2.14mg
Sodium	252.67mg

FRENCH TOAST

SERVES 3
2 SLICES PER
SERVING

NUTRIENT ANALYSIS*

Calories	132.14kcal
Protein	7.07gm
Carbohydrate	22.09gm
Total Fat	1.37gm
Saturated	0.37gm
Polyunsaturated	0.40gm
Monounsaturated	0.46gm
Cholesterol	0.64mg
Sodium	267.90mg

* Without Apple-Almond Butter.

3 large egg whites, lightly beaten
6 slices cinnamon-raisin bread
Vegetable oil spray
2 tablespoons Apple-Almond Butter (see page 38)

Place egg whites in a medium pie plate. Place two slices of bread into pie plate and let soak 5 to 10 seconds; turn bread over and let soak another 5 to 10 seconds. Remove from plate and set aside. Repeat with remaining slices of bread.

Coat a nonstick skillet with vegetable oil spray. Heat skillet over medium-high heat. When skillet is hot, add the prepared slices of bread. Brown evenly on both sides. Serve with a teaspoonful of Apple-Almond Butter on each slice of bread.

BREAKFAST TOAST

SERVES 1
2 SLICES PER
SERVING

NUTRIENT ANALYSIS

Calories	166.13kcal
Protein	5.28gm
Carbohydrate	25.04gm
Total Fat	6.10gm
Saturated	0.90gm
Polyunsaturated	3.23gm
Monounsaturated	1.46gm
Cholesterol	0.71mg
Sodium	306.15mg

2 slices whole-wheat bread
1 teaspoon acceptable vegetable oil
½ teaspoon nonfat "butter" granules
Ground cinnamon to taste (optional)

Preheat broiler. Lightly toast bread. Brush one side of each slice with oil and sprinkle with "butter" granules. Add cinnamon if desired. Place 3 to 4 inches from broiler, "buttered"-side up, and toast again 30 to 60 seconds, or until nicely browned.

CHEESE DANISH

1 whole-wheat pita, approximately 7 inches in
    diameter
½ cup lowfat cottage cheese, drained
1 tablespoon raisins
1 teaspoon honey
Pumpkin pie spice to taste

Preheat oven to 350° F.
    Cut pita in half and toast lightly 3 to 4 minutes.
In a small bowl, mix cottage cheese, raisins, honey
and spice. Spoon into warm pita pockets. Place on
baking sheet or aluminum foil and bake 3 to 4
minutes. Serve immediately.

SERVES 1

*This Cheese Danish will be
filling even to a person
with a hearty appetite. If
you want to watch your
calories, just eat half the
Danish.*

**NUTRIENT
ANALYSIS***

Calories	355.75kcal
Protein	23.41gm
Carbohydrate	57.12gm
Total Fat	3.37gm
Saturated	1.56gm
Polyunsaturated	0.59gm
Monounsaturated	0.73gm
Cholesterol	9.07mg
Sodium	876.10mg

* For entire recipe.

CORNBREAD DRESSING

SERVES 7
ABOUT ¾ CUP
PER SERVING

When it comes to dressing, everyone seems to have a favorite recipe. Here's a winner with real Southern flavor.

NUTRIENT ANALYSIS

Calories	230.25kcal
Protein	8.66gm
Carbohydrate	36.14gm
Total Fat	6.50gm
Saturated	0.97gm
Polyunsaturated	3.18gm
Monounsaturated	1.86gm
Cholesterol	2.42mg
Sodium	349.34mg

¼ cup water
1½ cups chopped celery
1 cup chopped onion (about 1 medium)
3 cups cornbread crumbs, approximately half of the
    Southern-Style Cornbread recipe (see page 203)
4 slices stale or toasted whole-grain bread, cut into
    cubes
1 teaspoon rubbed sage
¼ cup chopped fresh parsley
1 teaspoon poultry seasoning
1½ cups homemade Chicken Stock (see page 263)
2 large egg whites, lightly beaten
Vegetable oil spray
1 tablespoon acceptable margarine

Preheat oven to 350° F.

In a small saucepan, boil the water. Add celery and onion and cook 2 to 3 minutes, or until soft. In a medium bowl, toss cornbread crumbs, bread cubes, sage, parsley and poultry seasoning to mix well. Add chicken stock and egg whites and mix again. Pour the celery, onions and cooking liquid into the bowl and mix well.

Spray a 2-quart casserole with vegetable oil spray. Pour mixture into prepared casserole and dot with margarine. Bake, uncovered, 30 minutes. Serve immediately.

CORN CRISPS

6 corn tortillas

Preheat oven to 350° F.

Stack the tortillas and cut into six wedges. Lay tortilla pieces on baking sheet so they do not overlap. Bake 15 to 20 minutes. Chips should be crisp and lightly brown. Serve warm or allow to cool and store in an airtight container.

SERVES 6
6 WEDGES
PER SERVING

Try these in place of regular corn chips. But watch out, it's hard to stop at just a few!

NUTRIENT ANALYSIS

Calories	47.81kcal
Protein	1.54gm
Carbohydrate	9.13gm
Total Fat	0.81gm
Saturated	0.09gm
Polyunsaturated	0.42gm
Monounsaturated	0.18gm
Cholesterol	0.00mg
Sodium	37.99mg

PITA CRISPS

SERVES 4
8 WEDGES
PER SERVING

Try these thin and crunchy Pita Crisps for a nutritious snack. They're easy to make and taste a lot like crackers.

NUTRIENT ANALYSIS

Calories	102.17kcal
Protein	3.82gm
Carbohydrate	19.92gm
Total Fat	0.54gm
Saturated	0.08gm
Polyunsaturated	0.25gm
Monounsaturated	0.05gm
Cholesterol	0.00mg
Sodium	207.64mg

2 whole-wheat pitas, approximately 7 inches in diameter

Preheat oven to 350° F.

Divide each pita into two circles. Stack pita circles on top of each other. Cut the stack into eight wedges. Put pita pieces on a baking sheet so they do not overlap. Bake 5 to 8 minutes, or until lightly browned. Watch carefully to prevent them from burning. Serve warm or allow to cool and store in an airtight container.

CROUTONS

2 tablespoons olive oil
4 slices whole wheat bread, cut into ¼-inch cubes
    (stale bread works well)
1 clove garlic, crushed

In a heavy, nonstick skillet, heat oil over medium-high heat. Add bread cubes and garlic. Sauté cubes, stirring frequently and shaking the pan, until the cubes are golden brown, 8 to 10 minutes. Remove and discard garlic.

Store croutons in an airtight container.

**SERVES 16
2 TABLESPOONS
PER SERVING**

These croutons add a special crunch to soups and salads.

**NUTRIENT
ANALYSIS***

Calories	242.89kcal
Protein	5.34gm
Carbohydrate	24.31gm
Total Fat	15.00gm
Saturated	2.14gm
Polyunsaturated	1.70gm
Monounsaturated	10.31gm
Cholesterol	0.70mg
Sodium	263.79mg

* For entire recipe.

SEASONED BREAD CRUMBS

SERVES 16
1 TABLESPOON
PER SERVING

This is a good staple to have on hand. It perks up ordinary steamed vegetables, adds crunch to broiled fish, and garnishes soups or salads. These bread crumbs also make a tasty topping for casseroles.

NUTRIENT ANALYSIS

Calories	24.11kcal
Protein	1.43gm
Carbohydrate	3.24gm
Total Fat	0.73gm
Saturated	0.38gm
Polyunsaturated	0.08gm
Monounsaturated	0.20gm
Cholesterol	1.49mg
Sodium	66.32mg

4 slices whole wheat bread
1 tablespoon dried parsley flakes
½ teaspoon dried basil
½ teaspoon dried oregano
1 teaspoon dried onion flakes
¼ cup grated Parmesan cheese

Preheat oven to 275° F.

Arrange bread slices in a single layer on a baking sheet. Bake 15 to 20 minutes, or until crisp and dry. Break slices into pieces and reduce to crumbs using a blender or a food processor, or by placing bread pieces in a plastic bag and crushing with a rolling pin. Add remaining ingredients and stir to mix well.

Store refrigerated in an airtight container.

Desserts

Angel Food Cake
Fresh Apple Streusel Cake
Carrot Cake
Orange Snack Cake
Basic Pie Dough
Pumpkin Pie
French Apple Tart
Apple-Almond Flavored Yogurt Pie
Meringue Pie Shell with Sherbet
Baklava
Chocolate Soufflé with Vanilla Sauce
Mocha Cheesecake
Coffee Liqueur Clouds
Mock Whipped Cream
Orange Fluff
Strawberries Romanoff
Frozen Banana Mousse
Tapioca Pudding
Blueberry Pudding
White Grape Juice Gelatin Dessert
Coffee Shake
Frozen Orange Cream
Very Berry Sorbet
Melon with Sherbet
Frozen Grape Treats
Yogurt-Fruit Cup
Cherries Jubilee
Broiled Grapefruit with Port Wine
Baked Apples
Meringues
Cocoa-Almond Meringue Kisses
Gingerbread Bars
Chewy Oatmeal Squares
Oatmeal Crisps

ANGEL FOOD CAKE

1 cup cake flour
10 large egg whites*
1 teaspoon cream of tartar
1 teaspoon vanilla extract
½ teaspoon almond extract
1 cup sugar

MAKES 1 CAKE
SERVES 12

NUTRIENT ANALYSIS

Calories	106.78kcal
Protein	3.36gm
Carbohydrate	22.74gm
Total Fat	0.06gm
Saturated	0.01gm
Polyunsaturated	0.03gm
Monounsaturated	0.00gm
Cholesterol	0.00mg
Sodium	58.92mg

Preheat oven to 350° F.

Sift flour and set aside.

In a large mixing bowl, beat egg whites until foamy. Add cream of tartar, vanilla and almond extracts. Beat until very stiff, but not dry. Add sugar, 2 tablespoons at a time, and continue to beat just until the mixture is smooth. Using a spatula, gently fold in flour.

Pour the batter into an ungreased, 10-inch tube pan. Draw a knife through the batter to remove any large air bubbles. Place the pan in the lower third of the oven and bake 45 minutes, or until cracks feel dry and top springs back when touched lightly.

When cake is done, remove it from the oven and invert the pan. If the tube in the center of the pan is not high enough for the inverted cake to be suspended in the air, use a heatproof funnel or a thin-necked soda bottle on which to rest the pan. Let the cake hang and cool for 1½ hours.

Remove the cake from its perch and slide a sharp knife inside the edges of the pan to release the cake.

* Remember, even a single drop of egg yolk will prevent egg whites from rising, so separate eggs very carefully, one at a time.

FRESH APPLE STREUSEL CAKE

MAKES 1 BUNDT CAKE
SERVES 20

Lowfat cakes are hard to find, but you can make one yourself. One taste will convince you that it was well worth the effort!

NUTRIENT ANALYSIS

Calories	289.06kcal
Protein	4.25gm
Carbohydrate	42.53gm
Total Fat	12.09gm
Saturated	1.47gm
Polyunsaturated	6.34gm
Monounsaturated	3.63gm
Cholesterol	0.00mg
Sodium	139.46mg

Vegetable oil spray

STREUSEL TOPPING
¼ cup pecans, chopped
3 tablespoons all-purpose flour
3 tablespoons sugar
2 tablespoons acceptable vegetable oil
1 teaspoon ground cinnamon

CAKE
2 cups whole-wheat flour
2 cups all-purpose flour
½ teaspoon salt
½ teaspoon baking soda
1 tablespoon baking powder
½ teaspoon ground cloves
2 teaspoons ground cinnamon
¾ cup acceptable vegetable oil
1¾ cups firmly packed brown sugar
6 large egg whites
1 4½-ounce jar strained applesauce (baby food)
1 tablespoon vanilla extract
2½ cups chopped fresh apples (about 3 medium)
2 tablespoons fresh lemon juice
¼ cup chopped pecans

Preheat oven to 350° F. Spray a nonstick Bundt pan with vegetable oil spray.

In a small bowl, mix ingredients for streusel topping until crumbly. Sprinkle topping over the bottom of prepared Bundt pan and set aside.

In a large bowl, sift together flours, salt, baking soda, baking powder, cloves and cinnamon. Mix until evenly distributed. Set aside.

In another large bowl, mix oil, brown sugar, egg whites, applesauce and vanilla with an electric mixer until fully blended and smooth.

In a small bowl, mix together apples and lemon

juice. Add the flour mixture and apple-lemon mixture alternately to the liquid mixture, beginning and ending with the flour. Fold nuts into the batter, being careful not to overmix.

Pour batter evenly into prepared pan. Bake on middle rack of oven for 55 minutes, or until a cake tester inserted into the center of the cake comes out moist, but not wet. Remove from oven and let cool on wire rack 5 minutes. Remove cake from pan, and after it has cooled, wrap with aluminum foil to retain moisture.

CARROT CAKE

MAKES 1 BUNDT
CAKE WITH
APPROXIMATELY
2 CUPS TOPPING
SERVES 20

This cake tastes marvelous and is healthful too. Watch it disappear! Instead of a lot of fat, strained carrots add moisture.

CAKE

Vegetable oil spray
2 cups whole-wheat flour
2 cups all-purpose flour
½ teaspoon salt
½ teaspoon baking soda
1 tablespoon baking powder
1 teaspoon ground allspice
2 teaspoons ground cinnamon
¾ cup acceptable vegetable oil
1¾ cups firmly packed brown sugar
6 large egg whites
1 4½-ounce jar strained carrots (baby food)
1 tablespoon vanilla extract
2 cups grated carrots, packed (about 6 carrots)
½ cup crushed pineapple, drained
2 tablespoons fresh lemon juice
¼ cup chopped walnuts

TOPPING

1 cup part-skim ricotta cheese
¾ cup Double-Thick Yogurt (see page 262)
¾ cup confectioners' sugar
Grated rind of 1 lemon
1 teaspoon vanilla extract

Preheat oven to 350° F. Spray a nonstick Bundt pan with vegetable oil spray.

In a large bowl, sift together flours, salt, baking soda, baking powder, allspice and cinnamon. Mix until evenly distributed. Set aside.

In another large bowl, combine oil, brown sugar, egg whites, strained carrots and vanilla. Mix until fully blended and no lumps remain.

Place the grated carrots, pineapple and lemon juice in another bowl. Mix well. Add the flour mixture and carrot-pineapple mixture alternately to the liquid mixture, beginning and ending with the flour. Stir in nuts, being careful not to overmix.

Pour batter evenly into prepared pan. Bake on middle rack of oven for 55 minutes, or until a cake tester inserted into the center comes out moist, but not wet. Remove from oven and let cool on wire rack 5 minutes. Remove cake from pan, and when completely cooled, wrap with aluminum foil to retain moisture.

Place all topping ingredients in a large bowl. Using an electric mixer, mix for about 1 minute, or until no lumps remain. Refrigerate for 30 minutes before serving. Place a dollop of topping on each slice of cake.

NUTRIENT ANALYSIS*

Calories	298.00kcal
Protein	6.60gm
Carbohydrate	46.16gm
Total Fat	10.54gm
Saturated	1.83gm
Polyunsaturated	5.65gm
Monounsaturated	2.99gm
Cholesterol	4.11mg
Sodium	175.01mg

* Includes 1 tablespoon of topping.

ORANGE SNACK CAKE

**MAKES 1
9 × 13-INCH CAKE
SERVES 12**

**NUTRIENT
ANALYSIS**

Calories	382.49kcal
Protein	4.86gm
Carbohydrate	58.27gm
Total Fat	15.20gm
Saturated	2.34gm
Polyunsaturated	6.17gm
Monounsaturated	5.81gm
Cholesterol	0.00mg
Sodium	310.71mg

Vegetable oil spray
1 cup quick-cooking oats
1½ cups boiling water
2 cups all-purpose flour
1 teaspoon baking powder
1 teaspoon baking soda
1 teaspoon ground cinnamon
¼ teaspoon salt (optional)
½ cup acceptable margarine, 1 stick,
   at room temperature
½ cup sugar
¾ cup lightly packed brown sugar
3 large egg whites
¼ cup frozen orange juice concentrate
1 teaspoon vanilla extract

TOPPING
¼ cup acceptable margarine, ½ stick
¾ cup lightly packed brown sugar
2 tablespoons orange juice concentrate
½ cup finely chopped walnuts or pecans

Preheat oven to 350° F. Grease a 9 × 13-inch cake pan with vegetable oil spray.

In a small bowl, combine oats and boiling water; set aside. In another bowl, mix flour, baking powder, baking soda, cinnamon and salt. Set aside.

In a large bowl, cream together margarine and sugars until light and fluffy. Beat in egg whites, orange juice concentrate and vanilla. Blend in flour mixture alternately with oats, beginning and ending with flour.

Pour into greased pan and bake 25 to 30 minutes, or until cake springs back when lightly pressed. Remove cake from oven and preheat broiler.

To make the topping, combine margarine, brown sugar and orange juice concentrate in a

small saucepan. Bring to a boil and cook 1 minute, over medium-high heat, stirring constantly. Remove from heat and stir in nuts. Spread topping evenly over warm cake; place under broiler for 1 minute, or until golden brown. Topping can burn easily. Watch it carefully! Allow to cool on rack before cutting.

BASIC PIE DOUGH

2 cups all-purpose flour
¼ teaspoon salt
½ cup acceptable margarine, 1 stick
7 to 9 tablespoons ice water

MAKES 2 9-INCH PIE SHELLS OR 1 DEEP-DISH PIE SHELL AND TOP CRUST

In a large bowl, combine flour and salt. Using a pastry blender, lightly cut the margarine into the flour until the mixture resembles coarse meal. Add water, a few tablespoons at a time, and mix lightly and quickly until pastry forms a ball.

If you need only one pie shell, just cut this recipe in half.

Divide pastry into two balls and form into two flat circles about 1-inch thick. Cover with plastic wrap and refrigerate at least 1 hour.

On a floured surface, roll each ball into a 12-inch circle. (The pastry can be rolled between sheets of floured wax paper or on a pastry sheet.) Place pastry in pie dish. (Folding the pastry in half before lifting helps prevent stretching or tearing.) Trim or flute the edges and prick the bottom of each shell lightly with a fork.

For a baked pie shell (to be filled later), bake in a preheated 400° F. oven. For a partially baked crust, bake 8 to 10 minutes. For a fully baked crust, bake 10 to 15 minutes, or until edges are light brown.

To prevent the crust from puffing up or losing shape during baking, cover pastry with wax paper and weigh it down with dried beans or an aluminum-foil pie plate.

NUTRIENT ANALYSIS*

Calories	1644.85kcal
Protein	25.05gm
Carbohydrate	176.05gm
Total Fat	92.88gm
Saturated	15.46gm
Polyunsaturated	31.67gm
Monounsaturated	41.40gm
Cholesterol	0.00mg
Sodium	1753.51mg

* For entire recipe.

PUMPKIN PIE

**MAKES 1
9-INCH PIE
SERVES 8**

Evaporated skim milk is very low in fat, yet rich in taste and texture. Use it in cooking in place of whole milk or cream. To make this tasty dessert attractive, serve each slice with a dollop of Creamy Topping (see page 193).

**NUTRIENT
ANALYSIS**

Calories	211.57kcal
Protein	6.30gm
Carbohydrate	33.93gm
Total Fat	6.12gm
Saturated	1.04gm
Polyunsaturated	1.99gm
Monounsaturated	2.62gm
Cholesterol	0.22mg
Sodium	177.11mg

9-inch unbaked pie shell (use ½ recipe Basic Pie Dough, see page 225)
½ cup firmly packed dark brown sugar
1 teaspoon ground cinnamon
1 teaspoon ground ginger
¼ teaspoon ground nutmeg
Pinch of ground cloves
1 16-ounce can pumpkin puree
1¼ cups evaporated skim milk
3 large egg whites

Preheat oven to 350° F.

Bake pie crust until lightly browned, about 10 minutes. Remove from oven and let cool to room temperature.

Preheat oven to 450° F.

In a large bowl, beat all filling ingredients until no lumps remain. Pour into pie shell and bake 10 minutes. Reduce heat to 325° F. and bake 50 minutes more, or until a knife inserted in the center comes out clean.

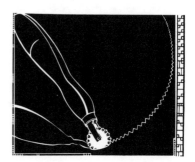

FRENCH APPLE TART

Pie dough for 1 pie shell (use ½ recipe Basic Pie
  Dough, see page 225)
½ cup unsweetened applesauce, divided
1 pound apples, quartered, cored and thinly sliced
2 tablespoons confectioners' sugar

Preheat oven to 350° F.

Prepare dough according to recipe. After chilling, roll the dough into a 12½- to 13-inch circle. Place on a flat, 12-inch round baking pan. Trim away extra dough from the sides. Prick dough with a fork in several places.

Brush dough with half the applesauce. Begin to arrange apple slices in a circular design, overlapping the pieces, starting from the outer edge. Arrange a second inner ring of apple slices overlapping the outer circle. Continue the pinwheel design until the whole surface is covered. Apples will flatten during baking. Brush surface of apples with remaining applesauce.

Bake 20 to 25 minutes, or until apples are golden and crust edge is crisp. Sprinkle with confectioners' sugar and serve immediately.

**MAKES 1
12-INCH PASTRY
SERVES 8**

This elegant way to serve fruit is easy to prepare. Since the tart must be served immediately after baking, it's a good idea to assemble it ahead of time and refrigerate it. Then bake it just before serving.

**NUTRIENT
ANALYSIS**

Calories	150.82kcal
Protein	1.71gm
Carbohydrate	23.40gm
Total Fat	6.02gm
Saturated	1.00gm
Polyunsaturated	2.03gm
Monounsaturated	2.60gm
Cholesterol	0.00mg
Sodium	109.92mg

APPLE-ALMOND FLAVORED YOGURT PIE

MAKES 1 9-INCH PIE SERVES 8

This pie looks beautiful and tastes much richer than it is. The apple juice concentrate gives it a sweet-but-not-too-sweet flavor. Of course it's great for dessert, but why not have a slice for breakfast, too?

NUTRIENT ANALYSIS

Calories	175.13kcal
Protein	6.48gm
Carbohydrate	38.66gm
Total Fat	0.90gm
Saturated	0.11gm
Polyunsaturated	0.04gm
Monounsaturated	0.03gm
Cholesterol	1.13mg
Sodium	121.50mg

CRUST

1¼ cups whole-grain, wheat-and-barley nugget cereal
¼ cup frozen apple juice concentrate, defrosted
1 tablespoon ground cinnamon

FILLING

1 envelope unflavored gelatin (1 tablespoon)
⅓ cup cold water
½ cup frozen apple juice concentrate, defrosted
2¼ cups plain nonfat yogurt
¼ cup honey
½ teaspoon ground cinnamon
½ teaspoon almond extract

GARNISH

1 dozen red seedless grapes, halved
1 dozen green seedless grapes, halved

Preheat oven to 350° F.

In a bowl, combine cereal, juice concentrate and cinnamon; mix until all cereal nuggets are coated. Press onto the bottom and sides of a 9-inch pie plate. Bake 5 minutes, remove from oven and let cool to room temperature.

To make the filling, sprinkle unflavored gelatin over cold water in a small bowl. Let stand for a few minutes. Pour juice concentrate into a small saucepan. Heat to boiling, add to gelatin and stir until completely dissolved. In another bowl, whisk together yogurt, honey, cinnamon and almond extract until well blended. Add gelatin-juice mixture to yogurt mixture and whisk together until thoroughly blended. Pour into crust, refrigerate overnight and serve cold.

Before garnishing, score the pie into eighths. That way you can avoid placing grape halves on the slicing lines—making slicing and serving much easier. Arrange grapes in two circles or any other pattern you like. If grapes are out of season, garnish with canned fruit such as mandarin oranges or dark, sweet, pitted cherries.

MERINGUE PIE SHELL WITH SHERBET

Vegetable oil spray
2 large egg whites*
⅛ teaspoon cream of tartar
½ cup sugar
½ teaspoon white vinegar
½ teaspoon vanilla extract
2 cups sherbet, any flavor

MAKES 1 9-INCH PIE SERVES 8

This elegant dessert is light and delicious. Try substituting ice milk or fresh fruit fillings for a different effect.

Preheat oven to 275° F. Lightly spray a 9-inch pie plate with vegetable oil spray.

In a large bowl, beat egg whites and cream of tartar with an electric beater until stiff peaks form. Add sugar 2 tablespoons at a time, beating well after each addition. To test if sugar is completely dissolved, rub meringue mixture between fingers; if grainy, continue beating. Add vinegar and vanilla; beat well to blend.

Spoon meringue into prepared pie plate, heaping the mixture higher along the sides so that it resembles a large nest. Bake 1 hour. Reduce heat to 250° F. and bake another 30 minutes, or until meringue is firm and crisp, but not brown.

Let cool to room temperature. Spoon sherbet evenly into pie shell. Serve immediately.

NUTRIENT ANALYSIS

Calories	119.76kcal
Protein	1.37gm
Carbohydrate	26.82gm
Total Fat	0.96gm
Saturated	0.59gm
Polyunsaturated	0.03gm
Monounsaturated	0.28gm
Cholesterol	3.38mg
Sodium	38.05mg

* Remember that even a single drop of egg yolk will prevent egg whites from rising, so separate eggs very carefully, one at a time.

BAKLAVA

SERVES 12
1 SLICE PER
SERVING

*Ready for a new taste
treat? Try this traditional
Greek favorite. It is made
with phyllo, a paper-thin
dough that is available in
most large supermarkets
and specialty groceries. It
is frozen in 1-pound
packages of about 24
sheets. Phyllo should be
defrosted in the
refrigerator. Unopened,
the defrosted dough will
keep for a month, if
refrigerated. Refreezing
can make the dough
crumbly. When working
with the dough, keep it
covered with a damp cloth
to prevent drying.*

**NUTRIENT
ANALYSIS**

Calories	195.49kcal
Protein	2.89gm
Carbohydrate	34.86gm
Total Fat	6.11gm
Saturated	0.88gm
Polyunsaturated	2.67gm
Monounsaturated	2.04gm
Cholesterol	0.00mg
Sodium	54.84mg

1 cup raisins
⅓ cup finely chopped pecans or walnuts
8 sheets phyllo dough
¼ cup acceptable margarine, ½ stick, melted
½ cup honey
2 teaspoons ground cinnamon

Preheat oven to 350° F.

In a small bowl, mix raisins and nuts. Set aside.

Lightly brush every other sheet of phyllo with melted margarine and stack the sheets on top of each other. Spread raisin-nut mixture over the phyllo, leaving a 1-inch border on all sides. Drizzle honey over the top and sprinkle with cinnamon.

Roll lengthwise, jelly-roll fashion, and place on a nonstick baking sheet, making sure that the ends of the roll are tucked under and the seam-side faces down. Brush the top lightly with remaining margarine. Cut through the pastry to the raisin-nut mixture, at 1½-inch intervals, to provide vents for steam to escape. Bake 20 to 30 minutes, or until light golden brown. Slice, using vent lines as guides.

This recipe freezes well. Prepare as above but omit the final brushing with margarine, and the baking. Freeze overnight on a baking sheet, then wrap well in freezer paper or foil. To prevent the pastry from getting soggy, do not defrost before baking. Place on a baking sheet, brush with margarine and bake 35 to 45 minutes, or until golden.

CHOCOLATE SOUFFLÉ WITH VANILLA SAUCE

Vegetable oil spray
⅓ cup fresh orange juice
⅓ cup sugar
4 large egg whites*
¼ cup unsweetened cocoa powder
2 tablespoons orange liqueur
¾ cup vanilla ice milk, softened

SERVES 6
5 OUNCES PER SERVING

This wonderful chocolate soufflé uses cocoa instead of chocolate. Cocoa is a great way to get that chocolaty flavor without the fat. Its unique topping makes this dessert taste just like the high-fat counterpart.

Preheat oven to 300° F. Grease six 5-ounce custard cups with vegetable oil spray.

In a small saucepan, cook orange juice and sugar over medium-high heat until mixture has a syrupy consistency, about 3 to 4 minutes, stirring occasionally. Remove from heat and reserve.

In a large bowl, beat egg whites until stiff, but stop before dry peaks form. Pour syrup over the egg whites and continue beating for 2 minutes. Add cocoa and liqueur and beat only until well mixed. Pour into prepared custard cups. Bake 12 minutes, or until soufflés are puffed. Do not overbake, or soufflés will become tough.

To serve, spoon 2 tablespoons softened vanilla ice milk into the center of each soufflé. Serve immediately.

* Remember, even a single drop of egg yolk will prevent egg whites from rising, so separate eggs very carefully, one at a time.

NUTRIENT ANALYSIS

Calories	116.95kcal
Protein	3.68gm
Carbohydrate	22.14gm
Total Fat	1.74gm
Saturated	1.05gm
Polyunsaturated	0.06gm
Monounsaturated	0.55gm
Cholesterol	2.05mg
Sodium	46.00mg

MOCHA CHEESECAKE

**MAKES 1
9-INCH PIE
SERVES 10**

With this recipe, you can indulge in cheesecake on a cholesterol-lowering diet. Double-Thick Yogurt and part-skim ricotta cheese replace the high-fat cream cheese found in most cheesecakes. Also, egg whites and cocoa powder are used instead of whole eggs and chocolate. The result is a delectable cake that tastes sinful but isn't. It freezes well if wrapped tightly before freezing.

To make a vanilla cheesecake with a hint of orange flavor, omit the cocoa and coffee liqueur.

**NUTRIENT
ANALYSIS***

Calories	301.51kcal
Protein	19.13gm
Carbohydrate	97.71gm
Total Fat	5.11gm
Saturated	2.93gm
Polyunsaturated	0.40gm
Monounsaturated	1.43gm
Cholesterol	17.40mg
Sodium	269.62mg

* Excluding garnish.

CRUST
Vegetable oil spray
4 slices whole-wheat bread, toasted
3 tablespoons wheat germ
2 tablespoons unsweetened cocoa powder
2 large egg whites
¼ cup honey
1½ teaspoons vanilla extract
1½ teaspoons coffee liqueur

FILLING
2 cups Double-Thick Yogurt (see page 262)
2 cups part-skim ricotta cheese
2 large egg whites
2 tablespoons all-purpose flour
⅔ cup sugar
Grated rind of ½ navel orange
1 tablespoon vanilla extract
2 tablespoons unsweetened cocoa powder
1 tablespoon coffee liqueur

GARNISH
Fresh fruit, thinly sliced (optional)

Preheat oven to 300° F. Spray a 9-inch springform pan with vegetable oil spray.

Break bread into quarters and place in the workbowl of a food processor fitted with a metal blade. Process into fine crumbs. In a medium bowl, mix bread crumbs, wheat germ, cocoa, egg whites, honey, vanilla and liqueur until coarse and moist. Using a fork, press mixture evenly in the bottom of the prepared pan. Bake 10 minutes, or until firm to the touch. Cool on wire rack.

In the workbowl of a food processor fitted with a metal blade, process yogurt, ricotta cheese, egg whites, flour, sugar, orange rind, vanilla, cocoa and liqueur until fully blended, scraping the sides of the bowl as needed.

Pour batter into prepared pan and bake on middle rack of oven 1 hour. Turn off the heat and let cake remain in the oven 15 minutes more. Remove from oven and let cool. Chill in refrigerator for at least 3 hours, or preferably overnight, before removing sides of pan.

Garnish with fresh fruit, if desired. Serve chilled or at room temperature.

COFFEE LIQUEUR CLOUDS

¾ cup part-skim ricotta cheese
2 tablespoons Mock Whipped Cream (see page 234)
¼ teaspoon ground cinnamon
2 tablespoons coffee liqueur
3 tablespoons confectioners' sugar
1 11-ounce can mandarin oranges, drained

GARNISH
Ground cinnamon

In a blender or the workbowl of a food processor fitted with a metal blade, thoroughly mix ricotta cheese, Mock Whipped Cream, ¼ teaspoon cinnamon, confectioners' sugar and coffee liqueur. Blend until smooth. Set aside.

Divide mandarin oranges evenly into five dessert dishes, and top each with ½ cup of cheese mixture. Garnish with ground cinnamon. Serve chilled.

SERVES 5
ABOUT ½ CUP PER SERVING

Go ahead—indulge in a rich dessert! Just make sure you use this recipe—all the flavor is here, but the fat isn't.

NUTRIENT ANALYSIS

Calories	124.00kcal
Protein	5.08gm
Carbohydrate	17.95gm
Total Fat	3.50gm
Saturated	1.90gm
Polyunsaturated	0.39gm
Monounsaturated	0.98gm
Cholesterol	11.67mg
Sodium	54.00mg

MOCK WHIPPED CREAM

MAKES 2 CUPS
SERVES 32
1 TABLESPOON
PER SERVING

Use this light, tasty topping in place of whipped cream or prepackaged nondairy whipped topping.

NUTRIENT ANALYSIS

Calories	20.00kcal
Protein	0.44gm
Carbohydrate	1.68gm
Total Fat	1.28gm
Saturated	0.17gm
Polyunsaturated	0.75gm
Monounsaturated	0.31gm
Cholesterol	0.19mg
Sodium	6.00mg

1 teaspoon gelatin
2 teaspoons cold water
3 tablespoons boiling water
½ cup ice water
½ cup nonfat dry milk
3 tablespoons sugar
3 tablespoons acceptable vegetable oil

Chill a small mixing bowl.

In another small bowl, soften gelatin with cold water. Add boiling water, stirring constantly until gelatin is completely dissolved. Cool until tepid.

Place ice water and nonfat dry milk in chilled mixing bowl. Beat at high speed of electric mixer until stiff peaks form. Continue beating and add sugar, oil and gelatin.

Place in freezer for approximately 15 minutes, then transfer to refrigerator until ready to use. Stir before using to retain creamy texture.

ORANGE FLUFF

1 envelope unflavored gelatin (1 tablespoon)
¼ cup cold water
½ cup boiling water
½ cup sugar
1 cup orange juice
8 tablespoons Mock Whipped Cream (see page 234)
1 tablespoon finely grated orange rind

GARNISH
2 kiwis, 2 peaches or 6 fresh strawberries, sliced
6 small sprigs of mint (optional)

In a small bowl, sprinkle gelatin over cold water. Let stand 2 to 3 minutes.

In another small bowl, mix sugar and boiling water. Add gelatin mixture; stir until dissolved. Add orange juice. Place bowl in refrigerator or over ice water and allow to chill, stirring occasionally, until the mixture thickens, 8 to 10 minutes. Add Mock Whipped Cream and beat vigorously with a hand beater. Continue beating 8 to 10 minutes, or until mixture is fluffy and doubles in volume. Fold in orange peel.

Spoon mixture into a serving bowl or individual glasses and chill until set. Garnish with sliced fruit and mint before serving.

SERVES 6
½ CUP PER SERVING

NUTRIENT ANALYSIS*

Calories	109.00kcal
Protein	1.89gm
Carbohydrate	22.75gm
Total Fat	1.55gm
Saturated	0.20gm
Polyunsaturated	0.89gm
Monounsaturated	0.37gm
Cholesterol	0.26mg
Sodium	10.00mg

* Based on recipe without garnish.

STRAWBERRIES ROMANOFF

SERVES 4
1 CUP PER
SERVING

This great dessert can also be served as a breakfast treat; just leave out the liqueur and top with crunchy whole-grain cereal. For flavor variety, try substituting other fresh fruit.

NUTRIENT
ANALYSIS

Calories	219.82kcal
Protein	7.88gm
Carbohydrate	69.25gm
Total Fat	3.36gm
Saturated	0.33gm
Polyunsaturated	0.61gm
Monounsaturated	1.50gm
Cholesterol	2.00mg
Sodium	92.79mg

SAUCE

1 cup Double-Thick Yogurt (see page 262)
¼ cup firmly packed brown sugar
½ teaspoon ground cinnamon
1 teaspoon vanilla extract
2 tablespoons strawberry liqueur (optional)

2 pints fresh strawberries, about 24 ounces, washed, hulled and cut into bite-size pieces

GARNISH

2 tablespoons pecan pieces, lightly toasted

In a small bowl, whisk sauce ingredients until fully mixed. Refrigerate for at least 1 hour to make the sauce slightly firm.

Divide berries evenly in four dessert dishes. Spoon ¼ cup sauce over each serving. Top with nuts and serve immediately.

FROZEN BANANA MOUSSE

3 ripe bananas
¼ cup part-skim ricotta cheese
3 tablespoons skim milk
Pinch ground nutmeg

Peel and place bananas in a heavy plastic bag. Freeze at least 6 hours. Remove from freezer and cut each into five or six pieces. In the workbowl of a food processor fitted with a metal blade, process banana pieces and remaining ingredients, scraping sides occasionally, until smooth and creamy. Serve immediately.

SERVES 3
⅔ CUP PER SERVING

NUTRIENT ANALYSIS

Calories	121.72kcal
Protein	3.62gm
Carbohydrate	25.13gm
Total Fat	2.03gm
Saturated	1.16gm
Polyunsaturated	0.14gm
Monounsaturated	0.49gm
Cholesterol	6.16mg
Sodium	32.57mg

TAPIOCA PUDDING

3 tablespoons quick-cooking tapioca
⅓ cup sugar
2 large egg whites, lightly beaten
2¾ cups skim milk
¾ teaspoon vanilla extract
Pinch ground nutmeg

GARNISH
¼ cup slivered almonds, toasted

In a 2-quart saucepan, mix tapioca, sugar, egg whites and milk and let stand 5 minutes. Bring mixture just to a boil over medium heat, stirring constantly. Remove from heat and stir in vanilla and nutmeg. Cover with plastic wrap and let stand at room temperature 20 minutes. Stir and pour into individual serving dishes.

Garnish with 1 tablespoon slivered almonds per serving. Serve warm or chilled.

SERVES 4
ABOUT ⅔ CUP PER SERVING

NUTRIENT ANALYSIS

Calories	203.78kcal
Protein	8.88gm
Carbohydrate	32.37gm
Total Fat	4.55gm
Saturated	0.55gm
Polyunsaturated	0.80gm
Monounsaturated	2.94gm
Cholesterol	3.37mg
Sodium	113.38mg

BLUEBERRY PUDDING

SERVES 4
ABOUT ⅔ CUP
PER SERVING

The sweetener in this
recipe is apple juice
concentrate. That's a good
way to cut down on
processed sugar.

**NUTRIENT
ANALYSIS**

Calories	139.88kcal
Protein	7.62gm
Carbohydrate	22.46gm
Total Fat	3.34gm
Saturated	0.47gm
Polyunsaturated	1.74gm
Monounsaturated	0.70gm
Cholesterol	0.00mg
Sodium	13.75mg

1 tablespoon unflavored gelatin, 1 envelope
¼ cup boiling water
10 ounces tofu, drained
5 tablespoons apple juice concentrate, defrosted
½ teaspoon vanilla extract
1 tablespoon firmly packed brown sugar
½ teaspoon ground cinnamon
1 pint fresh blueberries, rinsed, drained and
  divided, about 16 ounces

Dissolve gelatin in boiling water, stirring until
crystals disappear.

In a blender or the workbowl of a food processor
fitted with a metal blade, blend dissolved gelatin,
tofu, apple juice concentrate, vanilla, brown sugar,
cinnamon and 1 cup of blueberries until smooth.
Pour pudding into a bowl; fold in remaining cup of
blueberries. Cover with plastic wrap and refrigerate
for 4 hours, or until set. Serve cold.

WHITE GRAPE JUICE GELATIN DESSERT

2 to 3 dozen seedless green grapes, chilled
1 envelope unflavored gelatin (1 tablespoon)
1 tablespoon sugar
2 cups white grape juice

Divide the grapes among four dessert dishes or wineglasses; set aside. In a medium bowl, mix gelatin with sugar. In a small saucepan, heat juice to boiling. Add to gelatin-sugar mixture and stir until gelatin is completely dissolved. Pour ½ cup gelatin liquid into each dessert dish or wineglass. Refrigerate 3 to 4 hours, or until mixture is slightly set. Serve cold.

SERVES 4
½ CUP PER SERVING

NUTRIENT ANALYSIS

Calories	116.77kcal
Protein	2.46gm
Carbohydrate	27.96gm
Total Fat	0.23gm
Saturated	0.08gm
Polyunsaturated	0.06gm
Monounsaturated	0.00gm
Cholesterol	0.00mg
Sodium	6.06mg

COFFEE SHAKE

1 quart decaffeinated coffee
2 cups vanilla ice milk, tightly packed

In blender, process coffee and ice milk until fully mixed. Serve, icy cold, in tall glasses.

SERVES 4
1 ¼ CUPS PER SERVING

NUTRIENT ANALYSIS

Calories	127.30kcal
Protein	3.45gm
Carbohydrate	20.79gm
Total Fat	3.76gm
Saturated	2.34gm
Polyunsaturated	0.14gm
Monounsaturated	1.09gm
Cholesterol	12.25mg
Sodium	70.00mg

FROZEN ORANGE CREAM

SERVES 6
½ CUP PER
SERVING

3 cups vanilla ice milk, tightly packed
½ cup frozen orange juice concentrate
1 teaspoon vanilla extract

The vanilla extract enhances the sweetness of this dish without adding calories.

In a blender or the workbowl of a food processor fitted with a metal blade, blend all ingredients until fully mixed. Spoon mixture into dessert cups. Cover with plastic wrap and freeze for about 2 hours. If you freeze it longer, remove the dish from the freezer 10 minutes before serving to allow it to thaw slightly.

NUTRIENT
ANALYSIS

Calories	160.21kcal
Protein	4.01gm
Carbohydrate	28.45gm
Total Fat	3.80gm
Saturated	2.34gm
Polyunsaturated	0.15gm
Monounsaturated	1.09gm
Cholesterol	12.20mg
Sodium	70.55mg

VERY BERRY SORBET

SORBET

1½ cups frozen no-sugar-added blackberries,
   slightly defrosted
1 teaspoon frozen orange juice concentrate
2 teaspoons water
1 teaspoon brandy or cognac (optional)

GARNISH

Fresh mint sprigs (optional)

In a blender or the workbowl of a food processor
fitted with a metal blade, process sorbet ingredients
until smooth, scraping sides as needed. Garnish
with mint, if desired. Serve immediately.

*This dish can be frozen. About 15 minutes before serv-
ing, remove from freezer and let defrost until it's soft
enough to serve.*

SERVES 2
½ CUP PER
SERVING

*This slightly tart sorbet is a
perfect complement to
Frozen Banana Mousse
(see page 237). For an
elegant presentation, try
combining them in
alternating layers in
parfait glasses.*

**NUTRIENT
ANALYSIS**

Calories	66.73kcal
Protein	0.83gm
Carbohydrate	14.95gm
Total Fat	0.43gm
Saturated	0.00gm
Polyunsaturated	0.00gm
Monounsaturated	0.00gm
Cholesterol	0.00mg
Sodium	0.13mg

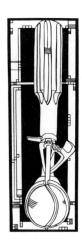

MELON WITH SHERBET

SERVES 6

Serve this dessert in glasses with pretty frosted rims.

1 small honeydew melon, cut in half and seeded
4 oranges or 2 cups strawberries
2 tablespoons confectioners' sugar, sifted
12 ounces rainbow sherbet, six 2-ounce scoops

GARNISH
Mint sprigs

NUTRIENT ANALYSIS

Calories	223.55kcal
Protein	3.37gm
Carbohydrate	53.64gm
Total Fat	1.48gm
Saturated	0.72gm
Polyunsaturated	0.08gm
Monounsaturated	0.35gm
Cholesterol	3.97mg
Sodium	54.62mg

With a melon baller, scoop out flesh of melon. Section oranges or slice strawberries. Combine melon and oranges or stawberries in a bowl and chill.

Place confectioners' sugar in a pie plate. Dampen rims of six dessert glasses and then dip rims individually in confectioners' sugar.

Divide fruit mixture among glasses, top each with a scoop of sherbet and garnish with a sprig of mint.

Serve immediately.

FROZEN GRAPE TREATS

SERVES 4
8 GRAPES PER SERVING

32 seedless green grapes
32 seedless red grapes

Place individual grapes in a flat pan and cover with foil. Freeze for at least 2 hours. Transfer grapes to a freezer bag and seal tightly until ready to serve.

Do not bite into frozen grapes; just suck on them and let them thaw in your mouth.

NUTRIENT ANALYSIS

Calories	50.44kcal
Protein	0.48gm
Carbohydrate	13.77gm
Total Fat	0.28gm
Saturated	0.09gm
Polyunsaturated	0.08gm
Monounsaturated	0.01gm
Cholesterol	0.00mg
Sodium	1.60mg

YOGURT-FRUIT CUP

1 16-ounce can sliced peaches or pears, packed in
   fruit juice
16 ounces lowfat vanilla yogurt
2 tablespoons finely chopped almonds
½ teaspoon ground cardamom

Drain and divide fruit among six small dessert bowls. Top with yogurt and sprinkle lightly with nuts and cardamom. Serve immediately.

SERVES 6

This offers a new twist to a back-to-basics favorite. You'll like the fragrant touch of cardamom.

NUTRIENT ANALYSIS

Calories	121.01 kcal
Protein	4.39gm
Carbohydrate	22.19gm
Total Fat	2.23gm
Saturated	0.67gm
Polyunsaturated	0.30gm
Monounsaturated	1.15gm
Cholesterol	3.21mg
Sodium	46.59mg

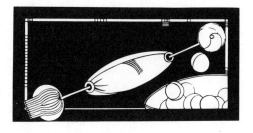

CHERRIES JUBILEE

SERVES 4
1 CUP PER
SERVING

What an elegant finale to a dinner party!

NUTRIENT ANALYSIS

Calories	299.13kcal
Protein	5.79gm
Carbohydrate	53.88gm
Total Fat	5.82gm
Saturated	3.55gm
Polyunsaturated	0.27gm
Monounsaturated	1.67gm
Cholesterol	18.37mg
Sodium	108.54mg

1 16-ounce can dark, sweet, pitted cherries
¼ cup apple juice
1 tablespoon cornstarch
2 tablespoons brandy or rum
3 cups vanilla ice milk

Drain syrup from cherries and mix with apple juice.

In a small bowl, mix cornstarch and 2 tablespoons of juice until no lumps remain.

In a small saucepan over high heat, bring remaining liquid to a boil and reduce heat to medium. Add cornstarch mixture, stirring constantly. Let mixture return to a boil and cook about 1 minute, or until thickened. Add brandy, stir in cherries, and ignite.

Pour over individual portions of ice milk. Serve immediately.

BROILED GRAPEFRUIT
WITH PORT WINE

2 grapefruit
2 tablespoons port wine

SERVES 4
**½ GRAPEFRUIT
PER SERVING**

Preheat broiler.

Cut grapefruit into halves. Trim a thin section off the uncut end of each half so the grapefruit can sit without wobbling. Section the grapefruit. Place grapefruit in a baking pan, sprinkle with wine, place pan about 2 inches from the broiler and broil about 5 minutes. Watch carefully to keep them from burning.

Port wine adds a tantalizing flavor to grapefruit. Try this dish as an appetizer or dessert.

**NUTRIENT
ANALYSIS**

Calories	57.64kcal
Protein	0.90gm
Carbohydrate	12.64gm
Total Fat	0.15gm
Saturated	0.01gm
Polyunsaturated	0.03gm
Monounsaturated	0.01gm
Cholesterol	0.00mg
Sodium	0.29mg

BAKED APPLES

SERVES 4

**NUTRIENT
ANALYSIS**

Calories	120.30kcal
Protein	0.77gm
Carbohydrate	27.67gm
Total Fat	0.37gm
Saturated	0.11gm
Polyunsaturated	0.11gm
Monounsaturated	0.01gm
Cholesterol	0.00mg
Sodium	6.40mg

¼ *cup port wine*
¼ *cup frozen apple juice concentrate, defrosted*
¼ *cup raisins*
¼ *teaspoon ground cinnamon*
4 *baking apples, preferably red Rome apples*

Preheat oven to 350° F.

In a small saucepan, heat wine and juice concentrate until mixture begins to boil. Turn heat off and add raisins and cinnamon. Stir, cover and let sit for 15 minutes.

Core each apple, leaving the last half-inch on the bottom intact. If necessary, slice off a small section from the bottom of each apple so that it does not fall over. Take a paring knife and score around the apple, about ½-inch from the bottom. Peel from top down to scored line to prevent splitting. Place apples in a glass baking dish so they are not touching. Stuff with the juice-soaked raisins, spooning remaining juice evenly over apples. Put water in the dish to a depth of ⅓ inch, cover with aluminum foil and bake 20 minutes. Remove the foil and bake another 20 minutes. Serve warm.

MERINGUES

Vegetable oil spray
4 large egg whites*
⅛ teaspoon cream of tartar
1 cup sugar
1 teaspoon white vinegar
½ teaspoon vanilla extract

Preheat oven to 275° F. Line two large baking sheets with wax paper, then spray lightly with vegetable oil spray.

In a large bowl, beat egg whites and cream of tartar with an electric beater until stiff peaks form. Add sugar, 2 tablespoons at a time, beating well after each addition. To test if sugar is completely dissolved, rub meringue mixture between fingers; if grainy, continue beating. Add vinegar and vanilla; beat well to blend.

Drop mixture by heaping tablespoonfuls about 2 inches apart on prepared baking sheets. Spread each spoonful into a 2½-inch circle, pushing the mixture against the edges to resemble a nest. Bake 45 minutes. Reduce heat to 250° F. and bake about 15 minutes more, until each meringue is firm and crisp, but not brown.

Remove from wax paper while warm, and allow to cool on a rack. Store in an airtight container.

* *Remember, even a single drop of egg yolk will prevent egg whites from rising, so separate eggs very carefully, one at a time.*

**SERVES 20
1 SHELL PER
SERVING**

For an elegant dessert, fill these with fresh fruit or vanilla ice milk and Blueberry Sauce (see page 196).

NUTRIENT ANALYSIS

Calories	41.61kcal
Protein	0.67gm
Carbohydrate	9.67gm
Total Fat	0.00gm
Saturated	0.00gm
Polyunsaturated	0.00gm
Monounsaturated	0.00gm
Cholesterol	0.00mg
Sodium	11.41mg

COCOA-ALMOND MERINGUE KISSES

SERVES 14
2 KISSES PER SERVING

These meringues are crispy on the outside and chewy on the inside.

NUTRIENT ANALYSIS

Calories	60.17kcal
Protein	1.32gm
Carbohydrate	11.27gm
Total Fat	1.44gm
Saturated	0.29gm
Polyunsaturated	0.21gm
Monounsaturated	0.86gm
Cholesterol	0.00mg
Sodium	12.59mg

Vegetable oil spray
3 large egg whites*
⅛ teaspoon cream of tartar
¾ cup sugar
3 tablespoons unsweetened cocoa powder
½ teaspoon vanilla extract
¼ cup sliced almonds

Preheat oven to 325° F. Spray two large baking sheets with vegetable oil spray.

In a large bowl, beat egg whites and cream of tartar until stiff peaks form. Add sugar, 2 tablespoons at a time, beating well after each addition. Add cocoa and vanilla, beat well to blend. Fold in almonds.

Drop mixture by tablespoonfuls onto prepared baking sheets. Bake 25 minutes, or until meringues are crisp on the outside. Remove from baking sheets immediately, and allow to cool on a rack. Store in an airtight container.

* Remember, even a single drop of egg yolk will prevent egg whites from rising, so separate eggs very carefully, one at a time.

GINGERBREAD BARS

Vegetable oil spray
6 tablespoons acceptable unsalted margarine, at
  room temperature
1 cup dark brown sugar, firmly packed
2 large egg whites
¼ cup molasses
1¼ cups all-purpose flour
1 cup whole-wheat flour
¼ cup dry skim milk powder
¾ teaspoon baking powder
¾ teaspoon baking soda
¾ teaspoon powdered ginger
½ teaspoon ground cinnamon
½ teaspoon ground nutmeg
⅛ teaspoon ground cloves
½ cup coarsely chopped walnuts

SERVES 15
2 BARS PER
SERVING

The wonderful, spicy aroma of these cookies baking will have the whole family lined up in the kitchen. They're great any time, and they freeze well.

NUTRIENT ANALYSIS

Calories	198.51kcal
Protein	3.47gm
Carbohydrate	31.75gm
Total Fat	6.97gm
Saturated	1.10gm
Polyunsaturated	3.18gm
Monounsaturated	2.27gm
Cholesterol	0.20mg
Sodium*	76.42mg

* Will increase if using regular margarine.

Preheat oven to 350° F. Spray a 12½ × 8-inch baking pan with vegetable oil spray.

In a large bowl, beat margarine at medium speed until creamy. Add brown sugar and beat at high speed until light, 1 to 2 minutes. Beat in egg whites. Add molasses and beat until no lumps remain.

In a separate bowl, sift together flours, dry skim milk powder, baking powder, baking soda, ginger, cinnamon, nutmeg and cloves. Add sifted ingredients to margarine mixture and blend thoroughly. Stir in nuts and mix well. The dough will be sticky.

Place the dough in center of prepared pan. Using a spatula or wet hands, spread dough evenly in pan. Place pan on center rack of oven and bake 25 minutes.

Allow to cool at least 5 minutes. Cut into 30 bars and store in an airtight container.

CHEWY OATMEAL SQUARES

SERVES 18
2 SQUARES PER
SERVING

This recipe and the one
following are two versions
of a favorite. Make them
both and see which you
like best.

NUTRIENT
ANALYSIS

Calories	127.72kcal
Protein	1.59gm
Carbohydrate	13.16gm
Total Fat	8.05gm
Saturated	1.02gm
Polyunsaturated	4.66gm
Monounsaturated	1.86gm
Cholesterol	0.00mg
Sodium	10.21mg

Vegetable oil spray
½ cup acceptable vegetable oil
½ cup firmly packed brown sugar
1 4½-ounce jar strained applesauce (baby food)
1 teaspoon vanilla extract
2 cups quick-cooking oats
⅓ cup chopped walnuts
½ teaspoon baking powder
1 teaspoon ground cinnamon

Preheat oven to 325° F. Spray a 9-inch square pan with vegetable oil spray.

In a mixing bowl, combine oil, brown sugar, applesauce and vanilla. Add oats, walnuts, baking powder and cinnamon. Mix until blended.

Press mixture evenly and firmly into prepared pan. Bake 20 to 25 minutes, or until edges are golden brown. Cut into 36 squares while hot. Allow to cool in pan. Store in an airtight container.

OATMEAL CRISPS

Vegetable oil spray
$\frac{1}{2}$ cup acceptable vegetable oil
$\frac{1}{2}$ cup firmly packed brown sugar
1 tablespoon honey
1 teaspoon vanilla extract
2 cups quick-cooking oats
$\frac{1}{2}$ teaspoon baking powder
1 teaspoon ground cinnamon

**SERVES 18
2 SQUARES PER
SERVING**

**NUTRIENT
ANALYSIS**

Calories	114.59kcal
Protein	1.25gm
Carbohydrate	12.03gm
Total Fat	6.65gm
Saturated	0.86gm
Polyunsaturated	3.74gm
Monounsaturated	1.65gm
Cholesterol	0.00mg
Sodium	10.00mg

Preheat oven to 325° F. Spray a 9-inch square pan with vegetable oil spray.

In a mixing bowl, combine oil, brown sugar, honey and vanilla. Add oats, baking powder and cinnamon. Mix until blended.

Press mixture evenly and firmly into prepared pan. Bake 20 to 25 minutes, or until edges are golden brown. Cut into 36 squares while hot. Allow to cool in pan. Store in a container with a loose-fitting lid.

Beverages

Orange Juice and Club Soda Cooler
Orange-Strawberry Juice Froth
Orange-Banana Shake
Spiced Apple Cider

ORANGE JUICE AND CLUB SODA COOLER

¼ cup frozen orange juice concentrate
3 cups club soda
Crushed ice

GARNISH
4 strawberries or 4 sprigs fresh mint

In a 2-quart pitcher, combine orange juice concentrate and club soda. Stir and serve immediately over crushed ice. Garnish each glass with a strawberry or a fresh mint sprig.

**SERVES 4
1 CUP PER
SERVING**

**NUTRIENT
ANALYSIS**

Calories	24.73kcal
Protein	0.40gm
Carbohydrate	5.89gm
Total Fat	0.08gm
Saturated	0.00gm
Polyunsaturated	0.00gm
Monounsaturated	0.00gm
Cholesterol	0.00mg
Sodium	29.37mg

ORANGE-STRAWBERRY JUICE FROTH

2 cups orange juice
1½ cups apricot nectar
1 cup frozen, sweetened strawberries

In blender, process ingredients for about 20 seconds, or until smooth and frothy. Serve immediately.

**SERVES 6
¾ CUP PER
SERVING**

**NUTRIENT
ANALYSIS**

Calories	113.53kcal
Protein	1.05gm
Carbohydrate	29.07gm
Total Fat	0.16gm
Saturated	0.02gm
Polyunsaturated	0.05gm
Monounsaturated	0.04gm
Cholesterol	0.00mg
Sodium	4.00mg

ORANGE·BANANA SHAKE

**SERVES 2
1 CUP PER
SERVING**

Cool. Refreshing. Fruity.
Delicious. And lowfat, too.

**NUTRIENT
ANALYSIS**

Calories	132.54kcal
Protein	4.36gm
Carbohydrate	29.59gm
Total Fat	0.38gm
Saturated	0.15gm
Polyunsaturated	0.06gm
Monounsaturated	0.05gm
Cholesterol	1.53mg
Sodium	53.32mg

1 cup orange juice
1 small, ripe banana
¼ cup instant nonfat milk powder
½ cup ice cubes
¼ cup club soda

In blender, process orange juice, banana, milk powder and ice cubes until mixture is thick and ice cubes are crushed. Add club soda, stir and serve immediately.

SPICED APPLE CIDER

12 whole allspice
6 whole cloves
2 quarts apple juice or apple cider
1 quart water
3 tea bags, regular or decaffeinated
½ orange with peel, thinly sliced
½ lemon with peel, thinly sliced
2 cinnamon sticks
Ground allspice to taste

GARNISH
1 orange with peel, thinly sliced
1 lemon with peel, thinly sliced

SERVES 16
¾ CUP PER
SERVING

*A warm fire. A cozy
room. A comfy chair. This
holiday favorite completes
the scene.*

NUTRIENT
ANALYSIS

Calories	71.05kcal
Protein	0.37gm
Carbohydrate	17.55gm
Total Fat	0.21gm
Saturated	0.04gm
Polyunsaturated	0.05gm
Monounsaturated	0.02gm
Cholesterol	0.00mg
Sodium	4.36mg

Place whole allspice and cloves in tied cheesecloth packet. In a saucepan, bring apple juice or cider, water, tea bags, orange, lemon, cinnamon and cheesecloth packet to a boil. Reduce heat and simmer 3 minutes. Remove cheesecloth packet, tea bags and orange and lemon slices. Simmer 5 additional minutes. Add ground allspice to taste.

Serve hot or chilled. Garnish with fresh slices of orange and lemon.

Basics and Techniques

Defatted Cheddar Cheese
Double-Thick Yogurt
Fish Stock—See Poached Fish and Fish Stock, page 93
Chicken Stock
Beef Stock

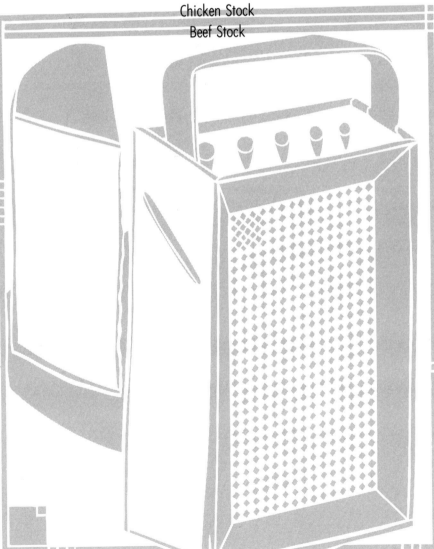

DEFATTED CHEDDAR CHEESE

Vegetable oil spray
4 ounces sharp cheddar cheese or another natural
cheese such as Monterey Jack or Gouda, cut into
½-inch cubes

MAKES 3 ½ OUNCES

This recipe shows how to separate cheese from some of its fat. You can do it in the oven or the microwave. Either way, this clever technique produces a tasty cheese that is lower in fat than commercially prepared cheeses. Use it when your recipe calls for cheddar cheese.

Oven Method: Preheat oven to 450° F.

Select an ovenproof 5- or 6-inch-diameter pan or bowl. Spray thoroughly with vegetable oil spray. Place cheese in greased bowl and add cool tap water to barely cover. Bake 20 minutes, stirring every 5 minutes. Remove from oven and let cool for about 15 minutes. Pour into a fine sieve and rinse under cool running water for about a minute to wash away remaining surface fat. Remove liquid by pressing the palm of your hand against the cheese in the sieve. Refrigerate and use within 3 to 4 days.

Microwave Method: Select a 5- or 6-inch-diameter bowl suitable for a microwave oven. Spray thoroughly with vegetable oil spray. Place cheese in greased bowl and add cool tap water to barely cover. Microwave on high setting 3 minutes, or until cheese is completely melted, stirring after each minute of cooking. Remove from oven and let cool for about 10 minutes. Pour into a fine sieve and rinse for about 15 seconds under cool running water to wash away remaining surface fat. Remove liquid by pressing the palm of your hand against the cheese in the sieve. Refrigerate and use within 3 to 4 days.

NUTRIENT ANALYSIS*

Calories	201.00kcal
Protein	30.30gm
Carbohydrate	0.20gm
Total Fat	8.80gm
Saturated	6.90gm
Polyunsaturated	0.20gm
Monounsaturated	1.80gm
Cholesterol	20.60mg
Sodium	163.00mg

* For entire recipe, using cheddar cheese.

DOUBLE-THICK YOGURT

MAKES 2 CUPS

Yogurt is one of the staples of a heart-healthful way of cooking. It is used in the Mocha Cheesecake (see page 232), the Beef or Venison Stroganoff (see page 137) and other recipes in this book. This recipe works best when using a yogurt that contains no gelatin, so read the label carefully.

1 quart plain nonfat yogurt

Place a double-thick layer of fine-mesh cotton cheesecloth or paper coffee filters inside a colander, which does not rust. Place the colander in a bowl, leaving enough space for about 2 cups of whey to drain out of the colander. Pour the yogurt into the cheesecloth-lined colander and refrigerate for 8 hours. This will yield 2 cups of firm yogurt and 2 cups of drained whey.

Reserve the whey and use it as a substitute in recipes calling for skim milk, such as in baking bread. (See Honey-Nut Bread, page 202, Potato Bread, page 204, etc.)

NUTRIENT ANALYSIS*

Calories	504.00kcal
Protein	52.16gm
Carbohydrate	69.76gm
Total Fat	1.60gm
Saturated	0.96gm
Polyunsaturated	0gm
Monounsaturated	0.32gm
Cholesterol	16.00mg
Sodium	680.00mg

* For entire recipe.

CHICKEN STOCK

3 pounds chicken, skinned and all visible fat
   removed
3 quarts water
1 medium onion, coarsely chopped
2 stalks celery, chopped
2 large carrots, chopped
1 teaspoon whole peppercorns, or to taste
½-inch piece peeled, fresh ginger, chopped
   (optional)
1 bay leaf
1 teaspoon dried thyme

In a large stockpot, bring all ingredients to a boil over medium-high heat. Reduce heat and simmer, partially covered, for at least 1 hour, or until chicken is tender. Frequently skim the froth off the top. Remove chicken and strain stock. (The chicken meat can be used in salads.)

To defat stock, refrigerate until the fat hardens on the surface, then remove and discard. The stock may gel during refrigeration; this is natural.

To defat commercially prepared canned chicken stock, store cans in the refrigerator to allow fat to harden. Remove and discard the fat before using the stock.

MAKES 2 ½ QUARTS

Canned chicken stock is no match for homemade. This stock is more flavorful and lower in fat and sodium than canned is. Because good stock is essential to so many recipes, prepare a large batch, freeze it in ice cube trays and then transfer the cubes to plastic freezer bags to be used as needed.

NUTRIENT ANALYSIS*

Calories	318.70kcal
Protein	29.70gm
Carbohydrate	38.30gm
Total Fat	5.70gm
Saturated	1.50gm
Polyunsaturated	1.30gm
Monounsaturated	1.50gm
Cholesterol	68.00mg
Sodium	326.80mg

* For entire recipe.

BEEF STOCK

MAKES 2 QUARTS

Roasting the bones gives the stock a rich flavor and color. You can, however, skip this step and combine the bones with the remaining ingredients to make a good stock. Defat and freeze the stock for future use. After tasting this, you may never want to buy another can of stock!

NUTRIENT ANALYSIS*

Calories	399.98kcal
Protein	34.61gm
Carbohydrate	50.63gm
Total Fat	7.22gm
Saturated	2.66gm
Polyunsaturated	0.42gm
Monounsaturated	2.66gm
Cholesterol	80.26mg
Sodium	235.55mg

* For entire recipe.

4 pounds beef or veal bones
3 quarts water
1 medium onion, coarsely chopped
3 large carrots, chopped
6 sprigs fresh parsley
1 teaspoon whole peppercorns, or to taste
4 cloves garlic, halved
1 bay leaf
2 whole cloves
1 teaspoon thyme
½ teaspoon celery seeds

Preheat oven to 400° F.

Place bones in a roasting pan and bake 30 minutes, turning once. Discard accumulated fat.

Transfer bones and remaining ingredients to a large stockpot. Bring mixture to a boil over medium-high heat. Reduce heat and simmer, partially covered, at least 4 hours. Frequently skim the froth off the top.

Using a colander or a large sieve lined with a layer of cheesecloth, strain stock.

To defat stock, refrigerate until the fat hardens on the surface, then remove and discard. The stock may gel during refrigeration; this is natural.

To defat commercially prepared canned beef stock, store cans in the refrigerator to allow fat to harden. Remove and discard fat before using the stock.

APPENDIX

Appendix A.

LIPOPROTEINS: THE VEHICLES OF CHOLESTEROL

Tiny particles in your blood called lipoproteins carry cholesterol and other fats to various parts of the body. Some are dangerous. Others are innocuous or even beneficial. The dangerous lipoproteins filter into the walls of your small arteries, allowing cholesterol to build up, a condition called atherosclerosis. Heavy build-up can cause the blood flow to become blocked, resulting in heart attack or stroke. Conversely, other lipoproteins may actually remove excess cholesterol from the arteries. That's why it's important to know which is which.

Low Density Lipoproteins (LDL)
In most people, the majority of blood cholesterol is carried in low density lipoproteins, or LDL. LDL is the "bad guy" of lipoproteins; it's the kind that enters artery walls to cause atherosclerosis. Your doctor can more accurately judge your coronary risk by determining the amount of cholesterol carried by your LDL. This is referred to as LDL-cholesterol.

If your LDL-cholesterol is over 160 milligrams per 100 ml of blood (mg/dl), it's considered high risk. If it's between 130 and 160, it's borderline high risk. A desirable LDL-cholesterol is below 130.

The relationship between the blood cholesterol level and LDL-cholesterol level varies. Your doctor can't predict your LDL-cholesterol from a blood cholesterol test. People with high blood cholesterol should have a lipoprotein analysis, too, especially since LDL-cholesterol level is a much more accurate predictor of coronary risk.

High Density Lipoproteins (HDL)
Typically, one third to one fourth of the cholesterol in the blood is carried in high density lipoproteins, or HDL. HDL is the "good guy" among lipoproteins; a high blood level seems to protect against heart attack.

We're not sure exactly how HDL works, but some authorities believe that it removes excess cholesterol from the arteries to prevent the buildup of cholesterol in the artery wall. So a high level of HDL-cholesterol reduces your risk of heart attack, while a low level increases it.

HDL-cholesterol levels for men usually range from 40 to 50 mg/dl. For women, levels of 50 to 60 mg/dl are normal. If your blood level is below 35 mg/dl, your HDL-cholesterol is abnormally low and is a major cardiac risk factor for you.

Reduced HDL-cholesterol levels can be caused by a number of factors. The most common are cigarette smoking, obesity and lack of exercise. Fortunately, all can be corrected, resulting in an increased HDL level and a reduced heart attack risk. Having a high level of triglycerides in your blood also reduces HDL-cholesterol, which may be why most people with high triglycerides are at increased risk for heart attack.

Some drugs (e.g., beta-blockers) used to treat high blood pressure lower blood HDL. Male sex hormones (androgens), progesterone and anabolic steroids all lower HDL levels. People who take anabolic steroids to build muscles may be setting themselves up for heart attacks later in life. Female sex hormones (estrogens) raise HDL-cholesterol. This difference between male and female sex hormones may be one reason why men are more prone to heart attack than women.

Very Low Density Lipoproteins (VLDL)

Blood cholesterol that is not present in LDL or HDL is found in very low density lipoproteins, VLDL for short. Very low density lipoproteins have the additional job of carrying most of the blood triglycerides. Chemically, triglycerides are what most people know as fat. In fact, most body fat occurs in the form of triglycerides. (Table fats like butter, margarine and vegetable oil are triglycerides, too.) Normally, triglycerides are removed from VLDL during circulation, and serve as a source of energy for muscle activity. After triglycerides are removed, the lipoprotein particles remaining are triglyceride-poor and are called VLDL remnants, which are further broken down to produce LDL. Thus, cholesterol-rich low density lipoproteins are the end products of VLDL metabolism.

Authorities are divided on whether very low density lipoproteins are "bad guys" in the sense of contributing to the buildup of cholesterol-laden plaque in the arteries. Many investigators believe that VLDL can enter the coronary arteries and deposit cholesterol. If they're right, it means that VLDL-cholesterol may contribute to atherosclerosis in the same way that LDL-cholesterol does.

The blood triglyceride level is an indirect measure of VLDL-cholesterol. A simple way to estimate VLDL-cholesterol is to divide the blood triglyceride by five. An increased blood triglyceride level could, therefore, reflect a high risk by indicating an elevated VLDL-cholesterol. Indeed, more than one fourth of all patients who've had heart attacks have triglyceride levels that are abnormally high (over 250). Authorities aren't certain whether that relationship is because of abnormally high VLDL-cholesterol levels or reduced levels of HDL-cholesterol, which often results from elevated triglyceride levels. The fact is, both may contribute to atherosclerosis.

Blood triglyceride levels can be high for any number of reasons, including overweight, high alcohol consumption, diabetes and various inherited disorders of triglyceride metabolism.

Appendix B.

HOW DIET AFFECTS YOUR CHOLESTEROL LEVEL

BLOOD CHOLESTEROL–RAISING FACTORS IN THE DIET

Three major factors in the diet raise the blood cholesterol level; these are saturated fats, cholesterol, and obesity. Each of these factors will be examined.

Saturated Fat

Fats are composed mainly of triglycerides, which in turn are composed mainly of fatty acids. The latter fall into three categories: saturated fatty acids, monounsaturated fatty acids and polyunsaturated fatty acids. Of these three, only the saturated fatty acids raise blood cholesterol. The term "saturated fat" is shorthand for the more accurate term "saturated fatty acid."

Foods high in saturated fatty acids come from both animal and plant sources. Animal-based foods containing lots of saturated fats include butter, beef tallow, lard and poultry fat. Fish also contains a small amount. Plant-based oils containing saturated fats are coconut oil, palm kernel oil and palm oil.

Research shows that, for an average person, the intake of 1 gram of saturated fatty acid increases blood cholesterol by about 1 milligram per deciliter of blood (mg/dl). This response, however, varies from person to person. Some people are unusually sensitive to saturated fatty acids and show striking increases in blood cholesterol when saturates are ingested. Others experience less dramatic increases. Many people with high blood cholesterol seem to be especially sensitive to saturated fats, which partially explains their cholesterol levels.

There are several different kinds of saturated fatty acids, and some types raise the blood cholesterol more than others. Fatty acids present in butter, coconut oil, palm oil and palm kernel oil are the worst offenders for raising blood cholesterol. The fatty acids in cocoa butter and meat fats such as beef tallow and lard raise the blood cholesterol less, but they still contain significant portions of blood cholesterol–raising saturates.

Dietary Cholesterol

Another dietary substance that raises blood cholesterol is the cholesterol found in many of the foods we eat. It is important to distinguish between dietary cholesterol and blood cholesterol; the two are not the same.

Cholesterol in the diet comes exclusively from animal products. The richest sources are egg yolks and organ meats. Some cholesterol is found in all meats, poultry, fish and animal fats, such as butter and lard. For most Americans, dietary cholesterol sources are divided evenly among eggs, meat and animal fats like butter.

The effect of dietary cholesterol on blood cholesterol levels has been a subject of much controversy and dispute. Many research studies show that a diet high in cholesterol raises the blood cholesterol level, but the amount of that increase varies from person to person. Moreover, the response can vary even within a single person from one time to another. On the average, however, for every 250 milligrams of cholesterol habitually consumed in the diet the blood cholesterol rises by about 10 mg/dl. Most of this increase occurs in the LDL-cholesterol, the type of cholesterol most likely to build up in your arteries.

Obesity

Another way that diet can raise blood cholesterol is by taking in more calories than the body burns, a situation that leads to obesity. When the cholesterol level of an obese person is elevated, the increase is usually found in both LDL-cholesterol and VLDL-cholesterol. In contrast, the level of HDL or "good guy" cholesterol is usually low. (For a discussion of these types of cholesterol and their significance, see Appendix A.)

The ways in which excessive intakes of saturated fatty acids, cholesterol and total calories raise the blood cholesterol are outlined in Figure 1. The left panel shows how the body reduces the amounts of LDL and VLDL in the blood: Both VLDL remnants and LDL are removed primarily through the function of LDL receptors in the liver, which are extremely important for reducing LDL or "bad guy" cholesterol. The receptors are special proteins located on the surface of liver cells. They work by binding both VLDL remnants and LDL and pulling them out of the blood.

FIGURE 1

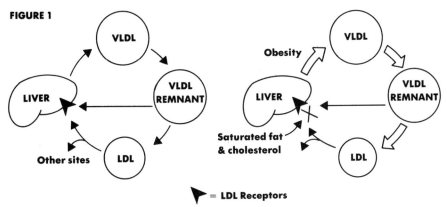

The right panel of Figure 1 shows how this LDL and VLDL removal process is changed by a cholesterol-raising diet. When the diet is rich in cholesterol, the excess cholesterol makes its way into the liver. As the liver receives more dietary cholesterol, it partially shuts down the production of LDL receptors, which leads to reduced removal of LDL-cholesterol from the blood.

Moreover, saturated fatty acids seem to increase the ability of dietary cholesterol to decrease the production of LDL receptors. That's how both dietary cholesterol and saturated fatty acids decrease LDL and VLDL removal and increase the blood's LDL-cholesterol level.

Obesity overloads the liver with calories, causing it to make more VLDL, which is transformed in excess into LDL. When obesity is combined with a high intake of saturated fatty acids and cholesterol, the blood level of LDL-cholesterol is doubly increased.

This combination of obesity and an excessive intake of cholesterol and saturated fatty acids is common among Americans. In some people it leads to a borderline cholesterol problem, whereas in others a serious one.

BLOOD CHOLESTEROL–LOWERING FACTORS IN THE DIET

In contrast to the nutrients that raise the blood cholesterol levels, there are others that have no effect on it. Nutrients that help reduce blood cholesterol levels include polyunsaturated fatty acids, monounsaturated fatty acids and carbohydrates. By substituting these nutrients for ones containing saturated fatty acids and dietary cholesterol, you can help decrease your blood cholesterol level.

Polyunsaturated Fatty Acids

There are two types of polyunsaturates. One is composed of Omega-6 fatty acids, found in many vegetable oils such as safflower oil, sunflower seed oil, soybean oil and corn oil. The other type is composed of Omega-3 polyunsaturates, which are found in high amounts in some fish and fish oils. The American diet is typically very low in Omega-3 polyunsaturates. Polyunsaturates of all kinds account for about 6 to 7 percent of our total caloric intake, and most of those polyunsaturates are of the Omega-6 type. When polyunsaturated Omega-6 fatty acids are substituted for saturated fatty acids, total blood cholesterol and LDL-cholesterol levels fall. The evidence that Omega-3 fatty acids will do this is limited.

Monounsaturated Fatty Acids

Monounsaturates are found primarily in olive oil, rapeseed (canola) oil and in high-monounsaturated forms of sunflower seed oil and safflower oil. For many years, monounsaturates were thought to be neutral, neither raising nor lowering blood cholesterol. Recent research suggests that monounsaturates do in fact lower LDL-cholesterol as much as polyunsaturates when used in place of saturated fatty acids in the diet.

Carbohydrates

Dietary carbohydrates occur in three types: simple sugars known as monosaccharides and disaccharides; digestible complex carbohydrates, otherwise known as starches; and indigestible complex carbohydrates called fiber. Some types of fiber, particularly the soluble type, may lower blood cholesterol. Examples of these are pectins, psyllium and certain gums. One such gum is beta-glucon, present in oat products and beans. A high intake (15 to 25 grams per day) of soluble fiber has been reported to slightly lower blood cholesterol levels. High intakes can produce gastrointestinal side effects, but improved tolerance usually is achieved after prolonged usage. The major sources of digestible complex carbohydrates and fiber are plant foods such as vegetables, fruits, legumes and grains, along with their products—breads and pastas.

Appendix C.

THE AMERICAN HEART ASSOCIATION/NATIONAL HEART, LUNG, AND BLOOD INSTITUTE DIETS

These eating plans are designed to help you lower your blood cholesterol. The recommended dietary change is presented in two stages—the Step-One and Step-Two Diets. These eating patterns are low in saturated fatty acids and cholesterol.

Since weight reduction will be necessary for many individuals, sample eating plans are included for both reducing and maintaining weight. The weight-maintenance calorie eating plans are 2000 and 2500 calories for men and 1600 and 2000 calories for women. The 1600-calorie eating plan will achieve weight reduction for many men. The 1200-calorie eating plan is intended for weight reduction for women.

THE STEP-ONE DIET

The Step-One Diet will put you on the road to lowering your blood cholesterol.

FOOD GROUPS

In this eating plan, foods are categorized in seven groups according to fat, carbohydrate, protein and calories. The food groups are:

1. Meat, Poultry and Seafood
2. Eggs
3. Dairy Products
4. Fats and Oils
5. Breads, Cereal, Pasta and Starchy Vegetables
6. Vegetables and Fruits
7. Optional Foods—Desserts, Sweets and Alcohol

Within a food group, the foods contain similar amounts of nutrients. Initially, a food scale, measuring cups and measuring spoons may help determine portion sizes.

| | DAILY | PORTIONS | | |
| **SAMPLE EATING PLANS FOR STEP-ONE DIETS*** | | | | |
FOOD GROUP	2500 CALORIES	2000 CALORIES	1600 CALORIES	1200 CALORIES
Meat, Poultry and Seafood	6 ounces	6 ounces	6 ounces	6 ounces
Eggs, Whole	3/week	3/week	3/week	3/week
Dairy Products	4	3	3	2
Fats and Oils	8	6	4	3
Bread, Cereal, Pasta and Starchy Vegetables	10	7	4	3
Vegetables	4	4	4	4
Fruits	5	3	3	3
Optional Foods	2	2	2	0

* Your physician or dietitian should recommend the appropriate calorie plan for you.

Meat, Poultry and Seafood

This food group averages about 60 calories, 3 grams of fat, 1 of which is saturated, and 25 milligrams of cholesterol per ounce. These foods provide protein, phosphorus, vitamins B_6 and B_{12}, and other vitamins and minerals. Red meats are also good souces of iron and zinc.

Eat no more than 6 ounces of cooked meat, fish or poultry each day. An easy way to divide this is into two 3-ounce servings. Or, divide it into one 2-ounce serving and one 4-ounce serving. The following general guidelines for portion sizes are based on 3-ounce servings. The size of a 3-ounce portion of cooked meat (such as a roast) is comparable to a deck of cards or the palm of your hand.

APPROPRIATE FOOD	PORTION SIZE*
Beef (trimmed of visible fat)	
1 small hamburger patty	3 ounces
1 piece cooked meat about the size of a deck of cards	3 ounces
¾ cup diced meat	3 ounces
Veal (trimmed of visible fat)	
1 medium chop	3 ounces
Pork (trimmed of visible fat)	
1 medium chop	3 ounces
Lamb (trimmed of visible fat)	
2 small chops	3 ounces
Poultry (without skin)	
½ chicken breast	3 ounces
1 chicken leg and thigh	3 ounces
½ Cornish hen	3 ounces
Seafood	
¾ cup flaked fish	3 ounces
¼ pound fish fillet	3 ounces
Approximately 12 medium shrimp	3 ounces
Approximately 10 medium scallops	3 ounces
Approximately 10 medium oysters	3 ounces

* Meat loses about 25 percent of its weight during cooking (e.g., 4 ounces raw will be about 3 ounces cooked).

FAT AND CHOLESTEROL INFORMATION

- Many processed meats (luncheon meat, wieners and sausage) are high in saturated fatty acids.
- "Prime" grade, heavily marbled and fatty meats are high in saturated fatty acids.
- Liver, brains, heart, kidney and sweetbreads are high in cholesterol and should be limited.
- Shellfish contains less fat than does meat or poultry. Although shrimp and crayfish are relatively high in cholesterol, they can be eaten occasionally.

Eggs

Eggs are good sources of protein, phosphorus, vitamins A, D, B$_6$, B$_{12}$ and other vitamins and minerals. Egg yolks are high in cholesterol, while egg whites contain no cholesterol. Three egg yolks per week are allowed in the Step-One

Diet. One large egg has about 79 calories, 6 grams of fat, 2 of which are saturated, and 213 to 220 milligrams of cholesterol. Cholesterol-free egg substitutes can be used to further reduce dietary cholesterol.

HOW EGGS ADD UP

EGG-CONTAINING FOODS	APPROXIMATE PORTION OF WHOLE EGG
Beverages	
Eggnog (½ cup)	¼
Breads	
Cornbread (⅑ of 9 × 9-inch pan)	¼
Muffin (1)	⅒
Pancakes, 4-inch (2)	¼
Desserts	
Baked custard or crème brûlée (6-ounce custard cup)	½
Chocolate, lemon meringue or pumpkin pie (⅛ of 9-inch pie)	⅓
Pound cake (1/12 of loaf)	¼
Sponge cake (1/12 of 9 × 9-inch cake)	½
Tapioca pudding (½ cup)	⅓
Yellow or chocolate 2-layer cake (1/16 of 9-inch cake)	⅛
Main Dishes	
Cheese soufflé (1 cup)	½
Chicken salad (½ cup)	⅓
Corn pudding (½ cup)	½
Egg salad	1 to 2
Omelet (depends on size)	1 to 3
Salad Dressings	
Mayonnaise (¼ cup)	¼
Thousand Island (¼ cup)	⅓

Dairy Products

These dairy products average about 90 calories, 3 grams of fat, 2 of which are saturated, and 11 milligrams of cholesterol per portion. Milk and most milk products provide calcium (they are the major source of calcium in the American diet), riboflavin, protein and vitamins A, B_6 and B_{12}. Fortified (with vitamins A and D) lowfat or skim milk products have essentially the same nutrients (except fat) as whole-milk products. However, they have less fat and fewer calories.

APPROPRIATE FOOD	PORTION SIZE
Milk and Yogurt	
Skim or 1-percent milk	1 cup
Nonfat or lowfat plain yogurt	1 cup
Cheese	
Dry, grated cheese, e.g., Parmesan or Sap Sago (1 tablespoon)	¼ ounce
Lowfat cheese, 5 grams fat or less per ounce (¼ cup diced)	1 ounce
Lowfat or dry-curd cottage cheese	½ cup
Mozzarella, part-skim	1 ounce
Ricotta cheese from whole milk	1 ounce
Frozen Desserts	
Frozen lowfat yogurt	½ cup
Ice milk	½ cup
Sherbet (see "Optional Foods")	

FAT AND CHOLESTEROL INFORMATION

- Cream substitutes—nondairy coffee creamers, sour-cream substitutes and whipped toppings often contain coconut, palm or palm kernel oil and are therefore high in saturated fatty acids. Read labels carefully.

Fats and Oils

Some of these foods are high in vitamins A or E; all are high in fat and calories. One portion from the "Fats and Oils" food group averages about 5 grams of fat, 1 of which is saturated, 45 calories and negligible cholesterol.

APPROPRIATE FOOD	PORTION SIZE
Margarines	
Margarine with liquid oil listed as the first ingredient	1 teaspoon
Diet margarine	2 teaspoons
Nuts and Seeds	
Chopped nuts, except coconut	1 tablespoon
Seeds, any variety (without shells)	1 tablespoon
Salad Dressings	
French, Italian, Thousand Island or mayonnaise-type salad dressing	1 tablespoon
Mayonnaise	2 teaspoons
Shortening	
Soybean oil	1 teaspoon

APPROPRIATE FOOD	PORTION SIZE
Other Fats	
Olives	10 small or 5 large
Peanut butter	2 teaspoons
Avocado	⅛ medium
Vegetable Oils	
Safflower, corn, sunflower, soybean, olive, canola	1 teaspoon

FAT AND CHOLESTEROL INFORMATION

- Chocolate, coconut, coconut oil, palm kernel oil and palm oil contain more saturated than unsaturated fat. When selecting commercial food items containing these ingredients, choose only those that provide fatty acid information on the label. The foods you buy should contain more polyunsaturated than saturated fatty acids. Currently, information about monounsaturated fatty acids is not listed on the nutrition label.

Bread, Cereal, Pasta and Starchy Vegetables

The foods in this group contain an average of 80 calories, 1 gram of fat with negligible saturated fatty acids and cholesterol per portion. Lowfat soups are included in this group. Whole-grain or enriched foods provide B vitamins and iron. They also provide protein and, in vegetarian diets, are a major source of this nutrient. Whole-grain products also contribute magnesium, folacin and fiber.

APPROPRIATE FOOD	PORTION SIZE
Breads	
Bagel	½
Bread sticks, 4 inches long × ½-inch diameter	2
Bread, white, whole wheat, rye, oatmeal, pumpernickel	1 slice
Croutons, plain bread cubes	1 cup
English muffin	½
Hamburger or hot dog bun	½

(continued)

APPROPRIATE FOOD	PORTION SIZE
Breads (continued)	
Pita, 6-inch diameter	½
Roll, plain (1 ounce)	1
Tortilla, corn, 6-inch diameter	1
Quick Bread (1 serving = 1 Bread + 1 Fat)	
Banana bread (16 slices/loaf)*	1 slice
Biscuit (2 inches across)*	1
Cornbread (muffin)*	1
Pancake (4-inch diameter)*	1
Waffle (9-inch diameter)*	¼
Crackers	
Animal crackers	8
Graham crackers, 2½-inch square	3
Matzoth, 4 × 6-inch	¾ ounce
Melba toast	5 slices
Oyster crackers	24
Popcorn (popped, no fat added)	3 cups
Pretzels	¾ ounce
Saltine crackers	6
Cereal, Pasta and Rice	
Bran cereals	⅓ cup
Cooked cereal, bulgur, grits	½ cup
Flake-type cereal, ready-to-eat, unsweetened	1 cup
Pasta	½ cup
Rice	⅓ cup
Starchy Vegetables	
Baked beans	¼ cup
Corn	½ cup
Corn on cob, 6 inches long	1
Dry beans, peas, lentils	⅓ cup
Green peas	½ cup
Lima beans	½ cup
Potato, baked (3 ounces)	1
Potato, mashed	½ cup
Squash, acorn or butternut	¾ cup
Sweet potato or yam	⅓ cup

* Prepared with skim milk, unsaturated oil, egg substitute or egg white. If whole egg is used, count as part of egg allowance.

APPROPRIATE FOOD	PORTION SIZE
Commercial Soup, Prepared with Water**	
Bouillon, broth, consumme	As desired
Chicken noodle, gazpacho, minestrone,	
onion, tomato, vegetarian	1 cup
Beef noodle, chicken rice, chunky-style,	
turkey noodle, oyster stew, split pea	¾ cup

** Homemade soups made low in fat (made with skim milk, removing fat from meat, etc.) may be counted as the same portions as commercial soups of a similar type. If milk is used in the preparation, count as part of dairy allowance.

FAT AND CHOLESTEROL INFORMATION

- Canned or dehydrated varieties of soup should have no more than 2 grams of fat per cup.
- If skim or 1-percent milk is used in preparing soup, count ½ cup milk per 1 cup soup as part of dairy group.
- Cream soup is usually prepared with whole milk or cream in restaurants.

Vegetables and Fruits

An average portion of vegetables has about 25 calories. An average portion of fruit has about 60 calories. Nearly all vegetables and fruits are low in fat, and none contains cholesterol. Vegetables and fruits are important sources of vitamins A and C, and fiber. Dark green and deep yellow vegetables are good sources of vitamin A. Most dark green vegetables, if not overcooked, are important sources of vitamin C, as are citrus fruits (oranges, grapefruit, tangerines and lemons), melons, berries and tomatoes. Dark green vegetables are also valued for riboflavin, folacin, iron and magnesium. Certain greens—collards, kale, mustard, turnip and dandelion—provide calcium.

APPROPRIATE FOOD

Vegetables

1 portion = ½ cup raw or cooked
Many vegetables have negligible fat and few calories and can be used as desired. Some suggestions include: cabbage, celery, Chinese cabbage, cucumbers, green onion, peppers, mushrooms, radishes, zucchini and salad greens such as endive, escarole, lettuce, romaine and spinach.

Fruit and Juice

1 portion = ½ cup or 1 medium-size piece of fresh fruit

Optional Foods (Desserts, Sweets and Alcohol)
Any one of the homemade desserts (cakes, cookies and pies) made with acceptable ingredients listed below has about 285 calories and 6 to 10 grams of fat. The amounts listed count as *two portions* of optional foods.

Any one of the sweets on the list contains about 75 calories and 0 to 1 gram of fat. Each counts as *one portion* of optional foods.

Any one portion of the listed alcoholic beverages contains ½ ounce ethanol and 90 to 150 calories. Count each as *one portion* of optional foods.

APPROPRIATE FOOD	PORTION SIZE
Desserts*	
2-layer cake, frosted (1⁄12 of cake)	1 slice
Sheet cake, frosted (2¼ × 2½ ×	
1½-inch piece or 1⁄20 of 9 × 13-inch cake)	1 slice
Cupcake, frosted (average size)	1
Oatmeal raisin cookies	4
Double-crust fruit pie (1⁄8 of 9-inch pie)	1 slice
Sweets	
Angel food cake (1⁄24 of cake)	1 slice
Candy made primarily with sugar (e.g.,	
candy corn, gumdrops, mints and hard candy)	¾ ounce
Carbonated beverage (sweetened)	6 fluid ounces
Fruit-flavored gelatin (sweetened)	½ cup
Fruit ice	1⁄3 cup
Gingersnaps	2
Lemonade (sweetened)	6 fluid ounces
Newton-type cookie	1
Sherbet	1⁄3 cup
Sugar, syrup, honey, jam, preserves or	
marmalade	1½ tablespoons
Alcoholic Beverages	
Beer	12 fluid ounces
80-proof spirits (bourbon, gin, rum, Scotch, tequila, vodka and	
whiskey)	1½ fluid ounces
Wine, red or white	4 fluid ounces

* Prepared with egg whites, egg substitute, skim or 1-percent milk, and vegetable oil or margarine. Each "dessert" serving counts as two optional food portions.

Free Foods

These foods and drinks contain fewer than 20 calories and no fat per portion. Items that have no portion size specified need not be limited. The others should be eaten in moderation—the portion sizes will guide you.

APPROPRIATE FOOD	PORTION SIZE
Drinks	
Bouillon or broth without fat*	
Carbonated drinks, sugar-free **	
Carbonated water	
Club soda *	
Cocoa powder, unsweetened	1 tablespoon
Coffee or tea	
Drink mixes, sugar-free**	
Tonic water, sugar-free**	
Sweet Substitutes **	
Candy, hard, sugar-free	
Gelatin, sugar-free	
Gum, sugar-free	
Jam or jelly, sugar-free	2 teaspoons
Pancake syrup, sugar-free	
Sugar substitutes (saccharin or aspartame)	
Fruits	
Cranberries, unsweetened	½ cup
Rhubarb, unsweetened	½ cup
Condiments	
Horseradish	
Ketchup	1 tablespoon
Mustard	
Pickles, dill, unsweetened*	
Salad dressing, oil-free	
Taco sauce	
Vinegar	

* High in sodium. Look for seltzers or soda with no salt added.
** Sweet substitutes are listed for the benefit of those following diabetic diets.

SAMPLE MENU—STEP-ONE DIET

2500 CALORIES PER DAY

BREAKFAST	**FOOD GROUP PORTIONS**
Pineapple juice (1 cup)	2 Fruits
Oatmeal (1 cup) with	2 Breads
Banana (½) and	1 Fruit
Milk, 1-percent (1 cup)	1 Dairy
Whole wheat toast (2 slices) with	2 Breads
Margarine (2 teaspoons)	2 Fats
Coffee or tea	

LUNCH	
Hamburger sandwich:	
Lean ground beef, broiled (3 ounces)	3 Meats
Mozzarella cheese, part-skim (1 ounce)	1 Dairy
Hamburger bun (1)	2 Breads
Lettuce (1 leaf)	Free
Tomato (1 slice)	Free
Relishes:	
Carrot curls (½ carrot)	1 Vegetable
Broccoli florets (1 cup)	1 Vegetable
Fresh Bartlett pear (1)	1 Fruit
Milk, 1-percent (1 cup)	1 Dairy

DINNER	
Broiled salmon (3 ounces) with dill and	3 Meats
Margarine (2 teaspoons)	2 Fats
Rice (1 cup) with	3 Breads
Margarine (2 teaspoons)	2 Fats
Steamed snow peas with onion slices (1 cup)	2 Vegetables
Cantaloupe cubes (⅓ melon)	1 Fruit
Roll (1) with	1 Bread
Margarine (2 teaspoons)	2 Fats
Devil's food cake with frosting (1 slice)	2 Optional
Milk, 1-percent (1 cup)	1 Dairy

NUTRIENT ANALYSIS   2509 Calories (distributed as follows):

18% Protein	30% Fat	160 mg Cholesterol*
52% Carbohydrate	8% Saturated fatty acids	2073 mg Sodium

* Cholesterol is less than 300 mg because an egg is not included.

SAMPLE MENU—STEP·ONE DIET

2000 CALORIES PER DAY

BREAKFAST	FOOD GROUP PORTIONS
Orange juice (1 cup)	2 Fruits
Poached egg (1)	1 Egg
Whole wheat toast (2 slices) with	2 Breads
Margarine (2 teaspoons)	2 Fats
Milk, 1-percent (1 cup)	1 Dairy
Coffee or tea	

LUNCH

Roast beef sandwich:	
Lean roast beef (3 ounces)	3 Meats
Whole wheat bread (2 slices)	2 Breads
Mayonnaise (2 teaspoons)	1 Fat
Lettuce (1 leaf)	Free
Cottage cheese, lowfat (½ cup) with	1 Dairy
Zucchini sticks (4)	1 Vegetable
Grapes (15)	1 Fruit
Graham crackers (3 squares)	1 Bread
Milk, 1-percent (1 cup)	1 Dairy

DINNER

Baked chicken breast (3 ounces) with	3 Meats
Onions and mushrooms (½ cup)	1 Vegetable
Steamed green peas (½ cup)	1 Bread
Steamed carrot strips (½ cup)	1 Vegetable
Tossed salad:	
Lettuce (1 cup)	Free
Tomato wedges (1 tomato)	1 Vegetable
Cucumber slices (¼ cucumber)	Free
Italian salad dressing (2 tablespoons)	2 Fats
Roll (1) with	1 Bread
Margarine (1 teaspoon)	1 Fat
Orange sherbet (⅓ cup)	1 Optional
White wine (4 fluid ounces)	1 Optional

NUTRIENT ANALYSIS   2024 Calories (distributed as follows):

23% Protein	30% Fat	473 mg Cholesterol*
43% Carbohydrates	8% Saturated fatty acids	2853 mg Sodium
4% Alcohol		

* Cholesterol is greater than 300 mg because an egg is included as breakfast.

SAMPLE MENU—STEP-ONE DIET
1600 CALORIES PER DAY

BREAKFAST	**FOOD GROUP PORTIONS**
Grapefruit (½)	1 Fruit
Bagel (1) with	2 Breads
Margarine (1 teaspoon)	1 Fat
Milk, 1-percent (1 cup)	1 Dairy
Coffee or tea	

LUNCH	
Broiled chicken thigh (2 ounces)	2 Meats
Tossed salad:	
Lettuce (1 cup)	Free
Cauliflower (4) with radishes (2)	1 Vegetable
Mushroom slices (4 mushrooms)	Free
Oil and vinegar dressing	
Olive oil (1 teaspoon)	1 Fat
Vinegar (2 teaspoons)	Free
Saltine crackers (6)	1 Bread
Nectarine (1)	1 Fruit
Milk, 1-percent (1 cup)	1 Dairy

DINNER	
Braised pot roast (4 ounces) with	4 Meats
Tomatoes, canned (½ cup)	1 Vegetable
Green bell pepper strips (½ cup)	Free
Diced onion (2 tablespoons)	Free
Steamed broccoli spears (½ cup)	1 Vegetable
Carrot-raisin salad:	
Shredded carrot (½ cup)	1 Vegetable
Raisins (2 tablespoons)	1 Fruit
Mayonnaise (2 teaspoons)	1 Fat
Roll (1) with	1 Bread
Margarine (1 teaspoon)	1 Fat
Gingersnap cookies (4)	2 Optional
Milk, 1-percent (1 cup)	1 Dairy

NUTRIENT ANALYSIS   1615 Calories (distributed as follows):

24% Protein	30% Fat	207 mg Cholesterol*
46% Carbohydrate	9% Saturated fatty acids	1775 mg Sodium

* Cholesterol is less than 300 mg because an egg is not included.

SAMPLE MENU—STEP·ONE DIET
1200 CALORIES PER DAY

BREAKFAST	FOOD GROUP PORTIONS
Fresh strawberries (1 cup)	1 Fruit
Plain lowfat yogurt (1 cup)	1 Dairy
Whole wheat toast (1 slice) with	1 Bread
Margarine (1 teaspoon)	1 Fat
Coffee or tea	

LUNCH

Open-face sandwich:	
Lowfat cheese (1 ounce)	1 Dairy
Lean ham (2 ounces)	2 Meats
Tomato (1 slice)	Free
Whole wheat bread (1 slice)	1 Bread
Relishes	
Carrot sticks (4) with green bell pepper rings (2)	1 Vegetable
Apple (1)	1 Fruit

DINNER

Broiled sirloin steak (4 ounces)	4 Meats
Pasta (½ cup) with herbs and	1 Bread
Margarine (1 teaspoon)	1 Fat
Steamed green beans (½ cup)	1 Vegetable
Steamed beets (½ cup)	1 Vegetable
Tossed salad:	
Assorted greens (1 cup)	Free
French salad dressing (1 tablespoon)	1 Fat
Fresh Bartlett pear (1)	1 Fruit

NUTRIENT ANALYSIS   1224 Calories (distributed as follows):

25% Protein	30% Fat	163 mg Cholesterol*
45% Carbohydrate	9% Saturated fatty acids	1993 mg Sodium

* Cholesterol is less than 300 mg because an egg is not included.

THE STEP-TWO DIET

The Step-Two Diet is usually recommended for people whose blood cholesterol level did not decrease sufficiently on the Step-One Diet. These individuals need to make additional changes in their eating plans to reach the blood cholesterol goal recommended by their physicians. The Step-Two Diet will help them do that.

Food Groups

In this eating plan, as in the Step-One Diet, foods are categorized in seven groups according to fat, carbohydrate, protein and calories.

Changes in food choices are needed for four food groups. The general changes are as follows:

1. Meat, Poultry and Seafood—Choose the very leanest.
2. Eggs—Limit egg yolks to one per week.
3. Dairy Products—Select nonfat products, skim milk and cheese with 2 grams of fat or less per ounce.
4. Fats and Oils—Use margarine or oils, but no shortening.

No changes are needed for the other three food groups. Accordingly, the information for these categories is the same as for the Step-One Diet and will be found on the preceding pages.

SAMPLE EATING PLANS FOR STEP-TWO DIETS*

	DAILY PORTIONS			
FOOD GROUP	2500 CALORIES	2000 CALORIES	1600 CALORIES	1200 CALORIES
Meat, Poultry and Seafood	6 ounces	6 ounces	6 ounces	6 ounces
Eggs, Whole	1/week	1/week	1/week	1/week
Dairy Products	3	2	2	2
Fats and Oils	8	7	5	3
Bread, Cereal, Pasta and Starchy Vegetables	10	8	5	4
Vegetables	5	4	4	4
Fruits	7	4	3	3
Optional Foods	2	2	2	0

* Your physician or dietitian should recommend the appropriate calorie plan for you.

Meat, Poultry and Seafood

This group averages 55 calories, 2 grams of fat, of which 0.8 grams are saturated, and 25 milligrams of cholesterol per ounce. To reduce the amount of saturated fatty acids and cholesterol in the meat group, only the leanest cuts are allowed. Shrimp and organ meats should be limited because of their cholesterol content.

Eat no more than 6 ounces of cooked meat, fish or poultry each day. An easy way to divide this is into two 3-ounce servings. Or, divide it into one 2-ounce serving and one 4-ounce serving. The following general guidelines for portion sizes are based on 3-ounce servings. The size of a 3-ounce portion of cooked meat (such as a roast) is comparable to a deck of cards or the palm of your hand.

APPROPRIATE FOOD	PORTION SIZE*
Beef (trimmed of visible fat)	
1 small hamburger patty**	3 ounces
1 piece cooked meat about the size of a deck of cards	3 ounces
¾ cup diced meat	3 ounces
Veal (trimmed of visible fat)	
1 medium chop	3 ounces
Pork (trimmed of visible fat)	
1 medium chop	3 ounces
Lamb (trimmed of visible fat)	
2 small chops	3 ounces
Poultry (without skin)	
½ chicken breast	3 ounces
1 chicken leg and thigh	3 ounces
½ Cornish hen	3 ounces
Seafood	
¾ cup flaked fish	3 ounces
¼ pound fish fillet	3 ounces
Approximately 10 medium scallops	3 ounces
Approximately 10 medium oysters	3 ounces

* Meat loses about 25 percent of its weight during cooking (e.g., 4 ounces raw will be about 3 ounces cooked).
** Note: To assure the leanest ground meat, select a lean cut, such as a round steak, and have it ground.

FAT AND CHOLESTEROL INFORMATION

- Regular "ground" meat (even extra lean) has more fat than is allowed in the Step-Two Diet. Select a lean meat cut, such as round steak, and have it trimmed and ground.
- Avoid liver and other organ meats since they are high in cholesterol.

- Shrimp and crayfish have about twice as much cholesterol as beef and chicken and should be limited in the Step-Two Diet.
- Combine large portions of pasta, rice, legumes and vegetables with small amounts of lean meat, poultry or seafood to get a complete protein source with less fat and fewer calories.

Eggs

To achieve the necessary reduction in cholesterol and saturated fatty acids, *limit egg yolks to one per week.* One large, whole egg contains 6 grams of fat, 2 grams of which are saturated, and 213 to 220 milligrams of cholesterol. Cholesterol-free egg substitutes can be used to further reduce dietary cholesterol.

Dairy Products

This group of dairy products differs from the group in the Step-One Diet because the types of dairy products are limited here. An average portion of this group has 80 calories, 2 grams of fat, of which 1 gram is saturated, and 9 milligrams of cholesterol. To achieve the necessary reduction in saturated fatty acids in this food group, choose only skim milk, nonfat dairy products and cheese with 2 grams of fat or less per ounce.

APPROPRIATE FOOD	PORTION SIZE
Milk and Yogurt	
Skim milk*	1 cup
Nonfat or lowfat plain yogurt	1 cup
Cheese	
Lowfat or dry-curd cottage cheese	½ cup
Lowfat cheese, 2 grams fat or less per ounce	1 ounce
Frozen Desserts	
Frozen lowfat yogurt	½ cup
Sherbet (see Optional Foods)	

* 1-percent milk has 2.2 grams fat per cup more than skim milk. If skim milk is unacceptable to you, adjust the eating plan to allow 1-percent milk. One way to do this is by eliminating 1 serving of fats and oils from your eating plan.

FAT AND CHOLESTEROL INFORMATION

- Cream substitutes—nondairy coffee creamers, sour-cream substitutes and whipped toppings often contain coconut, palm or palm kernel oil and are therefore high in saturated fatty acids. Read labels carefully.

Fats and Oils

An average portion from this group contains 45 calories, 5 grams of fat, with less than 1 gram of saturated fatty acids. To reduce saturated fatty acids, margarine (stick or tub) is substituted for shortening.

APPROPRIATE FOOD	PORTION SIZE
Margarines	
Margarine with liquid oil listed as the first ingredient	1 teaspoon
Diet margarine	2 teaspoons
Nuts and Seeds	
Chopped nuts, except coconut	1 tablespoon
Seeds, any variety (without shells)	1 tablespoon
Salad Dressings	
French, Italian, Thousand Island or mayonnaise-type salad dressing	1 tablespoon
Mayonnaise	2 teaspoons
Other Fats	
Olives	10 small or 5 large
Peanut butter	2 teaspoons
Avocado	⅛ medium
Vegetable Oils	
Safflower, corn, sunflower, soybean, olive, canola	1 teaspoon

FAT AND CHOLESTEROL INFORMATION

- Chocolate, coconut, coconut oil, palm kernel oil and palm oil contain more saturated than unsaturated fatty acids. Look for the listing of these fats when you read package labels. Select only those that contain less saturated fatty acids than polyunsaturated fatty acids. Currently, information about monounsaturated fatty acids is not listed on the nutrition label.

SAMPLE MENU—STEP·TWO DIET
2500 CALORIES PER DAY

BREAKFAST	FOOD GROUP PORTIONS
Apple juice (1 cup)	2 Fruits
Corn flakes (1 cup) with	1 Bread
Sliced banana (1) and	2 Fruits
Milk, skim (1 cup)	1 Dairy
Whole wheat toast (2 slices) with	2 Breads
Margarine (2 teaspoons)	2 Fats
Coffee or tea	

LUNCH

Turkey sandwich:

Roast turkey breast (2 ounces)	2 Meats
Whole wheat bread (2 slices)	2 Breads
Mayonnaise (2 teaspoons)	1 Fat
Lettuce (1 leaf)	Free

Marinated raw vegetables:

Tomato wedges (1 tomato)	1 Vegetable
Green bell pepper rings (½ pepper)	Free
French salad dressing (2 tablespoons)	2 Fats
Nectarine (1)	1 Fruit
Graham crackers (6 squares)	2 Breads
Milk, skim (1 cup)	1 Dairy

DINNER

Roast beef (4 ounces)	4 Meats
Pasta (1 cup) with herbs and	2 Breads
Margarine (1 teaspoon)	1 Fat
Steamed green beans (1 cup)	2 Vegetables
Steamed yellow squash (½ cup)	1 Vegetable
Onion slices (½ cup)	1 Vegetable
Margarine (1 teaspoon) on vegetables	1 Fat
Orange slices (1 orange) with	1 Fruit
Raisins (2 tablespoons)	1 Fruit
Whole wheat bread (1 slice) with	1 Bread
Margarine (1 teaspoon)	1 Fat
Apple pie (1 slice)	2 Optional
Milk, skim (1 cup)	1 Dairy

NUTRIENT ANALYSIS   2526 Calories (distributed as follows):

17% Protein	26% Fat	173 mg Cholesterol*
57% Carbohydrate	6% Saturated fatty acids	2948 mg Sodium

* Cholesterol is less than 200 mg because an egg is not included.

SAMPLE MENU—STEP-TWO DIET

2000 CALORIES PER DAY

BREAKFAST	FOOD GROUP PORTIONS
Orange juice (1 cup)	2 Fruits
Cheese Omelet:	
Egg substitute (½ cup) with	Free
Lowfat cheese (1 ounce)	1 Dairy
Margarine (1 teaspoon)	1 Fat
Corn grits (½ cup)	1 Bread
Bagel (1) with	2 Breads
Margarine (1 teaspoon)	1 Fat
Coffee or tea	

LUNCH	
Barbecued beef sandwich:	
Lean beef (3 ounces)	3 Meats
Barbecue sauce (1 tablespoon)	Free
Hamburger bun (1)	2 Breads
Tossed salad:	
Lettuce (1 cup)	Free
Tomato wedges (1 tomato)	1 Vegetable
Shredded carrot (½ cup)	1 Vegetable
Green bell pepper strips (½ pepper)	Free
Italian salad dressing (2 tablespoons)	2 Fats
Grapes (15)	1 Fruit
Milk, skim (1 cup)	1 Dairy

DINNER	
Broiled filet of sole (3 ounces) with lemon and	3 Meats
Margarine (1 teaspoon)	1 Fat
Rice (⅔ cup) with	2 Breads
Margarine (1 teaspoon)	1 Fat
Steamed broccoli (½ cup) and	1 Vegetable
Cauliflower (½ cup)	1 Vegetable
Fresh strawberries (1 cup)	1 Fruit
Roll (1) with	1 Bread
Margarine (1 teaspoon)	1 Fat
White cake with frosting (1 slice)	2 Optional

NUTRIENT ANALYSIS 1996 Calories (distributed as follows):

21% Protein	27% Fat	153 mg Cholesterol*
52% Carbohydrate	6% Saturated fatty acids	2510 mg Sodium

* Cholesterol is less than 200 mg because an egg is not included.

SAMPLE MENU—STEP·TWO DIET
1600 CALORIES PER DAY

BREAKFAST	FOOD GROUP PORTIONS
Grapefruit juice (½ cup)	1 Fruit
Oatmeal (½ cup) with	1 Bread
Milk, skim (1 cup)	1 Dairy
Whole wheat toast (1 slice) with	1 Bread
Margarine (1 teaspoon)	1 Fat
Coffee or tea	

LUNCH

Tuna salad on lettuce:

Tuna, canned in water (½ cup)	2 Meats
Diced celery (¼ cup)	Free
Mayonnaise (4 teaspoons)	2 Fats
Lettuce (1 leaf)	Free

Relishes:

Broccoli florets (1 cup)	1 Vegetable
Tomato wedges (1 tomato)	1 Vegetable
Saltine crackers (6)	1 Bread
Apple (1)	1 Fruit

DINNER

Broiled sirloin steak (4 ounces)	4 Meats
New potatoes (½ cup) with parsley and	1 Bread
Margarine (1 teaspoon)	1 Fat
Steamed green beans (½ cup)	1 Vegetable
Steamed carrot strips (½ cup)	1 Vegetable
Watermelon chunks (1¼ cups)	1 Fruit
French bread (1 slice) with	1 Bread
Margarine (1 teaspoon)	1 Fat
Gingersnap cookies (4)	2 Optional
Milk, skim (1 cup)	1 Dairy

NUTRIENT ANALYSIS   1603 Calories (distributed as follows):

22% Protein	29% Fat	135 mg Cholesterol*
49% Carbohydrate	7% Saturated fatty acids	1684 mg Sodium

* Cholesterol is less than 200 mg because an egg is not included.

SAMPLE MENU—STEP-TWO DIET
1200 CALORIES PER DAY

BREAKFAST	FOOD GROUP PORTIONS
Fresh blueberries (1 cup)	1 Fruit
Plain nonfat yogurt (1 cup)	1 Dairy
English muffin (1) with	2 Breads
Margarine (1 teaspoon)	1 Fat
Coffee or tea	

LUNCH

Chef's salad:

Lettuce (2 cups)	Free
Tomato wedges (1 tomato)	1 Vegetable
Shredded carrot (½ cup)	1 Vegetable
Turkey (1 ounce)	1 Meat
Lean ham (2 ounces)	2 Meats
Lowfat cheese (1 ounce)	1 Dairy
French salad dressing (1 tablespoon)	1 Fat
Saltine crackers (6)	1 Bread
Fresh plums (2)	1 Fruit

DINNER

Roast chicken breast (3 ounces)	3 Meats
Steamed asparagus spears (½ cup)	1 Vegetable
Steamed yellow squash (½ cup)	1 Vegetable
Roll (1) with	1 Bread
Margarine (1 teaspoon)	1 Fat
Fresh peach (1)	1 Fruit

NUTRIENT ANALYSIS   1191 Calories (distributed as follows):

28% Protein	22% Fat	150 mg Cholesterol*
50% Carbohydrate	6% Saturated fatty acids	2636 mg Sodium

* Cholesterol is less than 200 mg because an egg is not included.

Appendix D.

A SIMPLE WAY TO CONTROL TOTAL FAT

When you modify your diet, instead of using the Step-One and Step-Two Diet exchange method described in Appendix C, you may want more precise information about individual foods. The "Grams of Fat Method" offered here provides this added precision. After using it for a while, you will become familiar with the foods that are highest in fat, saturated fatty acids and cholesterol. It will become easier for you to balance your intake of higher fat foods with those lower in fat. This is an important skill that will be helpful to you when eating away from home.

The method involves counting the grams of fat and saturated fatty acids consumed each day. Food selections should be made so that the grams of fat and saturated fatty acids are within your set goal. The table below shows fat and saturated fatty acids limits based on calorie levels for the Step-One and Step-Two Diets. The desired calorie level is based on whether you need to lose, gain or maintain weight, and your level of physical activity. As a guideline, typical calorie levels for men are 2000 to 2500 calories for weight maintenance, 1600 to 2000 for weight loss. For women, typical calorie levels are 1600 to 2000 for weight maintenance, 1200 to 1600 for weight loss.

The Food Table on the following pages shows the amount of fat and saturated fatty acids in foods. You can easily see which foods are low in fat and may be eaten often and which ones are high in fat and need to be avoided or eaten

FAT LIMITS BASED ON CALORIE LEVELS

CALORIE LEVEL	TOTAL FAT (GRAMS)	STEP-ONE: SATURATED FATTY ACIDS (GRAMS)	STEP-TWO: SATURATED FATTY ACIDS (GRAMS)
1200	40	13	9
1500	50	17	12
1800	60	20	14
2000	67	22	16
2200	73	24	17
2500	83	28	19
3000	100	33	23

infrequently. When you eat a high-fat food, you can compensate by selecting other very low-fat foods that day.

A food scale, measuring cups and measuring spoons will help you accurately determine portion sizes.

Numerous commercial products are available, many of which have nutrition information on the label. That information can be used along with the information offered here to help you reach your fat intake goals. (Where discrepancies between the two occur, accept the information listed on the label.) For example, the label below shows 5 grams of fat in each 4-ounce portion of spaghetti sauce.

SPAGHETTI SAUCE LABEL	
Nutrition information per serving	
Serving size	4 ounces (113 grams)
Servings per container	7⅞
Calories	130
Protein (grams)	2
Total carbohydrates (grams)	18
Fat (grams)	5

FOOD TABLE

Foods listed in the table are grouped under major headings that are similar to the ones on page 274. Foods listed under the subheading make it easy to compare values for similar foods.

ABOUT THE FOOD TABLE

A dash (—) means that a value could not be found although there is reason to believe that a measurable amount of the nutrient may be present.

ABBREVIATIONS USED IN THE TABLE			
cal.	calories	poly. fatty acid	polyunsaturated fatty acid
chol.	cholesterol	sat. fatty acid	saturated fatty acid
gm	gram	tbsp.	tablespoon
mg	milligram	tr	trace
Na	sodium	pkg.	package
oz.	ounce		

Note: Values have been rounded off; 0.5 or greater is rounded up; 0.4 or less is rounded down.

Food Description/Portion	Weight (gm)	Fat (gm)	Sat. Fatty Acid (gm)	Energy (cal.)	Chol. (mg)	Na (mg)
MEAT, POULTRY AND SEAFOOD						
Beef						
Lean only, average all grades, cooked (1 oz.)	28	2.9	1.1	63	25	18
Lean only, "Select" grade, cooked (1 oz.)	28	2.6	1.0	60	25	18
Lean only, "Choice" grade, cooked (1 oz.)	28	3.0	1.2	64	25	18
Lean only, "Prime" grade, cooked (1 oz.)	28	3.8	1.5	71	25	18
Flank steak, lean only, broiled (1 oz.)	28	4.2	1.8	69	20	19
Round steak, lean only, broiled (1 oz.)	28	2.3	0.8	55	23	18
Top loin steak, lean only, broiled (1 oz.)	28	2.7	1.1	59	22	19
Rib eye steak, lean only, broiled (1 oz.)	28	3.3	1.4	64	23	19
Chuck roast or steak, lean only, braised (1 oz.)	28	2.9	1.1	66	28	19
Tenderloin, lean only, broiled (1 oz.)	28	2.7	1.1	59	24	18
Arm roast or steak, lean only, braised (1 oz.)	28	2.9	1.1	66	28	19
Brain, simmered (1 oz.)	28	3.6	0.8	45	582	34
Ground beef, extra lean, broiled (1 oz.)	28	4.5	1.8	75	28	23
lean, broiled (1 oz.)	28	5.0	2.0	79	29	25
regular, broiled (1 oz.)	28	5.5	2.2	83	29	26
Heart, simmered (1 oz.)	28	1.6	0.5	49	55	18
Kidney, simmered (1 oz.)	28	1.0	0.3	41	110	38
Liver, braised (1 oz.)	28	1.4	0.5	46	110	30
Shortribs, lean only, braised (1 oz.)	28	5.1	2.2	84	26	17
Tongue, simmered (1 oz.)	28	5.9	2.5	80	30	17
Tripe (1 oz.)	28	1.1	0.6	28	27	13
Lamb						
Fore shank, braised (1 oz.)	28	1.7	0.4	53	29	21
Leg, shank portion, roasted (1 oz.)	28	1.9	0.5	51	25	19
Loin chops, broiled (1 oz.)	28	2.7	1.0	61	27	24
Rack, rib, roasted (1 oz.)	28	3.8	1.2	66	25	23
Pork						
Bacon, pan-fried, 4½ slices (1 oz.)	28	14.0	5.0	163	24	452
Canadian bacon, grilled (1 oz.)	28	2.4	0.8	52	16	438
Chitterlings, simmered (1 oz.)	28	8.2	2.9	86	41	11
Fresh pork, lean only						
center loin, fresh, broiled (1 oz.)	28	3.0	1.0	65	28	22
shoulder, arm picnic, roasted (1 oz.)	28	3.6	1.2	65	27	23
shoulder, Boston blade, roasted (1 oz.)	28	4.8	1.6	73	28	21
sirloin, fresh, broiled (1 oz.)	28	3.9	1.3	69	28	17
tenderloin, roasted (1 oz.)	28	1.4	0.5	47	26	19
whole leg, roasted (1 oz.)	28	3.1	1.1	62	27	18
Ham, boneless						
extra lean, roasted (1 oz.)	28	1.6	0.5	41	15	341
canned, extra lean, roasted (1 oz.)	28	1.4	0.5	39	8	322
canned, regular, roasted (1 oz.)	28	4.3	1.4	64	17	267
Liver, braised (1 oz.)	28	1.3	0.4	47	101	14
Spareribs, lean and fat, braised (1 oz.)	28	8.6	3.3	113	34	26

Food Description/Portion	Weight (gm)	Fat (gm)	Sat. Fatty Acid (gm)	Energy (cal.)	Chol. (mg)	Na (mg)
Veal						
Arm steak, braised (1 oz.)	28	1.4	0.3	55	45	27
Blade steak, braised (1 oz.)	28	1.6	0.4	56	46	30
Loin chop, braised (1 oz.)	28	2.4	0.7	64	46	25
Rib roast, cooked (1 oz.)	28	1.8	0.6	48	36	29
Luncheon Meat and Sausage						
Bologna, beef and pork (1 oz.)	28	8.0	3.0	89	16	289
Braunschweiger pork (1 oz.)	28	9.1	3.1	102	44	324
Chicken spread, canned (2 tablespoons)	26	3.3	—	55	—	—
Frankfurter						
beef and pork (1 oz.)	28	8.3	3.1	91	14	318
chicken (1 oz.)	28	5.5	1.6	73	28	388
Pepperoni, pork, beef (1 oz.)	28	12.5	4.6	141	—	578
Salad spread, ham, cured (2 tablespoons)	30	4.7	1.5	64	12	274
Salami, dry, pork, beef (1 oz.)	28	9.8	3.5	119	22	527
Sausage						
Italian, pork, cooked (1 oz.)	28	7.3	2.6	92	22	261
knockwurst, pork, beef (1 oz.)	28	7.9	2.9	87	16	286
pork, fresh, cooked (1 oz.)	28	8.8	3.1	105	24	366
liverwurst, pork (1 oz.)	28	8.1	3.0	93	45	244
Polish, pork (1 oz.)	28	8.1	2.9	92	20	248
Vienna, beef and pork, canned (1½ links)	28	7.1	2.6	79	15	270
Mixed Dishes with Meat, Poultry and Seafood						
Chicken à la king (1 cup)	245	34.3	12.9	468	220	760
Chicken and noodle casserole (1 cup)	240	18.5	5.9	367	—	600
Chili con carne, with beans, canned (1 cup)	255	15.6	7.5	339	—	1354
Chop suey, beef and pork, without noodles (1 cup)	250	17.0	8.5	300	—	1053
Chow mein, chicken, without noodles (1 cup)	250	10.0	2.4	255	—	718
Macaroni and cheese, homemade (1 cup)	200	22.2	11.9	430	—	1086
canned (1 cup)	240	9.6	4.2	228	—	730
Pâté, chicken liver (2 tablespoons)	26	3.4	—	52	—	—
Pizza, cheese (1 slice)	120	8.6	4.2	290	56	698
pepperoni (1 slice)	120	11.5	—	306	—	817
Pot pie, chicken (⅓ of 9-inch diameter)	232	31.3	10.3	545	56	594
beef (⅓ of 9-inch diameter)	210	30.5	7.9	517	42	596
Spaghetti with meatballs and tomato sauce, canned						
(1 cup)	250	10.8	2.2	258	—	1220
Stew, beef and vegetable (1 cup)	245	10.5	4.4	218	72	292
Chicken						
Light meat, without skin, stewed (1 oz.)	28	1.1	0.3	45	22	18
with skin, stewed (1 oz.)	28	2.8	0.8	57	21	18
Dark meat, without skin, stewed (1 oz.)	28	2.5	0.7	54	25	21
with skin, stewed (1 oz.)	28	4.2	1.6	66	23	20
Breast, meat only, stewed (3 oz.)	95	2.9	0.8	144	73	59
meat and skin, stewed (4 oz.)	110	8.2	2.3	202	83	68
fried with batter, meat and skin (5 oz.)	140	18.5	4.9	364	119	385

Food Description/Portion	Weight (gm)	Fat (gm)	Sat. Fatty Acid (gm)	Energy (cal.)	Chol. (mg)	Na (mg)
Chicken (cont'd)						
Drumstick, meat only, stewed (1½ oz.)	46	2.6	0.7	78	40	37
meat and skin, stewed (2 oz.)	57	6.1	1.7	116	48	43
fried with batter, meat and skin (2½ oz.)	72	11.3	3.0	193	62	194
Thigh, meat only, stewed (2 oz.)	55	5.4	1.5	107	49	41
meat and skin, stewed (2½ oz.)	68	10.0	2.8	158	57	49
fried with batter, meat and skin (3 oz.)	86	14.2	3.8	238	80	248
Wing, meat only, stewed (1 oz.)	24	1.7	0.5	43	18	18
meat and skin, stewed (1½ oz.)	40	6.7	1.9	100	28	27
fried with batter, meat and skin (1¾ oz.)	49	10.7	2.9	159	39	157
Boneless, canned in broth (1 oz.)	28	2.2	0.6	47	62	143
Frankfurter, chicken (1 oz.)	28	5.5	1.6	73	28	388
Giblets—gizzard, heart, liver (1 each)						
(2½ oz.)	68	3.6	1.1	112	243	40
(1 oz.)	28	1.5	0.5	47	101	17
Liver pâté, canned (2 tablespoons)	28	3.7	—	57	—	—
Roll, chicken, light (1 oz.)	28	2.1	0.6	45	14	166
Spread, chicken, canned (1 oz.)	28	3.3	—	55	—	—
Turkey						
Light meat						
meat only, roasted (1 oz.)	28	0.3	0.1	40	24	16
meat with skin, roasted (1 oz.)	28	2.4	0.7	46	22	18
Dark meat						
meat only, roasted (1 oz.)	28	1.2	0.4	46	32	22
meat with skin, roasted (1 oz.)	28	3.3	1.0	63	25	22
Turkey						
Ham, cured thigh meat (1 oz.)	28	1.4	0.5	37	—	283
Pastrami (1 oz.)	28	1.8	0.5	40	—	297
Roll, light and dark meat (1 oz.)	28	2.0	0.6	42	16	166
Frozen with gravy, 1 pkg.						
(5 oz.)	142	3.7	1.2	95	—	786
(1 oz.)	28	0.8	0.2	19	—	157
Giblets—gizzard, heart, liver (1 each)						
(5½ oz.)	158	8.0	2.4	264	660	92
(1 oz.)	28	1.4	0.4	47	119	17
Game						
Goose, domesticated						
meat only, roasted (1 oz.)	28	3.6	1.3	67	26	20
meat with skin, roasted (1 oz.)	28	6.2	2.0	86	26	20
Finfish						
Catfish, breaded and fried (1 oz.)	28	3.8	0.9	65	23	79
Cod, Atlantic, cooked, dry heat (1 oz.)	28	0.2	0.1	30	16	22
Eel, cooked, dry heat (1 oz.)	28	4.2	0.9	67	46	18
Fish sticks and portions, frozen and reheated (1 oz.)	28	3.4	0.9	76	31	163
Flounder, cooked, dry heat (1 oz.)	28	0.4	0.1	33	19	30
Grouper, cooked, dry heat (1 oz.)	28	0.4	0.1	33	13	15

Food Description/Portion	Weight (gm)	Fat (gm)	Sat. Fatty Acid (gm)	Energy (cal.)	Chol. (mg)	Na (mg)
Finfish (cont'd)						
Haddock, cooked, dry heat (1 oz.)	28	0.3	0.1	32	21	25
Halibut, cooked, dry heat (1 oz.)	28	0.8	0.1	40	12	20
Herring, pickled (1 oz.)	28	5.1	0.7	74	4	247
Mackerel, canned, drained solids (1 oz.)	28	1.8	0.5	44	22	107
Mackerel, cooked, dry heat (1 oz.)	28	5.0	1.2	74	21	24
Ocean Perch, cooked, dry heat (1 oz.)	28	0.6	0.1	34	15	27
Perch, cooked, dry heat (1 oz.)	28	0.3	0.1	33	33	22
Pike, Northern, cooked, dry heat (1 oz.)	28	0.3	tr	32	14	14
Pollack, Walleye, cooked, dry heat (1 oz.)	28	0.3	0.1	32	27	33
Pompano, cooked, dry heat (1 oz.)	28	3.4	1.3	60	18	22
Redfish (see Ocean Perch)						
Rockfish, cooked, dry heat (1 oz.)	28	0.6	0.1	34	13	22
Salmon, Chinook, smoked (1 oz.)	28	1.2	0.3	33	7	220 *
Salmon, Chum, canned, drained solids with bone (1 oz.)	28	1.6	0.4	40	11	138 **
Salmon, Coho, cooked, moist heat (1 oz.)	28	2.1	0.4	52	14	17
Salmon, Sockeye, canned, drained solids with bone (1 oz.)	28	2.1	0.5	43	12	153 **
Sardine, Atlantic, canned in oil, drained solids with bone (1 oz.)	28	3.2	tr	59	40	143
Sardine, Pacific, canned in tomato sauce, drained solids with bone (1 oz.)	28	3.4	0.9	50	17	117
Sea Bass, cooked, dry heat (1 oz.)	28	0.7	0.2	35	15	25
Scrod (see Cod, Atlantic)						
Snapper, cooked, dry heat (1 oz.)	28	0.5	0.1	36	13	16
Sole (see Flounder)						
Swordfish, cooked, dry heat (1 oz.)	28	1.5	0.4	44	14	33
Trout, rainbow, cooked, dry heat (1 oz.)	28	1.2	0.2	43	21	10
Tuna, light, canned in oil, drained solids (1 oz.)	28	2.3	0.4	56	5	100
Tuna, light, canned in water, drained solids (1 oz.)	28	0.1	0.1	37	—	101
Tuna, white, canned in oil, drained solids (1 oz.)	28	2.3	—	53	9	112
Tuna, white, canned in water, drained solids (1 oz.)	28	0.7	0.2	39	12	111
Tuna salad, prepared with light tuna in oil, pickle relish, salad dressing, onion, celery (½ cup)	103	9.5	1.6	192	14	412
Shellfish						
Clam, cooked, moist heat (1 oz.)	28	0.6	0.1	42	19	32
Crab, Alaskan king, cooked, moist heat (1 oz.)	28	0.4	tr	27	15	304
Crab, Alaskan king, imitation, made from surimi (1 oz.)	28	0.4	—	29	6	238
Crab, blue, cooked, moist heat (1 oz.)	28	0.5	0.1	29	28	79
Crab cakes, prepared with egg, fried in margarine (1 cake)	60	4.5	0.9	93	90	198
Crayfish, cooked, moist heat (1 oz.)	28	0.4	0.1	32	50	19
Lobster, northern, cooked, moist heat (1 oz.)	28	0.2	tr	28	20	108

* Regular lox has approximately 567 mg sodium per ounce.
** Value based on product with salt added.

Food Description/Portion	Weight (gm)	Fat (gm)	Sat. Fatty Acid (gm)	Energy (cal.)	Chol. (mg)	Na (mg)
Shellfish (cont'd)						
Oyster, eastern, cooked, breaded and fried (1 oz.)	28	3.6	0.9	56	23	118
Shrimp, cooked (1 oz.)	28	0.3	0.1	28	55	63
Shrimp, breaded and fried (4 large)	30	3.7	0.6	73	53	103
Shrimp, imitation, made from surimi (1 oz.)	28	0.4	—	29	10	200
Scallop, breaded and fried (2 large)	31	3.4	0.8	67	19	144
Fast Food						
Bacon cheeseburger (1)	150	27.3	—	464	68	660
Burrito (1)	174	13.6	—	392	56	1030
Cheeseburger: regular (1)	112	15.1	—	299	45	672
4-oz. patty (1)	194	31.4	—	524	105	1224
Eggs, scrambled (2)	95	14.7	—	175	346	226
Enchilada (1)	230	20.9	—	396	—	1332
English muffin sandwich with egg, cheese, bacon (1)	138	18.1	—	359	214	832
Fish sandwich, regular with cheese (1)	140	22.7	—	421	56	668
large (1)	170	26.7	—	469	90	621
French-fried potatoes (3 oz.)	85	14.2	—	274	14	152
Ham and cheese sandwich (1)	155	16.0	—	372	70	1118
Hamburger: regular (1)	98	11.1	4.0	245	32	463
double meat and double-decker roll (1)	190	29.6	10.0	524	78	893
4-oz. patty, regular roll (1)	174	21.1	7.0	444	71	762
4-oz. patty, large roll (1)	264	37.2	13.0	668	114	1019
Hot dog (1)	82	13.7	5.0	214	37	636
Hot fudge sundae (1)	165	10.9	—	312	18	177
Hushpuppy (3 pieces)	45	5.5	—	153	—	—
Onion rings (3 oz.)	85	15.6	—	285	16	485
Pancake, butter, syrup (3)	200	10.4	—	468	46	1020
Roast beef on bun (5 oz.)	150	13.4	4.0	347	56	756
Taco (1)	81	15.0	4.0	187	21	456
Tuna sub (1)	255	27.8	—	566	—	1288
Turnover, apple (1)	85	14.1	—	255	4	326
EGGS						
Whole, raw (1)	50	5.6	1.7	79	274	69
Yolk, raw (1)	17	5.6	1.7	63	272	8
White, raw (1)	33	tr	0.0	16	0	50
Fried in butter (1)	46	6.4	2.4	83	246	144
scrambled with butter and milk (1)	64	7.1	2.8	95	248	155
Egg substitute,* liquid (¼ cup)	60	2.0	0.4	50	1	106
frozen (¼ cup)	60	6.7	1.2	96	1	120
Omelet with butter and milk (1 egg)	64	7.1	2.8	95	248	155
DAIRY PRODUCTS						
Milk						
Buttermilk, cultured (1 cup)	245	2.2	1.3	99	9	257
Condensed, sweetened, canned (1 cup)	306	26.6	16.8	982	104	389
Evaporated, skim, canned (½ cup)	128	0.3	0.2	99	5	147
Evaporated, whole, canned (½ cup)	126	9.5	5.8	169	37	133

* Check label—several brands are fat-free.

Food Description/Portion	Weight (gm)	Fat (gm)	Sat. Fatty Acid (gm)	Energy (cal.)	Chol. (mg)	Na (mg)
Milk (cont'd)						
Hot cocoa, with whole milk (1 cup)	250	9.1	5.6	218	33	123
Malted milk beverage						
(1 cup whole milk + 2 to 3 heaping teaspoons						
malted milk powder)	265	9.9	6.0	236	37	215
Milk						
skim or nonfat (1 cup)	245	0.4	0.3	86	4	126
1-percent fat (1 cup)	244	2.6	1.6	102	10	123
2-percent fat (1 cup)	244	4.7	2.9	121	18	122
whole (1 cup)	244	8.2	5.1	150	33	120
whole, chocolate (1 cup)	250	8.5	5.3	208	30	149
Milkshake, vanilla, thick (11 oz.)	313	9.5	5.9	350	37	299
Yogurt						
Nonfat or skim, plain (1 cup)	227	0.4	0.3	127	4	174
Lowfat, plain (1 cup)	227	3.5	2.3	144	14	159
Whole, plain (1 cup)	227	7.4	4.8	139	29	105
Frozen Desserts						
Frozen yogurt (½ cup)	113	2.3	1.5	123	9	60
Ice cream, rich, 16% fat (½ cup)	74	11.8	7.4	175	44	54
Ice cream, regular, 10% fat (½ cup)	67	7.1	4.5	135	30	58
Ice milk, regular (½ cup)	66	2.8	1.8	92	9	53
Ice milk, soft serve (½ cup)	88	2.3	1.4	112	7	82
Sherbet, orange (½ cup)	97	1.9	1.2	135	7	44
Cream, Nondairy Creamers and Toppings						
Half & half cream (1 tablespoon)	15	1.7	1.1	20	6	6
Sour cream, real (1 tablespoon)	12	2.5	1.6	26	5	6
Whipped cream, pressurized (1 tablespoon)	3	0.7	0.4	8	2	4
Whipping cream, heavy, fluid (1 tablespoon)	15	5.6	3.5	52	21	6
Creamer, nondairy, liquid (1 tablespoon)	15	1.5	0.3	20	0	12
Creamer, nondairy, powder (1 teaspoon)	2	0.7	0.7	11	0	4
Dessert topping, nondairy, frozen (1 tablespoon)	4	1.0	0.9	13	0	1
Cheese*						
American (1 oz.)	28	8.9	5.6	106	27	406
Blue, Brie, Cheddar, Colby, Edam, Gouda, Gruyère,						
Monterey, Parmesan, Roquefort, Swiss (1 oz.)	28	9.4	6.0	114	30	176
Cheese spread, processed, American (1 oz.)	28	6.0	3.8	82	16	381
Cottage cheese, dry curd (½ cup)	73	0.3	0.2	62	5	10
lowfat, 1-percent fat (½ cup)	113	1.2	0.7	82	5	459
lowfat, 2-percent fat (½ cup)	113	2.2	1.4	101	9	459
creamed (½ cup)	105	4.7	3.0	109	16	425
Cream cheese, regular (1 oz.)	28	9.9	6.2	99	31	84
Cream cheese, Neufchâtel (1 oz.)	28	6.6	4.2	74	22	113
Mozzarella, part skim (1 oz.)	28	4.5	2.9	72	16	132
Ricotta, part skim milk (1 oz.)	28	2.2	1.4	39	9	35
Ricotta, whole milk (1 oz.)	28	3.7	2.4	49	14	24

* Many lowfat varieties are in grocery stores—check label.

Food Description/Portion	Weight (gm)	Fat (gm)	Sat. Fatty Acid (gm)	Poly Fatty Acid (gm)	Energy (Cal.)	Chol. (mg)	Na (mg)
FATS AND OILS							
Margarine							
Corn oil, stick (1 teaspoon)	5	3.8	0.6	0.8	34	0	44
Corn oil, tub (1 teaspoon)	5	3.8	0.7	1.5	34	0	51
Diet (2 teaspoons)	10	3.8	0.6	1.6	33	0	92
Safflower oil, tub (1 teaspoon)	5	3.8	0.4	2.1	34	0	51
Soybean, hydrogenated, tub (1 teaspoon)	5	3.8	0.6	1.3	34	0	51
Soybean, hydrogenated, whipped, tub (1 teaspoon)	5	2.9	0.6	0.3	26	0	48
Nuts (Approximately 3 Tablespoons)							
Almonds, dried	28	14.8	1.4	3.1	167	0	3
Brazil nuts, dried	28	18.8	4.6	6.9	186	0	0
Cashews, dry roasted	28	13.2	2.6	2.2	163	0	4
Chestnuts, roasted	28	0.3	0.1	0.1	68	0	1
Coconut, flaked, sweetened	28	9.0	8.0	0.1	126	0	76
Filberts/hazelnuts, dried	28	17.8	1.3	1.7	179	0	1
Macadamia nuts, oil roasted	28	21.7	3.3	0.4	204	0	2
Mixed nuts, dry roasted	28	14.6	2.0	3.1	169	0	3
Peanuts, oil roasted	28	14.0	1.9	4.4	165	0	4
Pecans, dried	28	19.2	1.5	4.8	190	0	0
Pistachio, dry roasted	28	15.0	1.9	2.3	172	0	2
Walnuts, Black	28	16.1	1.0	10.6	172	0	0
Walnuts, English, dried	28	17.6	1.6	11.1	182	0	3
Seeds (Approximately 3 Tablespoons)							
Pumpkin, squash, dried	28	13.0	2.5	5.9	154	0	5
Sesame, roasted and toasted	28	13.6	1.9	6.0	161	0	3
Sunflower, dried	28	14.1	1.5	9.3	162	0	1
Salad Dressing							
Blue cheese (1 tablespoon)	15	8.0	1.5	4.3	77	—	—
French (1 tablespoon)	16	6.4	1.5	3.4	67	—	214
Italian (1 tablespoon)	15	7.1	1.0	4.1	69	0	116
Mayonnaise (1 tablespoon)	14	11.0	1.6	5.7	99	8	78
Mayonnaise-type (1 tablespoon)	15	4.9	0.7	2.6	57	4	104
Sandwich spread, commercial (1 tablespoon)	15	5.2	0.8	3.1	60	12	—
Thousand Island (1 tablespoon)	16	5.6	0.9	3.1	59	5	109
Vinegar and oil (1 tablespoon)	16	8.0	1.5	3.9	72	0	0
Other Fats							
Bacon (see page 298)							
Butter (1 teaspoon)	5	4.1	2.5	0.2	36	11	41
Olives, green (10 small)	34	3.6	0.4	0.3	33	0	686
Olives, ripe (5 extra large)	28	3.3	0.4	0.3	30	0	193
Peanut butter, smooth (2 teaspoons)	11	5.5	0.9	1.6	63	0	52
Shortening, hydrogenated soybean and cottonseed (1 teaspoon)	4	4.3	1.1	1.1	38	0	—

Food Description/Portion	Weight (gm)	Fat (gm)	Sat. Fatty Acid (gm)	Poly Fatty Acid (gm)	Energy (Cal.)	Chol. (mg)	Na (mg)
Oil							
Canola (1 teaspoon)	5	4.5	0.3	1.5	40	0	0
Corn (1 teaspoon)	5	4.5	0.6	2.7	40	0	0
Olive (1 teaspoon)	5	4.5	0.6	0.4	40	0	0
Peanut (1 teaspoon)	5	4.5	0.8	1.4	40	0	0
Safflower (1 teaspoon)	5	4.5	0.4	3.4	40	0	0
Sesame (1 teaspoon)	5	4.5	0.6	1.9	40	0	0
Soybean (1 teaspoon)	5	4.5	0.7	2.6	40	0	0
Soybean/cottonseed (1 teaspoon)	5	4.5	0.8	2.2	40	0	0
Soybean, hydrogenated (1 teaspoon)	5	4.5	0.7	1.7	40	0	0
Sunflower (1 teaspoon)	5	4.5	0.5	3.0	40	0	0

Food Description/Portion	Weight (gm)	Fat (gm)	Sat. Fatty Acid (gm)	Energy (cal.)	Chol. (mg)	Na (mg)
BREADS, CEREALS, PASTA AND STARCHY VEGETABLES						
Breads, Pancakes and Waffles						
Bagel, 3-inch diameter (1)	100	2.6	—	296	—	360
Biscuit, made with milk, 2-inch diameter (1)	28	2.6	0.6	91	—	272
Bread, white (1 slice)	23	0.9	0.2	63	—	114
Bun, hamburger, 3½-inch diameter, or hot dog, 6 inches long (1)	40	2.2	0.5	119	—	202
English muffin, plain (half)	29	0.6	—	69	—	185
French toast (1 slice)	65	6.7	—	153	—	257
Muffin, bran, 2-inch bottom diameter (1)	40	3.9	1.2	104	—	179
Pancake, with egg, milk, 6-inch diameter × ½-inch thick (1)	73	5.3	1.9	164	—	412
Popover, 2¾-inch top, 2-inch bottom, 4 inches high in center (1)	40	3.7	1.3	90	—	88
Roll, hard, 3¾-inch diameter × 2 inches high (1)	50	1.6	0.4	156	—	313
Waffle, 9 × 9 × ⅝-inch square (1)	200	19.6	6.3	558	—	290
Crackers						
Bread sticks, 7¾ inches × ¾-inch diameter (5)	25	0.8	0.2	96	0	175
Cheese crackers (10)	31	6.7	2.6	150	—	325
Graham crackers, 2½-inch square (4 squares)	28	2.6	0.6	110	—	190
Saltine crackers (10)	28	3.4	0.8	123	—	312
Sandwich-type, cheese-peanut butter (4 sandwiches)	28	6.8	1.8	139	—	281
Zwieback crackers (4 pieces)	28	2.8	1.1	121	6	66

Food Description/Portion	Weight (gm)	Fat (gm)	Sat. Fatty Acid (gm)	Energy (cal.)	Chol. (mg)	Na (mg)
Cereal, Ready-to-Eat						
40% bran flakes (1 oz.)	28	0.5	0.0	93	0	264
Corn flakes (1 oz.)	28	0.1	0.0	110	0	351
Granola, homemade (1 oz.)	28	7.7	1.4	138	—	3
Grape-nuts (1 oz.)	28	0.1	0.0	101	0	197
Puffed wheat, plain (1 oz.)	28	0.4	0.0	104	0	2
Shredded wheat (1 large biscuit)	24	0.3	0.0	83	0	0
Wheat germ, plain, toasted (1 oz.)	28	3.0	0.5	108	0	1
Cereal, Cooked						
Corn grits, regular and quick (1 cup)	242	0.5	0.0	146	0	0 *
Cream of wheat, regular (1 cup)	251	0.5	0.0	134	0	2 *
Oatmeal, regular, quick and instant (1 cup)	234	2.4	0.4	145	0	1 *
Pasta and Rice, Cooked						
Noodles, chow mein, canned (1 cup)	45	10.6	2.0	220	5	450
Noodles, egg (1 cup)	160	2.4	—	200	50	3 *
Rice, white, brown or wild (1 cup)	205	0.2	0.0	223	0	4 *
Spaghetti (1 cup)	140	0.6	0.0	155	—	1 *
Starchy Vegetables						
Corn, lima beans, green peas, plantain, white potato, winter or acorn squash, yam or sweet potato (½ cup)		0.0	0.0	80	0	**
Prepared Vegetables						
Coleslaw/dressing with table cream (½ cup)	60	1.6	0.2	42	5	14
Corn pudding, whole milk, egg, butter (½ cup)	125	6.6	3.2	136	115	69
French fries						
oven-heated, cottage-cut (10)	50	4.1	1.9	109	0	23
fried in animal and vegetable fat (10)	50	8.3	3.4	158	6	108
Onion rings, frozen, oven-heated (7)	70	18.7	6.0	285	0	263
Potato chips (1 oz.)	28	10.1	2.6	148	0	133
Potato						
au gratin with whole milk, butter and cheese (½ cup)	122	9.3	5.8	160	29	528
candied sweet potatoes, brown sugar, butter, 2½ × 2-inch piece (1)	105	3.4	1.4	144	8	73
hashed brown, oil (½ cup)	78	10.9	4.2	163	—	19
mashed, whole milk, margarine (½ cup)	105	4.4	1.1	111	2	309
O'Brien, whole milk, butter (½ cup)	97	1.3	0.8	79	4	211
pancake, eggs, margarine (1)	76	12.6	3.4	495	93	388
potato sticks (1 oz.)	28	9.8	2.5	148	0	71
potato puff, vegetable oil (½ cup)	62	6.7	3.2	138	0	462
scalloped, whole milk, butter (½ cup)	122	4.5	2.8	105	14	409
salad, egg, mayonnaise (½ cup)	125	10.3	1.8	179	86	661

* Product cooked in unsalted water.
** Canned vegetables are high in sodium unless label states canned without salt.

Food Description/Portion	Weight (gm)	Fat (gm)	Sat. Fatty Acid (gm)	Energy (cal.)	Chol. (mg)	Na (mg)
Soup, Canned						
Bean with bacon, prepared with water (1 cup)	253	5.9	1.5	173	3	952
Beef broth or bouillon, ready-to-serve (1 cup)	240	0.5	0.3	16	tr	782
Beef, chunky-style, ready-to-serve (1 cup)	240	5.1	2.6	171	14	867
Chicken broth, prepared with water (1 cup)	244	1.4	0.4	39	1	776
Chicken, chunky-style, ready-to-serve (1 cup)	251	6.6	2.0	178	30	887
Chicken noodle, prepared with water (1 cup)	241	2.5	0.7	75	7	1107
Chicken rice, prepared with water (1 cup)	241	1.9	0.5	60	7	814
Chili beef, prepared with water (1 cup)	250	6.6	3.3	169	12	1035
Cream of chicken, prepared with water (1 cup)	244	7.4	2.1	116	10	986
Cream of mushroom, prepared with water (1 cup)	244	9.0	2.4	129	2	1031
Gazpacho, ready-to-serve (1 cup)	244	2.2	0.3	57	0	1183
Minestrone, prepared with water (1 cup)	241	2.5	0.5	83	2	911
Oyster stew, prepared with water (1 cup)	241	3.8	2.5	59	14	980
Split pea with ham, prepared with water (1 cup)	253	4.4	1.8	189	8	1008
Tomato, prepared with water (1 cup)	244	1.9	0.4	86	0	872
Tomato rice, prepared with water (1 cup)	247	2.7	0.5	120	2	815
Vegetarian vegetable, prepared with water (1 cup)	241	1.9	0.3	72	0	823
Baking Ingredients						
Cornmeal, dry (1 cup)	138	1.7	—	502	—	1
Cornstarch, not packed (1 tablespoon)	8	tr	0.0	29	—	tr
Flour, white (1 cup)	115	1.2	—	419	—	2

VEGETABLES AND FRUITS

Vegetables

Food Description/Portion	Weight (gm)	Fat (gm)	Sat. Fatty Acid (gm)	Energy (cal.)	Chol. (mg)	Na (mg)
All vegetables are low in fat and saturated fat (½ to 1 cup)		0.2	0.0	25	0	*
Fruits						
Apple, raw, 2¾-inch diameter (1)	138	0.5	0.1	81	0	1
Applesauce, canned, unsweetened (½ cup)	122	0.1	0.0	53	0	2
Apricots, medium, raw (4)	141	0.6	0.0	68	0	1
Banana, 9 inches long (half)	57	0.3	0.1	53	0	1
Blackberries, raw (¾ cup)	108	0.4	0.0	56	0	0
Cantaloupe (1 cup, cubes)	160	0.4	0.0	57	0	14
Cherries, sweet, raw (12)	82	0.8	0.2	59	0	0
Figs, medium, raw (2)	100	0.3	0.0	74	0	2
Fruit cocktail, canned, juice packed (½ cup)	124	0.1	0.0	56	0	4
Grapefruit (half)	123	0.1	0.0	37	0	0
Grapes, raw (15)	36	0.1	0.0	23	0	0
Honeydew melon (1 cup, cubes)	170	0.2	0.0	60	0	17
Kiwifruit (1 large)	91	0.4	0.0	55	0	4
Mango, raw (half)	104	0.3	0.0	68	0	2
Nectarine, 2½-inch diameter (1)	136	0.6	0.0	67	0	0
Orange, 2½-inch diameter (1)	131	0.2	0.0	62	0	0

* Sodium values vary from 2 to 63 mg per ½ cup cooked.
  Canned vegetables are higher in sodium than fresh or frozen.

Food Description/Portion	Weight (gm)	Fat (gm)	Sat. Fatty Acid (gm)	Energy (cal.)	Chol. (mg)	Na (mg)
Fruits (cont'd)						
Papaya (1 cup, cubes)	140	0.2	0.1	54	0	4
Peach, 2½-inch diameter (1)	87	0.1	0.0	37	0	0
Peaches, canned, water packed (2 halves)	154	0.1	0.0	36	0	6
Pear, raw (1)	166	0.7	0.0	98	0	1
Pineapple, raw (¾ cup)	116	0.5	0.0	58	0	2
Pineapple, canned, juice pack (⅓ cup)	83	0.1	0.0	50	0	1
Plum, raw, 2⅛-inch diameter (2)	132	0.8	0.1	72	0	0
Pomegranate (half)	77	0.2	0.0	52	0	3
Raspberries, raw (1 cup)	123	0.7	0.0	61	0	0
Strawberries, raw, whole (1¼ cup)	186	0.7	0.0	56	0	3
Tangerine, 2½-inch diameter (2)	168	0.3	0.0	74	0	2
Watermelon (1¼ cup, cubes)	200	0.9	0.0	63	0	4
Dried Fruits						
Apples, uncooked (4 rings)	26	0.1	0.0	62	0	22
Apricots, uncooked (7 halves)	25	0.1	0.0	58	0	2
Dates (2½)	21	0.1	0.0	57	0	1
Figs, uncooked (1½)	28	0.3	0.1	72	0	3
Prunes, uncooked (3)	25	0.1	0.0	60	0	1
Raisins (2 tablespoons)	21	0.1	0.0	62	0	2
Fruit Juices						
Apple juice (½ cup)	124	0.1	0.0	58	0	4
Cranberry juice cocktail (⅓ cup)	84	0.0	0.0	49	0	3
Grapefruit juice, unsweetened (½ cup)	124	0.1	0.0	47	0	2
Grape juice (⅓ cup)	84	0.1	0.0	52	0	2
Orange juice (½ cup)	125	0.3	0.0	55	0	1
Pineapple juice (½ cup)	125	0.1	0.0	70	0	1
Prune juice (⅓ cup)	85	0.0	0.0	60	0	4

DESSERTS AND SNACKS

	PORTION					
***AHA Cookbook* Quick Breads**	PORTION					
Banana bread (1/16 of loaf)	1 slice	4.0	0.6	132	0	172
Biscuit, oil and skim milk (2-inch)	1 biscuit	4.7	0.6	116	0	174
Cornbread muffin, oil and skim milk (2¼-inch)	1 muffin	4.8	0.6	125	0	171
French toast, 1 slice	1 serving	4.3	0.7	113	0	176
Muffin, egg white, oil (2¼-inch)	1 muffin	6.2	0.8	143	0	270
Waffle, whole wheat, oil and skim milk, approximately 4 inches square	1 waffle	5.6	0.9	127	55	101
***AHA Cookbook* Desserts**						
Cake, sheet, devil's food (1/20 of cake)	1 serving	7.7	1.1	179	1	137
minute fudge frosting	1 serving	2.4	0.5	61	0	35
Cake, white, 2-layer, made with oil, skim milk, egg white (1/16 of cake)	1 slice	6.0	1.2	197	1	143
seven-minute frosting	2 tbsp.	0.0	0.0	73	0	7
Cookies, raisin-oatmeal, made with oil, egg white	4 cookies	9.1	1.2	317	0	74

Food Description/Portion	Weight (gm)	Fat (gm)	Sat. Fatty Acid (gm)	Energy (cal.)	Chol. (mg)	Na (mg)
AHA *Cookbook* Desserts (cont'd)	**PORTION**					
Pie, apple, double crust						
crust made with oil, skim milk	⅛ of pie	8.5	1.1	179	0	309
apple filling	⅛ of pie	1.6	0.3	135	0	19
Cakes, Cookies, Pies and Other Baked Goods	**WEIGHT GM.**					
Brownies, with nuts and icing (⅙ of 7½ ×						
5¼ × ⅞-inch pan)	60	12.6	4.3	257	—	123
Cake, without frosting						
angel food (½ of 10-inch diameter)	60	0.1	0.0	161	0	170
devil's food, sheet cake (3 × 3 ×						
2-inch piece)	88	15.1	—	322	41	259
white, 2-layer (1/16 of 9-inch diameter)	53	8.5	2.2	198	3	171
Boston cream pie, 2-layer (½ of 8-inch						
diameter)	69	6.5	2.0	208	—	128
fruitcake (1/32 of 7-inch diameter)	43	7.1	1.6	167	60	83
pound cake (1/12 of 8½-inch loaf)	42	7.8	2.0	171	32	74
sponge cake (1/12 of 9¾-inch diameter)	66	3.8	1.2	196	7	110
yellow, 2-layer (1/16 of 9-inch diameter)	54	6.9	1.9	197	36	140
Cake frosting						
chocolate, prepared with milk and fat						
(1 tablespoon)	17	2.4	1.3	65	—	11
coconut with boiled frosting (1 tablespoon)	10	0.8	0.7	38	—	12
fudge made with water, from mix						
(1 tablespoon)	15	1.0	0.3	52	—	36
white boiled (1 tablespoon)	6	0.0	0.0	19	0	8
Cheesecake (1 portion)	100	19.2	—	302	170	222
Cookies, sandwich, 1¾-inch diameter (4)	40	9.0	2.4	198	—	193
chocolate chip, 2⅓-inch diameter (4)	40	12.0	3.4	206	—	139
fig bars (4)	56	3.1	0.9	200	—	141
gingersnaps, 2-inch diameter (4)	28	2.5	0.6	118	—	160
Cupcake, plain, no icing, 2½-inch diameter (1)	25	3.5	1.0	91	—	75
plain, with white uncooked icing, 2½-inch						
diameter (1)	35	4.1	1.1	128	—	79
Doughnut, cake type, 3⅝-inch diameter (1)	58	10.8	2.7	227	—	291
yeast type, 3¾-inch diameter (1)	42	11.3	2.8	176	—	99
Pastry, Danish, plain, 4¼-inch diameter × 1-inch						
thick (1)	65	15.3	4.5	274	—	238
Pastry, toaster, commercial (1)	52	6.0	—	203	—	239
Pie, apple, 2 crust (⅛ of 9-inch diameter)	118	13.1	3.4	302	—	355
custard (⅛ of 9-inch diameter)	114	12.7	4.3	249	—	327
pumpkin (⅛ of 9-inch diameter)	114	12.8	4.5	241	—	244
pecan (⅛ of 9-inch diameter)	103	23.6	3.3	431	—	228
cherry, 2 crust (⅛ of 9-inch diameter)	118	13.3	3.5	308	—	359
Pie crust, baked (⅛ of 9-inch diameter)	23	7.5	1.8	113	—	138

Food Description/Portion	Weight (gm)	Fat (gm)	Sat. Fatty Acid (gm)	Energy (cal.)	Chol. (mg)	Na (mg)
Candy						
Candy corn (approximately 20 pieces)	28	0.6	0.1	103	—	60
Caramels, plain or chocolate (1 oz.)	28	2.9	1.6	113	—	64
Chocolate coated peanuts (8 to 16)	28	11.7	3.0	159	—	17
Fudge, plain (1 oz.)	28	3.5	1.2	113	—	54
Gumdrops (1 oz.)	28	0.2	0.0	98	0	10
Hard candy (1 oz.)	28	0.3	0.0	109	0	9
Marshmallow (1 oz.)	28	tr	0.0	90	0	11
Milk chocolate, plain (1 oz.)	28	9.2	5.1	147	—	27
Milk chocolate, almond (1 oz.)	28	10.1	4.5	151	—	23
Mints, uncoated (1 oz.)	28	0.6	0.1	103	0	60
SAUCES AND GRAVIES						
Dehydrated Sauces						
Béarnaise, prepared with milk and butter (¼ cup)	64	17.1	10.4	175	47	316
Cheese, prepared with milk (¼ cup)	70	4.3	2.3	77	13	92
Hollandaise, prepared with milk and butter (¼ cup)	64	17.1	10.5	176	47	284
Mushroom, prepared with milk (¼ cup)	67	2.6	1.4	57	9	383
Sour cream, prepared with milk (¼ cup)	79	7.6	4.0	127	23	252
Stroganoff, prepared with milk and water (¼ cup)	74	2.7	1.7	68	10	457
Sweet and sour, prepared with water and vinegar (¼ cup)	78	0.0	0.0	74	0	195
White, prepared with milk (¼ cup)	66	3.4	1.6	60	9	199
Ready-to-Serve Sauces						
Barbecue (¼ cup)	63	1.1	0.0	47	0	510
Soy (1 tablespoon)	18	0.0	0.0	11	0	1029
Teriyaki (1 tablespoon)	18	0.0	0.0	15	0	690
Canned Gravy						
Au jus (¼ cup)	60	0.1	0.1	10	0	—
Beef (¼ cup)	58	1.4	0.7	31	2	29
Chicken (¼ cup)	60	3.4	0.8	47	1	344
Mushroom (¼ cup)	60	1.6	0.2	30	0	340
Turkey (¼ cup)	60	1.3	0.4	31	1	—
Dehydrated Gravy						
Au jus, prepared with water (¼ cup)	62	0.2	0.1	5	0	145
Brown, prepared with water (¼ cup)	65	0.1	0.0	22	tr	31
Chicken, prepared with water (¼ cup)	65	0.5	0.1	21	1	283
Mushroom, prepared with water (¼ cup)	64	0.2	0.1	18	0	351
Onion, prepared with water (¼ cup)	65	0.2	0.1	20	0	259
Pork, prepared with water (¼ cup)	64	0.5	0.2	19	1	309
Turkey, prepared with water (¼ cup)	65	0.5	0.1	22	1	375

REFERENCES FOR FOOD TABLE

USDA AGRICULTURE HANDBOOK NO. 8 SERIES

Series No.	Food Group Issued	Year
8-1	Dairy and Egg Products	1976
8-3	Baby Foods	1978
8-4	Fats and Oils	1979
8-5	Poultry Products	1979
8-6	Soups, Sauces and Gravies	1980
8-7	Sausages and Luncheon Meats	1980
8-8	Breakfast Cereals	1982
8-9	Fruits and Fruit Juices	1982
8-10	Pork Products	1983
8-11	Vegetables and Vegetable Products	1984
8-12	Nut and Seed Products	1984
8-13	Beef Products	1986
8-15	Finfish and Shellfish Products	1987

American Heart Association Cookbook. David McKay, Fourth Edition, 1984.

Breidenstein, Burdette C.: Nutrient Value of Meat. Food & Nutrition News, Vol. 59, No. 2, 1987.

Communication with USDA, 1987.

USDA Nutritive Value of American Foods in Common Units. Agricultural Handbook No. 456, 1975.

USDA Provisional Table on the Fatty Acids and Cholesterol Content of Selected Foods, 1984.

USDA Provisional Table on the Nutrient Content of Fast Foods, 1984.

Appendix E.

HINTS FOR STAYING WITH YOUR DIET

The tips presented here can help you achieve your dietary goal. The methods work well for success in a cholesterol-lowering diet as well as a weight reduction diet. Because human beings are creatures of habit, it's difficult to alter eating patterns overnight. In fact, people who make instantaneous changes usually revert to their old ways just as quickly. That's why we suggest that you ease into your new routine gradually. For example, if you never eat breakfast, don't start forcing yourself to do so right away. If you like having lunch in the cafeteria, you needn't force yourself to bring lunch from home; just start making more careful selections. By taking your time, you allow yourself to form new, positive habits that will eventually become just as firmly established as your old ones.

As you embark on your diet, it's also important to examine your old eating habits and understand your behaviors, attitudes and motivations. This will require reflection and discussion with other family members; for some, consultation with a Registered Dietitian is desirable. It may be helpful to keep a written record of your eating habits for a few days. As you reflect on those habits, look for signs of unconscious behaviors. Ask yourself the following questions:

- Do I eat compulsively?
- Do I use food to relieve anxiety or depression?
- Do I give in to social pressure from family or friends to eat foods that are wrong for me?
- Are there times when I overeat excessively or go on eating binges?

What you learn from your answers may help you as you change your eating behaviors. Your family is an important component in adopting a new diet. Unfortunately, your family and social environment may not provide easy access to the right foods. Nor is moral support from family members always available. You may find it necessary to have frank discussions with members of your family about the importance to you of your dietary changes. It you consult a Registered Dietitian, take your spouse or other family members along, so they'll understand your dietary requirements. Ideally, the whole family should be educated about the dangers of high blood cholesterol and should adopt a cholesterol-lowering diet. But whether or not you enlist their participation in your diet, do try to enlist their support.

HOW TO WIN AT LOSING

The biggest obstacles to losing weight and maintaining your normal weight are your own thoughts and habits. The following suggestions may help you. If you really want to lose weight, nothing can stop you—unless you let it.

Tips for Living at Your Best Weight

- Be your own cheerleader. It's okay to be proud of yourself when you succeed at new habits and make good choices. Argue with yourself when temptation appears. Know that your weight has nothing to do with whether you are loved or whether you are a good person.
- Analyze your environment and eliminate those things that stimulate you to choose the overweight way of life.
- Store food out of sight. Candy dishes and snack food on tables and countertops are big temptations.
- Get rid of tempting foods until you can handle having them around.
- Portion food onto plates in the kitchen rather than putting serving dishes on the table.
- Eat in a designated place and sit down. Eating while standing in front of the refrigerator or pantry contributes to overeating.
- Don't do other things when you eat. Just enjoy your food. Chew slowly. TV or reading are pleasant distractions that lead to nibbling snack foods.
- Find friends and neighbors who support and encourage your new lifestyle changes.
- Concentrate on maintaining a gradual weight loss. It's natural to reach a temporary plateau, but commit yourself to moving on—not gaining weight back.
- Plan your meals ahead of time. Don't leave important details to chance. Social engagements, holidays and business luncheons will always happen. There will always be depressing or upsetting episodes in life. You can always find an excuse for not getting more exercise. Plan out the kind of life you really want, and live it, every day.
- While you want lifelong changes, appreciate the smaller goals along the way. If you can't lose 5 pounds, you won't be able to lose 30. So, don't worry about losing 30 pounds; just work on each 5-pound segment.
- Set realistic goals. Remember that people lose weight at varying rates. Generally, 4 to 6 pounds per month is a safe, average weight loss. Cutting 500 calories a day or using up 500 calories by increasing physical activity will result in losing one pound a week. These figures are approximate. No two people respond exactly alike.
- Depriving yourself of special treats only makes you crave them. Plan to

enjoy a small treat once or twice a week. Yes, treats are possible on a cholesterol-lowering diet.

• Recording the food eaten daily helps most people lose weight—especially in the beginning. It's easy to forget small snack samples eaten while meals are being prepared. Stay aware by writing them down.

• The scale is a problem for many dieters. Some people want a reward if their weight is down. If their weight is up, they think, "What's the use, I might as well eat." Actually, the scale is a limited measurement. It can't distinguish between gaining muscle weight (while exercising) and losing fat weight. The scale weighs the natural fluctuations in body water and waste products the same as it weighs fat. Because of this, weigh yourself no more than once a week, preferably in the morning, without clothing and after going to the bathroom. Some find that keeping a weight grid is helpful in tracking progress. A calender can also be useful for recording weight, entering goals and jotting down progress notes.

• If you need support for your dieting efforts, find it. Consider individual consultations by a Registered Dietitian.

Eating Habits

If you want to win at losing weight, make these four minor changes in your eating habits:

• Learn to eat certain foods differently. Eat high-calorie foods in smaller portions and less often.

• Eat food for nourishment—not as a release for anger or for comfort.

• When you exercise more or less than usual, adjust the amount of food you eat to maintain your best weight. To lose weight you don't have to eat *diet* foods. That's a misconception. Just eat normal foods in smaller portions.

• To feel your best and control hunger, eat regularly. Divide your daily calorie allotment into three regular meals or six small meals.

Keep Moving

Before beginning an exercise program, check with your doctor. If he or she tells you there is no reason why you can't engage in moderate exercise, here are some ideas.

• Try to add a daily walk to your schedule. Start slowly and gradually build to 45 minutes or an hour. Use the time to relax, make plans and enjoy life. If you would rather swim or ride a bicycle, by all means do so. It's important to choose activities you enjoy.

• Look for ways to put more activity back into your life. Walk to the store or post office, or park farther away from your office or home. Take the stairs instead of the elevator. Turn off the TV and work outside or go dancing.

- To make your outdoor exercise safer and more enjoyable, wear good exercise shoes, comfortable clothing and a hat in hot weather. Be sure to drink plenty of water. Avoid exercising outdoors in very cold or very hot or humid weather. During hot weather, walk in the early morning or after the temperature drops in the evening.

Losing weight is not easy. It requires commitment and hard work. But once you reach your goal and learn to adopt a life-style that will keep you at your best weight, you'll forget you ever had to fight with being overweight.

WINNING FOR LIFE

After you lose the weight, you face the most important challenge to your weight-loss efforts—keeping it off. You'll be around food several times each day and at most social events, so you will be tempted by high-calorie foods and old habits. Sticking with your daily exercise also takes commitment.

You have to learn how to handle life's lapses, relapses and collapses. A *lapse* is a slight error or return to your overweight habits, the first instance of backsliding. For example, you may have a bad day and overeat, or skip a week of exercise. A *relapse,* on the other hand, is if you return to your former habits for several days or weeks. A *collapse* occurs if you are unable to reverse the negative trend, and you go back to old ways of eating and not exercising.

The critical thing to realize is that a lapse or even relapse *should not be seen as a failure,* but, instead, as a challenge to overcome. Use the following easy behaviors to help handle these times.

Identify Urges and High-Risk Situations

It is important to tell the difference between hunger (gnawing in your stomach and light-headedness) and urges (mental cravings for food). Hunger or low blood sugar tells you it is time to eat, either a meal or a small piece of fruit or glass of lowfat milk. Urges are another matter. They include situations like eating a large meal after you have several glasses of wine or eating candy to reward yourself after a stressful incident. You can handle these urges with some of the following techniques:

- Delayed gratification.

Delayed gratification is a behavioral tool that many people use successfully to stop their impulsive grabbing for food. It is a lesson in tolerance. When you feel the urge to eat, set a timer for 15 minutes and wait, or find something else to do, before eating. This will teach you to postpone your desire for food.

- ABC Theory.

Use behavior other than eating to help you find ways to respond to life's stresses. The theory works like this: if A happens (you have an argument with your spouse, for example), you always do B (you leave the argument with hard feelings) and this always causes C (you respond by gorging). How can you change this? Change A or B so that you don't have a reason to do C, or find a release for your frustrations other than eating, such as jogging, going for a walk or meditating.

Eat Like a Normal Person

By now you know that eating healthy to stay slim is not an exercise in starvation or self-deprivation, like crash dieting. It's a way of life in which you can look forward to enjoying mealtimes, not just enduring them.

When you reach your best weight, add about 200 calories of healthy food each day. Select some nutritious foods you have been eating during your weight loss period—fruits and vegetables, whole-grain products and lowfat dairy items. Save your rich favorites for special occasions. After four or five days, if you are still losing weight add several hundred more calories. By adding calories slowly, you will eventually be able to maintain your weight at your present exercise level. If you alter the amount of exercise, adjust your eating accordingly. Again, keeping a record of your food intake and exercise can make this process much easier.

Hints for Staying at Your Best Weight Forever

- Accept the idea that wise eating doesn't mean eating diet foods—it just means eating usual foods in smaller amounts.
- Stock up on good, fresh foods that make you look forward to meals. Make a shopping list, and always shop after a meal instead of on an empty stomach.
- Plan your meals, and don't leave your eating habits to chance. Before meals, parties and potlucks, decide what you can do to make it easier on yourself. Offer to bring a fresh fruit, a vegetable appetizer or a fruit dessert. If the meal will be later than usual, eat something before you go, such as a slice of lowfat cheese, lean meat or a piece of fruit, or drink a glass of lowfat milk.
- When confronted with a delicious banquet or dinner at a friend's house, use your head. There will always be special occasions. And it's okay to splurge occasionally, but don't eat everything in sight. Choose between the options. If the dinner is lasagna, green beans, tossed salad, garlic bread, wine and a special cherry dessert, don't panic. You can pick and choose what to eat. Most people face this situation often. One way to handle it might be to eat a medium serving of lasagna and salad and an extra serving of green beans. Then choose one from the bread, wine or dessert. Another way might be to eat a little of everything. Try to see if you can handle it. You'll find it works best to have your host or hostess serve only the small portion you want to eat. It is often too difficult to resist the urge to clean your plate when it is filled to the brim with large portions.

- When you feel hungry between meals, drink a glass of water, skim milk, iced tea, hot tea or coffee, or eat a piece of fruit. Then get out of the kitchen. Keep your mind and body busy.

- It is usually better to eat a little bit of a high-calorie food you crave than to avoid it for so long that you gorge on it when you finally decide to eat it. Eat a small amount, and leave it at that. If you don't trust yourself with just a small amount, don't eat any at all.

Staying Active as a Way of Life

Physical fitness and strength are abilities you have to learn, and you have to work at keeping them. Normally, your body slowly adjusts to the level of fitness needed to handle the lifestyle you choose. If you regularly exercise and stretch your muscles, they will become slightly larger, more flexible and stronger. Your body will carry oxygen, nutrients and blood more efficiently. It will also use more calories each day, so you can afford to eat more food. Unfortunately, however, these changes are reversible if your activity level slows down.

To keep up your enthusiasm for exercise, consider finding a partner or a class to exercise with so the session will be fun and the time will pass quickly. It is easy to talk yourself out of taking a walk when the weather isn't just right or when something else comes up. But if a friend knocks on your door and says, "Come on, let's go," it's hard to refuse.

Another tactic to help you continue lifelong exercise habits is to choose activities that fit easily into your present lifestyle. Why join a health club across town if you hate driving that far? Why buy a stationary bicycle to use in the basement when you know you haven't been near that room since you bought your house? Look for sports, activities, exercise partners and programs that you will enjoy and stick with.

Remember that you can increase your physical activity level without taking up organized sports or exercise programs. Try parking your car farther from the office to build walking into your day. Take the stairs instead of the elevator. Instead of spending an hour at a "sit down" lunch, bring a light lunch from home and go for a walk.

The Best You Can Be

When you learn and accomplish these techniques, your days of being overweight will be finished. You can enjoy shopping for clothes, the swimsuit season and dinner with friends without guilt or fear. These techniques will help you keep your weight off and are the tools you need to stay your best weight forever. This new lifestyle will always work for you. Why? Because you're in control.

Appendix F.

TIPS FOR DINING OUT

Americans are eating out more than ever before. In fact, more than half of all our meals take place in restaurants.

If you're a member of the group that enjoys letting someone else do the cooking, don't despair. A low-cholesterol, lowfat diet doesn't have to mean a lifetime of housebound meals. It just means taking the time to learn a few tips to heart-healthy restaurant dining.

- It takes a little more time to plan your selection when you're on a restricted diet. Start studying the menu before the waiter appears to avoid making split-second—and often regrettable—decisions.
- If your companions don't mind, have the waiter remove unnecessary temptations like butter.
- Don't be reluctant to ask the waiter about ingredients or preparation methods for the dishes you're not familiar with.
- Feel free to ask the waiter to make substitutions like green vegetables in place of french fries or a dry salad in place of mayonnaise-laden cole slaw.
- If you find it impossible to order from the menu without ruining your diet, ask the waiter if the chef could prepare a fruit or vegetable platter for you. Most are eager to please.
- Order all dressings and sauces on the side, so you can control your portions.
- Stay away from fried appetizers or creamy soups and begin your meal with broth-based soups such as minestrone or gazpacho instead.
- Salad bars can be your friend or foe depending on what you choose. Stay away from high-fat items such as grated cheese, cream dressings, chopped eggs and croutons.
- Try a squeeze of lemon on your salad instead of dressing.
- Stick to the basic guidelines of your diet as you choose an entree. Pick fish or chicken in place of fatty meats.
- Choose an entree that's broiled, baked, grilled, steamed or poached instead of fried.
- Ask to have your food prepared without butter or cream sauces.
- If you choose chicken, remove the skin before eating.
- If you choose meat, remove all visible fat.
- Order plenty of vegetable side dishes whenever possible. And be sure to ask the waiter to leave off any sauces or butter.

- If you order potatoes, choose baked, boiled or roasted instead of fried. And ask the waiter to skip the butter and sour cream.
- Order fresh fruit instead of cake or pie for dessert. Or pick a fruit sorbet in place of ice cream.
- If you go to an Oriental restaurant, try a stir-fried chicken or fish and vegetable dish. Better still, choose a steamed main dish. And be sure to ask for steamed instead of fried rice.
- If you go to an Italian restaurant, steer clear of white creamy sauces and opt for red marinara sauce instead. Try a fish selection or meatless pasta in place of an entree with sausage or meatballs. Ask for plain Italian bread instead of buttery garlic bread. And be sure to go easy on the grated Parmesan.

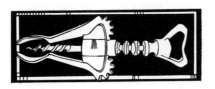

Appendix G.

DRUGS: WHEN DIET ALONE WON'T WORK

For some people, diet alone won't lower blood cholesterol sufficiently. For example, one in five hundred people has a genetic condition called familial hypercholesterolemia, which typically causes blood cholesterol levels to be over 300 mg/dl and often as high as 500. If you have this or a related condition, your doctor may prescribe drug therapy immediately.

In most cases, however, your physician will want you to try to lower your cholesterol through diet before considering drug treatment. If, after changing your diet, you're still unable to lower your LDL-cholesterol level to below 190, drugs may be an appropriate alternative. The same holds true if you have an LDL-cholesterol level between 160 and 190 in combination with coronary heart disease or other serious risk factors. But whatever the reason for resorting to medication, a change in diet should always go along with the drug treatment to maximize the effect.

The types of drugs used to lower cholesterol are varied and work in a number of different ways.

Bile Acid Binding Drugs. There are two drugs in this category: colestipol, known by the trade name Colestid, and cholestyramine, known by the trade name Questran. Cholestyramine was the drug used in the Coronary Primary Prevention Trial to prove the connection between lowering blood cholesterol and preventing heart attack.

Bile acid binding drugs stay within the intestinal tract and are not absorbed into the body. They act by binding to the bile acids, which are breakdown products of cholesterol. This binding action leads to more excretion of bile acids and hence to a more rapid breakdown of cholesterol in the liver; this in turn causes the liver to make more LDL receptors, thus allowing it to remove more cholesterol. At the usual dosage, two packets twice daily, these drugs typically lower blood cholesterol by 15 to 30 percent.

Both colestipol and cholestyramine exist in powder form and must be mixed with water or fruit juice. Colestipol comes in packages of 5 grams each or in bottles. Cholestyramine is currently available in packets, each containing 4 grams, or in large cans of bulk powder. Both are relatively expensive, but are less so when bought in bulk.

It may be easier to take the usual dosage for colestipol or cholestyramine if you start out with one package twice daily. In fact, some patients get sufficient results at this dosage. If your cholesterol is very high, you may be asked to take two packets three times a day. The packets are equivalent to measured scoops of the bulk powder.

The bile acid binding drugs sometimes cause gastrointestinal side effects, such as constipation, bloating, intestinal gas, feelings of stomach fullness and nausea. Constipation is a consequence of the bile acid's binding process, because, left in their natural state, bile acids are natural laxatives. A good way to control the constipation is to add more fiber to your diet with bran cereals, or fiber laxatives containing psyllium. Also, your physician may recommend a stool softener. Regular laxatives should not be used because prolonged use may produce side effects.

Many patients have some trouble taking bile acid binding drugs at first. If you're one of them, don't give up. Eventually, you'll adjust. Start at very low doses and work up the dose slowly. While these drugs are somewhat inconvenient to take, they've proven both safe and effective for preventing heart attacks.

Nicotinic Acid. This is an inexpensive drug that's been used for many years to treat high blood cholesterol. Nicotinic acid was used in a major clinical trial, the Coronary Drug Project, with patients who had suffered previous heart attacks. Throughout the trial, half took nicotinic acid and half took a placebo. Nicotinic acid was found to significantly reduce the recurrence rate of heart attack. Moreover, after 15 years, there were fewer deaths among the nicotinic-acid group.

Nicotinic acid works by reducing the formation of lipoproteins in the liver. In doing so, it lowers blood trigylcerides, VLDL-cholesterol and LDL-cholesterol; by lowering triglycerides it also raises the HDL-cholesterol.

The major problem with nicotinic acid is its troublesome side effects. One is a flushing of the skin, especially the face, which occurs several minutes after taking the drug. Itching and skin rash can also result. Finally, gastrointestinal problems can make the drug a poor choice for people who are prone to peptic ulcers. At the very least, this drug necessitates periodic monitoring through certain types of blood tests. There are other less common side effects, too. For some, the drug proves mildly toxic to the liver and has to be discontinued. It may also raise the blood uric acid level and possibly lead to gout; if you have gout, you probably should not take nicotinic acid. Additionally, nicotinic acid could make a diabetic condition worse.

If your doctor has prescribed nicotinic acid, be sure to avoid confusing it with the vitamin, nicotinamide, which is not effective for lowering cholesterol. Nicotinic acid comes in tablets of 50, 100 and 500 milligrams. It also comes in sustained-release pills that will reduce flushing but are also more expensive. Choose only one method, because switching back and forth between tablets and sustained release increases the likelihood of side effects.

Nicotinic acid is best started in very low doses that are easily tolerated. Commonly, one starts by taking one 50-milligram tablet three times a day. Another way is to take 100 milligrams after dinner to avoid the initial flushing during working hours. Flushing can sometimes be controlled by taking an aspirin 30 minutes before taking the drug. But with or without aspirin, tolerance to the flushing usually develops after several weeks.

After starting with a low dose, it is best to build the dosage slowly. For example, if you start with 50 milligrams three times daily, you could increase to 100 milligrams three times daily within a couple of days. By raising each dose in 50-milligram increments, you can reach a dosage of 1,000 to 1,500 milligrams three times daily over a period of three to four weeks. This is the dosage range you should aim for. There's little evidence that taking less than 1,000 milligrams a day is effective in lowering blood cholesterol. It's a good idea to take the drug after meals, never on an empty stomach.

Lovastatin. Known by the trade name Mevicor, lovastatin is a new type of drug used to lower blood cholesterol. It works by interfering with the formation of cholesterol in the liver, forcing the liver to utilize increased amounts of blood cholesterol. The liver then produces more LDL receptors to take LDL-cholesterol out of the bloodstream. The result is a major reduction in blood cholesterol, often by 30 to 40 percent. It's a much greater reduction than other drugs and requires only small doses of 40 to 80 milligrams a day. Because of its high effectiveness and low dose requirement, lovastatin is an extremely attractive drug for treating high blood cholesterol.

There remains, however, the crucial question of side effects. So far no serious effects have been observed, although one to five people in every hundred have some problem with the drug. A few have gastrointestinal complaints. Others have a high blood level of certain liver enzymes because the enzymes leak out of the liver cells. This change may reflect mild toxicity to the liver but can be reversed rapidly when the drug is stopped. In still others, enzymes from muscle cells escape into the bloodstream, resulting in mild muscle damage and occasional complaints of muscle soreness. This too is reversed when the drug is stopped. If you take lovastatin and develop sore muscles, report it immediately to your physician.

Some authorities are concerned that lovastatin might cause cataracts. There are certain theoretical reasons why this might occur, but so far, patients who take lovastatin have not reported increased incidences of cataracts. Nevertheless, if you are currently taking or plan to take lovastatin, it may be prudent to have the lenses of your eyes checked by an ophthalmologist now, and yearly thereafter, until it's definitely proven that lovastatin does not cause cataracts.

Lovastatin should not be viewed as an easy answer to high blood cholesterol. After all, the drug could have serious long-term, not-yet-detected side effects. Standard drugs, such as the bile acid binding medications, may be a preferable way to lower blood cholesterol when the level is not extremely high but diet alone is not enough. Still, for some patients with very high cholesterol, lovastatin may prove extremely beneficial. In the future, drugs similar to lovastatin will become available, but their basic action will be the same.

Gemfibrozil. Sold under the trade name of Lopid, gemfibrozil lowers blood triglycerides and raises HDL-cholesterol. To a lesser extent, it acts by lowering LDL-cholesterol, often accomplishing reductions of 8 to 15 percent. How gemfibrozil lowers the blood lipids is not well understood. In the Helsinki Heart Study, a large clinical trial, it reduced the risk of heart attacks among patients with high blood cholesterol. It was useful in treating patients with moderately elevated blood cholesterol who couldn't tolerate more potent drugs.

The typical dose of gemfibrozil is 600 milligrams twice a day. Patients taking this drug should be aware of certain dangers and side effects. The drug increases the risk of developing gallstones. It sometimes causes gastrointestinal discomfort or diarrhea. In some patients, gemfibrozil causes muscle pain similar to lovastatin. Others report a variety of other minor problems, but no life-threatening side effects have been reported.

Clofibrate. Sold under the name Atromid-S, clofibrate's actions are similar to gemfibrozil's. The two drugs are chemically related. Clofibrate, like gemfibrozil, proved effective in a clinical trial (the World Health Organization's Clofibrate Trial). Unfortunately, the trial also uncovered some possible side effects that may offset its benefit for coronary risk reduction. In the group treated with the drug, the number of non-heart-related deaths was greater than in the placebo group, which suggested to some that clofibrate has occasional serious side effects. However, there remains some skepticism about the validity of this finding, and the actual occurrence of serious side effects has not been proven. Nonetheless, since the publication of the trial's results, the use of the drug for treating high blood cholesterol has declined dramatically.

Probucol. Also known as Lorelco, probucol has been used for many years in the treatment of high blood cholesterol. The standard dose is 500 milligrams twice a day. It's generally well tolerated, and the side effects are few. Gastrointestinal discomfort and diarrhea occur in a few patients taking the drug.

Probucol can reduce total blood cholesterol by 10 to 15 percent. Unfortunately, it causes some reduction of the HDL-cholesterol as well as the LDL-cholesterol. This has led some investigators to question whether probucol provides any benefit for prevention of heart attack. To date, there have been no clinical trials carried out with probucol to determine whether it will actually prevent heart attack, but results of such trials should be available in a few years. Probucol usually is reserved for patients who cannot tolerate other cholesterol-lowering drugs.

Appendix H.

OTHER CORONARY RISK FACTORS

High blood cholesterol is one of many factors that can increase your coronary risk. If other risk factors are also present, the danger of heart attack may be significantly greater. That's why it's even more important for people with high blood cholesterol to eliminate or minimize other risks whenever possible.

Cigarette smoking. Heavy smoking is probably the worst of all risk factors for first heart attacks. Smoking doubles or triples your chance of heart attack. If you smoke two packs a day, your risk is twice as high as if you smoke one pack. As soon as you quit, that risk begins to drop. And within ten years after quitting, your chances of having a heart attack drop back to near normal.

High blood pressure. High blood pressure is dangerous because it has no symptoms. It's important to have your blood pressure checked regularly. If it's 140/90 or above, your doctor can help you control it through diet or medication.

A family history of heart attack. If your parent or sibling has had a heart attack, there's an increased chance that you will have one, too. High blood cholesterol tends to run in families. Consequently, if you find that your blood cholesterol is high, it's a good idea to urge your family members to be tested as well.

A previous heart attack. You are at greater risk of a second heart attack, regardless of whether other risk factors are present, if you've already had one.

Overweight or obesity. Excess body weight causes a reduction in HDL-cholesterol and may increase LDL-cholesterol. It also predisposes people to high blood pressure and adult diabetes. If you're one of the millions of Americans who are overweight, be aware that it is possible to lose weight and to maintain a desirable weight for life through exercise and diet. (See Appendix E, pages 312–317.) The table at right shows the proper weight range for your sex and height.

Diabetes. The 3 million Americans who have adult diabetes are major candidates for heart attack. In fact, heart attack is the number one killer of diabetic patients. Since the two risk factors of diabetes and overweight often go hand in hand, it's particularly important for diabetic patients to watch their diets and maintain their proper weights.

Lack of exercise. There is growing evidence that regular, vigorous physical activity protects against heart disease. It raises HDL-cholesterol and, in some individuals, reduces LDL-cholesterol as well as blood pressure. Exercise also reduces the danger of dying suddenly if you do have a heart attack. If you

DESIRABLE BODY WEIGHT RANGES

HEIGHT WITHOUT SHOES	WEIGHT WITHOUT CLOTHES MEN (LBS)	WOMEN (LBS)
4'10"	—	92–121
4'11"	—	95–124
5'0"	—	98–127
5'1"	105–134	101–130
5'2"	108–137	104–134
5'3"	111–141	107–138
5'4"	114–145	110–142
5'5"	117–149	114–146
5'6"	121–154	118–150
5'7"	125–159	122–154
5'8"	129–163	126–159
5'9"	133–167	130–164
5'10"	137–172	134–169
5'11"	141–177	—
6'0"	145–182	—
6'1"	149–187	—
6'2"	153–192	—
6'3"	157–197	—

Note: For women 18–25 years, subtract one pound for each year under 25.
Source: Adapted from the 1959 Metropolitan Desirable Weight Table.

decide to begin an exercise program, remember to consult your physician first, especially if you're middle aged or older and haven't exercised for a long time.

Stress. Social and professional stress may provoke other risk factors (for example, a rise in blood pressure or blood cholesterol), lead to excessive smoking or eating or, perhaps, induce coronary thrombosis. However, stress levels are difficult to measure, and responses to stress vary markedly. It has been suggested that persons with an overdeveloped sense of time urgency, drive or competitiveness are more prone to heart attack than those who are more complacent and do not respond excessively to social stresses. This is an issue that requires further investigation.

The male sex. Men are more prone to heart attack than women. While the reasons for this are not entirely clear, men tend to have higher levels of LDL-cholesterol and lower levels of HDL-cholesterol than women. Because of the higher coronary risk, men should pay particular attention to other risk factors. Nonetheless, heart disease is the number one killer of American women as well, particularly those past menopause.

Appendix I.

AMERICAN HEART ASSOCIATION AFFILIATES

**American Heart Association
National Center
Dallas, TX**

American Heart Association
Alabama Affiliate, Inc.
Birmingham, AL

American Heart Association
Alaska Affiliate, Inc.
Anchorage, AK

American Heart Association
Arizona Affiliate, Inc.
Phoenix, AZ

American Heart Association
Arkansas Affiliate, Inc.
Little Rock, AR

American Heart Association
California Affiliate, Inc.
Burlingame, CA

American Heart Association of
Metropolitan Chicago, Inc.
Chicago, IL

American Heart Association of
Colorado, Inc.
Denver, CO

American Heart Association
Connecticut Affiliate, Inc.
Wallingford, CT

American Heart Association
Dakota Affiliate, Inc.
Jamestown, ND

American Heart Association of
Delaware, Inc.
Wilmington, DE

American Heart Association
Florida Affiliate, Inc.
St. Petersburg, FL

American Heart Association
Georgia Affiliate, Inc.
Marietta, GA

American Heart Association
Hawaii Affiliate, Inc.
Honolulu, HI

American Heart Association of
Idaho, Inc.
Boise, ID

American Heart Association
Illinois Affiliate, Inc.
Springfield, IL

American Heart Association
Indiana Affiliate, Inc.
Indianapolis, IN

American Heart Association
Iowa Affiliate, Inc.
West Des Moines, IA

American Heart Association
Kansas Affiliate, Inc.
Topeka, KS

American Heart Association
Kentucky Affiliate, Inc.
Louisville, KY

American Heart Association
Greater Los Angeles Affiliate, Inc.
Los Angeles, CA

American Heart Association of
Louisiana, Inc.
Destrehan, LA

American Heart Association
Maine Affiliate, Inc.
Augusta, ME

American Heart Association
Maryland Affiliate, Inc.
Baltimore, MD

American Heart Association
Massachusetts Affiliate, Inc.
Needham Heights, MA

American Heart Association of
Michigan, Inc.
Lathrup Village, MI

American Heart Association
Minnesota Affiliate, Inc.
Minneapolis, MN

American Heart Association
Mississippi Affiliate, Inc.
Jackson, MS

American Heart Association
Missouri Affiliate, Inc.
Columbia, MO

American Heart Association
Montana Affiliate, Inc.
Great Falls, MT

American Heart Association
Nation's Capital Affiliate, Inc.
Washington, D.C.

American Heart Association
Nebraska Affiliate, Inc.
Omaha, NE

American Heart Association
Nevada Affiliate, Inc.
Las Vegas, NV

American Heart Association
New Hampshire Affiliate, Inc.
Manchester, NH

American Heart Association
New Jersey Affiliate, Inc.
North Brunswick, NJ

American Heart Association
New Mexico Affiliate, Inc.
Albuquerque, NM

American Heart Association
New York City Affiliate, Inc.
New York City, NY

American Heart Association
New York State Affiliate, Inc.
North Syracuse, NY

American Heart Association
North Carolina Affiliate, Inc.
Chapel Hill, NC

American Heart Association
Northeast Ohio Affiliate, Inc.
Cleveland, OH

American Heart Association
Ohio Affiliate, Inc.
Columbus, OH

American Heart Association
Oklahoma Affiliate, Inc.
Oklahoma City, OK

American Heart Association
Oregon Affiliate, Inc.
Portland, OR

American Heart Association
Pennsylvania Affiliate, Inc.
Camp Hill, PA

Puerto Rico Heart Association, Inc.
Hato Rey, Puerto Rico

American Heart Association
Rhode Island Affiliate, Inc.
Pawtucket, RI

American Heart Association
South Carolina Affiliate, Inc.
Columbia, SC

American Heart Association
Southeastern Pennsylvania
Affiliate, Inc.
Philadelphia, PA

American Heart Association
Tennessee Affiliate, Inc.
Nashville, TN

American Heart Association
Texas Affiliate, Inc.
Austin, TX

American Heart Association
Utah Affiliate, Inc.
Salt Lake City, UT

American Heart Association
Vermont Affiliate, Inc.
Shelburne, VT

American Heart Association
Virginia Affiliate, Inc.
Glen Allen, VA

American Heart Association
Washington Affiliate, Inc.
Seattle, WA

American Heart Association
West Virginia Affiliate, Inc.
Charleston, WV

American Heart Association
Wisconsin Affiliate, Inc.
Milwaukee, WI

American Heart Association of
Wyoming, Inc.
Cheyenne, WY

INDEX